Southerners on Film

Southerners on Film

Essays on Hollywood Portrayals Since the 1970s

Edited by ANDREW B. LEITER

McFarland & Company, Inc., Publishers
Jefferson, North Carolina, and London

LIBRARY OF CONGRESS CATALOGUING-IN-PUBLICATION DATA

Southerners on film : essays on Hollywood portrayals
   since the 1970s / edited by Andrew B. Leiter.
      p.   cm.
   Includes bibliographical references and index.

   ISBN 978-0-7864-4960-6
   softcover : 50# alkaline paper ∞

   1. Southern States — In motion pictures.   2. Identity
(Psychology) in motion pictures.   3. Culture in motion pictures.
4. Motion pictures — United States — History — 20th century.
I. Leiter, Andrew B., 1972 –
PN1995.9.S66S68   2011
791.43'65875 — dc23   2011023410

BRITISH LIBRARY CATALOGUING DATA ARE AVAILABLE

© 2011 Andrew B. Leiter. All rights reserved

*No part of this book may be reproduced or transmitted in any form
or by any means, electronic or mechanical, including photocopying
or recording, or by any information storage and retrieval system,
without permission in writing from the publisher.*

Front cover image: Robert Duvall as Euliss "Sonny" Dewey in
The Apostle, 1997 (October Films/Photofest)

Manufactured in the United States of America

*McFarland & Company, Inc., Publishers
   Box 611, Jefferson, North Carolina 28640
      www.mcfarlandpub.com*

To my sons, Robert and Charles

Contents

Introduction (*Andrew B. Leiter*)   1

I. Multiculturalism and Melodrama: Southern White Heroines of the 1980s (*Amy Corbin*)   15

II. You're Only as Good as Your Last Game: *Remember the Titans* Remembers Civil Rights (*Oliver Gruner*)   32

III. "Every Man Has the Right to Contribute a Verse": Representin' Black Masculinity and the South in Three Popular Hip Hop Films (*Courtney George*)   47

IV. "That Old-Timey Music": Nostalgia and the Southern Tradition in *O Brother, Where Art Thou?* (*Andrew B. Leiter*)   62

V. American Dreams and Country Music: *Nashville* and *Payday* (*Hugh Ruppersburg*)   76

VI. Gender, Regional Identity, and the Civil War: Politics of the North and South in *Sweet Home Alabama* and *Junebug* (*Landon Palmer*)   89

VII. The Screen Kallikak: White Trash for White Guilt in Post-Vietnam American Film (*C. Scott Combs*)   106

VIII. The Haunting of a Black Southern Past: Considering Conjure in *To Sleep with Anger* (*Phillip Lamarr Cunningham*)   123

IX. Practice in a Cemetery: Ross McElwee's North Carolina Documentaries (*Stephen Broomer*)   134

X. The *Junebug* Dilemma (*Bryan Giemza*)   147

XI. Imagined Realities: Appalachia, Arabia, and Orientalism in *Songcatcher* and *The Sheik* (*Thomas R. Britt* and *Usame Tunagur*)   161

XII.	*Adaptation* and *Sunshine State*: Nature and Nostalgia in Contemporary Florida Films (*Marlisa Santos*)	175
XIII.	Reel Horror: Louisiana's Vanishing Wetlands and the Threat of Hollywood (Mis)Representation (*Maria Hebert-Leiter*)	187
XIV.	An Aesthetic of Play: A Contemporary Cinema of South-Sploitation (*James A. Crank*)	204
XV.	"You Taste of America": *Talladega Nights*, *Deliverance*, and Southern Studies (*Tara Powell*)	217

About the Contributors — 231
Index — 235

Introduction

Andrew B. Leiter

At least two automobiles in my Pennsylvania town display bumper stickers that read, "Paddle faster, I hear banjos." The stickers are presumably humorous declarations of the drivers' affinity for canoeing or kayaking the area's extensive waterways, and the allusion — a distressing one for many bluegrass aficionados — refers, of course, to John Boorman's mountain adventure film, *Deliverance* (1972). For those who have seen the film, the bumper sticker immediately conjures up the sound of "Dueling Banjos," the scene of sadistic rape, and the infamous line, "Squeal like a pig." The enduring and widespread permutations of this filmic hillbilly violence are such that, even for those who have not seen the film, the bumper sticker reference to banjos suggests that one better hurry because an inbred hillbilly has bad intentions. While no one is likely to entertain the sensationalized violence of *Deliverance* or its grotesque stereotypes as realistic or representative depictions of Southern life, the association of the South with such images lingers as a common cultural touchstone for uneasy laughter at America's "backwards" region. The South has had a long and, at times, troubling history of filmic representation and, more so than any other American region, has offered a psychic space for the nation to entertain its various fantasies of racial and class identities. David O. Selznick's classic production *Gone with the Wind* (1939), for example, has entertained audiences for generations with Scarlett and Rhett's tempestuous love affair set against the epic backdrop of the Civil War and Reconstruction, but the film's tremendous cultural influence on popular conceptions of the South, as documented by Tara McPherson, Helen Taylor, and other scholars, both relies on and promulgates a highly romanticized version of American racial hierarchy. While such romanticized depictions of the antebellum world have not faded from American cultural consciousness, they have largely faded out of contemporary film.

One would be hard pressed to find a more iconic image of the South on film than Scarlett O'Hara. As the cinematic shadow of Scarlett and her voluminous dresses have receded in the face of more racially savvy audiences, however, the hillbilly or redneck image has remained central to popular constructions of Southern identities in contemporary film from the *Deliverance* banjoes to a toothless Cajun firefly in Disney's *The Princess and the Frog* (2009). For a collection of essays taking stock of post–civil rights era films that engage the South, a basic challenge exists in balancing the critical attention to the pervasive redneck image with the critical attention to the multitude of filmic Southern identities that are not grounded in the redneck image. The essays included in this collection were selected with the dual goals of contributing to the scholarship that addresses the continued cultural significance of the redneck image in its grotesqueries and subtleties, while simultaneously emphasizing the rich possibilities for critical consideration of the filmic South beyond these familiar parameters. This introduction provides a brief overview of the South on film with an emphasis on the redneck image as well as the plantation South and its decline (or, perhaps more accurately, its transition into Afrocentric plantation cinema) followed by a preview of the essays situated in the context of Southern studies and contemporary film.

Antebellum writers such as Augustus Baldwin Longstreet, George Washington Harris, and Johnson Jones Hooper entertained eastern audiences with their caricaturized accounts of rowdy life in the frontier South. The comic figures of old southwestern humor — Longstreet's Ransy Sniffle, Harris's Sut Lovingood, and Hooper's Captain Simon Suggs — have close kinfolk in the twentieth century work of such writers as Erskine Caldwell, whose bestselling novels *Tobacco Road* (1932) and *God's Little Acre* (1933) highlight the debilitating poverty and ignorance, as well as the sexual degeneracy, of the rural South. The presentation of the redneck South, with varying degrees of sensationalism, continued through the twentieth century and remains a prevalent literary conception of Southern identity. While popular redneck identity has some of its roots in literature, variations of the same image permeate almost every aspect of popular American culture of the last hundred years, including comic strips such as "Li'l Abner" and "Snuffy Smith"; animation such as the Bugs Bunny short "Hillbilly Hare" and Disney's "The Martins and the Coys" in *Make Mine Music* (1946); country, bluegrass, and rock music; television series such as *The Beverly Hillbillies*, *The Dukes of Hazzard*, and *Blue Collar TV*; and countless internet sites ridiculing, celebrating, and selling the redneck image. A simple search of *YouTube*, while I was writing this introduction, yielded over 60,000 results for redneck, 31,000 results for hillbilly, and nearly 14,000 for white trash.

More than any other medium, however, movies have shaped popular perceptions of the redneck South over the last hundred years. The early years of American cinema were rife with backwards mountain men, moonshine, and feuds. J. W. Williamson counts seventy-one hillbilly films in 1914 alone (179), and the hillbilly South has been a consistent aspect of American film through the decades from *Tol'able David* (1921) to the recent film adaptation of the television series *The Dukes of Hazzard* (2005). As Williamson and Anthony Harkins demonstrate, the hillbilly image has a geographical association with the southern mountains but is more fully defined in terms of cultural characteristics than in terms of geography (Williamson 16; Harkins 5). While popular imagination frequently affiliates the ignorant, poor, scofflaw, and primitive hillbilly stereotypes with the mountains, these same characteristics are likewise standard aspects of the broader Southern image. The murderous rednecks of *Easy Rider* (1969) and even *The Texas Chain Saw Massacre* (1974) have plenty in common with the hillbilly sadists of *Deliverance* but have no discernible ties to the mountains and, as C. Scott Combs notes in his essay for this collection, the redneck pawnshop owners and rapists of Quentin Tarantino's *Pulp Fiction* (1994) appear to be *Deliverance*-inspired Southern transplants to Los Angeles. Similarly, the dimwitted rustic, with his open mouth and vacant eyes, is a comedic staple of the Southern image, whether the setting is highland, lowland, or swampland. The cult favorite of *The Simpsons* fans, Cletus the Slack-Jawed Yokel is a compilation of any number of redneck stereotypes, but he lives in Springfield, Matt Groening's Everytown, USA. Such rednecks abroad can be found with increasing frequency throughout popular American culture and are indicative of an enduring and even expanding national fascination with "redneck behavior" as spectacle entertainment.

A sadistic hillbilly (Herbert "Cowboy" Coward) watches the infamous rape in John Boorman's *Deliverance* (1972, Warner Bros).

Similar to the image of the redneck South, the image of the romanticized plantation South had roots in the literature of the antebellum period and developed in subsequent fiction before becoming a familiar aspect of American cinema. Juxtaposed to the old southwestern humorists' portrayal of an ignorant and semi-barbaric South, plantation fiction tended to highlight an ideally ordered and genteel society of manners that engaged in slavery as a benign institution, and this image found popular proponents in such works as John Pendleton Kennedy's *Swallow Barn* (1832), Beverly Tucker's *The Partisan Leader* (1836), and Caroline Lee Hentz's *The Planter's Northern Bride* (1854). While the Civil War radically altered the reality of the South, the romanticized recreation of the Old South was standard practice in the Southern culture of the lost cause, and a generation after the war, the fiction of Thomas Nelson Page featured chivalrous planters, genteel ladies, and freedmen who reminisce of slavery as the good old days. More than seventy years after the war, Margaret Mitchell's monumental bestseller *Gone with the Wind* (1936) celebrated a similar version of the Old South and inspired the movie which remains the touchstone for popular conceptions of the romanticized plantation South.

By the time *Gone with the Wind* appeared in theaters in 1939, the South's romanticized identity had been thoroughly developed through three preceding decades of cinematic images. As Edward D. C. Campbell, Jr., has argued, the familiarity of Southern plantation subject matter was appealing in early cinema because films were generally short, and "the subject matter had to be instantly recognizable and present obvious character types" (12). Civil War dramas in particular were prevalent during the silent era and included such films as Burton King's *The Pride of the South* (1913), Herbert Brenon's *The Heart of Maryland* (1915), and William Desmond Taylor's *Her Father's Son* (1916), as well as numerous D. W. Griffith films such as *The Guerrilla* (1908), *His Trust* (1911), *The Battle* (1911), and *The Birth of a Nation* (1915). These films featured belles in love, gallants in battle, and — with the notable exception of *The Birth of a Nation*— slaves faithful in their servitude. Various other films, such as Otis Turner's *In Slavery Days* (1913), Oscar Apfel's *Cameo Kirby* (1914), and S. Rankin Drew's *Kennedy Square* (1916), engaged similar Southern images in antebellum settings. With the emergence of synchronized sound in the 1920s, musicals became a popular genre that both contributed to and relied upon idealized images of the South. Whether set in the antebellum or postbellum South, such films engaged audiences' familiarity with filmic conventions to establish romanticized Southern backdrops against which various stars displayed their talents: Buddy Rogers in *The River of Romance* (1929), Bing Crosby in *Mississippi* (1935), Shirley Temple and Bill "Bojangles" Robinson in *The Little Colonel* (1935) and *The Littlest Rebel* (1935), and Bobby Breen in *Way Down South* (1939), among many others. By 1939, then, audiences were familiar with the idealized plantation South featured in *Gone with the Wind*. Even Scarlett's self-centered and less-than-chaste Southern belle persona had predecessors in Richard Thorpe's *The Toy Wife* (1938) starring Luise Rainer and William Wyler's *Jezebel* starring Bette Davis (1938). *Gone with the Wind*, however, was the pinnacle of Hollywood's Old South, and it endures in that role seventy years later. With its combination of epic grandeur, action, Civil War realism, romance, and especially the magical interplay of Vivien Leigh and Clark Gable, the film enjoys iconic status that transcends other romanticized representations of the South.

In the wake of *Gone with the Wind*, romanticized films about the South became less frequent, and while such films as Edward H. Griffith's *Virginia* (1941), Disney's *Song of the South* (1946), and George Sidney's musical *Show Boat* (1951) continued to indulge in idealized images of the South, the developing cinematic trend, as Campbell and Jack Temple Kirby have demonstrated, emphasized a more decadent, gothic, and racist South. A number of factors likely contributed to the decline in films embracing a romanticized South, not the least of which was that the escapist tendencies in films during the Depression era gave way to more realistic representations of the region in the wake of World War II. Most importantly, however, the idealized South, which had always existed contemporaneously with popular and contradictory representations of the redneck South, was also now being challenged more emphatically on the racial front. Southern white versions of slavery and race relations had, of course, not gone uncontested in American popular culture. The antebellum period, in particular, witnessed a propagandistic struggle for control of the popular perception of slavery in America, and the most successful novel of the nineteenth century was Harriet Beecher Stowe's abolitionist sensation, *Uncle Tom's Cabin* (1852). Likewise, during the era of silent films, the NAACP protested against *The Birth of a Nation*, and the African American filmmaker Oscar Micheaux produced *Within Our Gates* (1920), which challenged Griffith's racist version of Reconstruction. Scholars of African American cinema and representation, including Donald Bogle, Manthia Diawara, and Mark A. Reid, among many others, have demonstrated that an African American cinematic tradition existed both counter to and independent of the American racist cinematic norms. For the most part, however, it would be after World War II and in conjunction with and subsequent to the civil rights and black pride movements of the next three decades that widespread revisionary representations of race relations would occur in popular American cinema.

Although the decline of the romanticized South has not been accompanied by the emergence of a single preeminent image of the South in film, the most prolific new grouping of films encompasses the numerous corrective films revising America's racial legacy to reflect the harsher realities of America's past that were glossed over in the first half of the twentieth century. In the 1970s, numerous Afro-centric considerations of American history, such as the film adaptation of Ernest Gaines's *The Autobiography of Miss Jane Pittman*

(1974), Richard Fleischer's *Mandingo* (1975), and the miniseries adaptation of Alex Haley's *Roots* (1977), contributed to the shift in popular perceptions of slavery and Reconstruction, and throughout the last thirty years, dozens of films have engaged slavery, segregation, and the civil rights struggle from a revisionary angle. In many ways these cinematic developments might be viewed as the legacy of nineteenth-century minstrelsy — the first full-fledged transatlantic popular culture according to W. T. Lhamon and Sarah Meer —

Mede (Ken Norton) and Blanche (Susan George) are slave and mistress who cross the color line in Richard Fleischer's *Mandingo* (1975, Dino De Laurentiis).

coming full circle from its origins in the plantation South. The popularity and influence of minstrelsy were such that the degrading tropes of blackface entertainment dominated popular cinematic representations of African Americans prior to World War II, remained influential throughout the later decades of the twentieth century and, as Spike Lee suggests in the new millennium minstrel show of *Bamboozled* (2000), may linger yet close to the surface of the American racial psyche.

This collection contributes to the existing scholarly work on the thematic intersections of film and Southern studies by addressing the dearth of critical attention to the image of the South in contemporary film. As such, some of the following essays address the cultural significance of the enduring redneck identity on film, while others consider films that engage Southern identities belying such easy categorization. Scholarly considerations of the South and film are heavily weighted toward films from the first half of the twentieth century. In part this may be attributed to the phenomenal cultural influence of *The Birth of a Nation* and *Gone with the Wind*, and in part this is due to the fact that three of the better book-length considerations of the South and film appeared in the late 1970s and early 1980s: Kirby's *Media-Made Dixie* (1978), Warren French's edited collection *The South and Film* (1981), and Campbell's *The Celluloid South* (1981). More recent book-length works have tended to derive from a single thematic focus. For example, Allison Graham's informative book *Framing the South* (2001) considers film and television during the civil rights era, while Bruce Chadwick and Simone Bachofner have addressed Civil War films in their respective books *The Reel Civil War* (2001) and *Hollywood Film and the Cultural Memory of the Civil War South* (2008). Larry Langman and David Ebner's *Hollywood's Image of the South* (2001) offers an exception to the trend of more focused thematic considerations of the South on film. While this useful filmography seeks to compile all films engaging the American South and arrange them thematically, the work does not offer analysis of the films. In short, a substantial need exists for critical works that engage the multi-faceted world of the contemporary filmic South.

Although redneck cinema has remained prominent and numerous films have rewritten America's racial narrative, these genres represent only two components of a multifaceted Southern presence in contemporary film. This collection of essays eschews holistic assertions about representations of the American South in popular culture. Never as cohesive in reality as it was in representation, the image of the South has grown increasingly less cohesive in the wake of the civil rights era as the legacy of slavery and segregation become less definitive factors in regional identity. One can certainly still identify additional thematic trends in contemporary Southern film: gothic, automotive, football, music, and so on. When the tendency of the last thirty five years has been the diversification of filmic considerations of the South, however, any attempts to establish a set of identifiable characteristics in Southern films would be necessarily limiting if not impossible. How does one categorize eclectic films like Robert Duvall's gem *The Apostle* (1998), Spike Jonze's experimental *Adaptation* (2002), or Andrew Douglas's surreal *Searching for the Wrong-Eyed Jesus* (2003)? Nor does this collection aspire toward any exhaustive consideration of the contemporary filmic South—a Sisyphean task at best. Rather, these essays represent an attempt to provide a cross-section of directions and developments in contemporary films representing the South from a variety of ethnic, thematic, and subregional perspectives.

Its reputation as slow to change notwithstanding, the American South has experienced transitions since national independence from frontier to antebellum South and on through Reconstruction, the segregation era, the civil rights era, and the post–civil rights era. Additionally labeled as the Old South, the New South, the industrial South, the agrarian South, the sunny South, the global South, and so on, the region's continuous transitions belie its reputation as stuck in its ways. The image of the South as slow to change only takes its significance from the region's relationship to the rest of the nation. For if anything has remained constant with the South, it is the region's image as not only "behind" the rest of the nation but as also reluctant to keep pace. This regional characterization, of course, is most notable and most accurate in terms of the white South's resistance to changes in racial hierarchy and perhaps less accurate in other areas, but the characterization permeates nearly every aspect of Southern popular image: economics, politics, religion, social policy, education, gender roles, criminal justice, environmental policy, and so on.

In popular representations of the South, regional and individual struggles with a changing world frequently provide dramatic and comedic impetus. The same might be said, of course, for many regions, but in addition to resisting and adapting to change in the South in uniquely "Southern" ways, the region often inhabits the role of foil for the nation as a whole and as such provides popular outlets for hilarity, nostalgia, horror, and disgust. The interchangeable redneck, hillbilly, and white trash stereotypes, for example, variously inspire this spectrum of emotions. The yokel comedy at the heart of countless films and shows extends from the South's presumed rural identification and resistance to the modern world that have amused Americans for generations. As a region popularly conceived as rural and adhering to a slower lifestyle and "traditional" values of family and work, Southern life has frequently been offered up as a nostalgic antidote to the fast-paced, materialistic, and morally adrift greater America in such television shows as *The Waltons* (1972–1981) and *The Andy Griffith Show* (1960–1968) and such movies as

Sweet Home Alabama (2002) and *Junebug* (2005). Yet as Harkins notes, only a fine line separates Ernest T. Bass, the hilariously uncontrollable mountain man of *The Andy Griffith Show*, from the sadistic hillbillies of *Deliverance*, who terrorize the middle class suburbanites during their nature escape from Atlanta, the South's foremost icon of modernization (184).

Various essays in this collection provide critical insight to filmic representations of the South in transition to modernity. Modern in this sense, however, is less temporal than conceptual and suggests that the South is becoming more "American" in nature and less distinctively Southern — a seemingly ubiquitous but never fully realized process throughout Southern history. While modern might be signified by electricity in Joel and Ethan Coen's *O Brother, Where Art Thou?* (2000), the sense of the South modernizing or catching up with the rest of America in other films entails transitions in commerce, racial hierarchy, cultural values, and so on. Some of the essays in this collection address filmic representations of the South in these transitions to "modernity" in various phases defined by such issues as integration, the emerging sunny South, and contemporary commercialism, and they do so by considering representations that proffer a holistic sense of Southern regional identity conflating with America. While the movies as discussed in these essays conceive of the South as a relatively homogenous region engaged in a frequently comedic and, at times, troubling merger with aspects of national identity, other essays focus on movies that address more particularized aspects of change in the South. The notion of a homogenous South identifiable by a set of regionally pervasive characteristics exists in popular imagination and in popular representations; however, such a unified identity has never been a realistic reflection of the region and has, perhaps, less concrete correlation to reality than ever in the contemporary South. Several essays in this collection engage films that offer a less cohesive regional understanding of change and instead emphasize a more specific vision of locale or identity in flux, whether demographically, economically, environmentally, or culturally. These essays indicate a mosaic of cinematic Southern identities vying with change in particularized locales and being treated with varying degrees of acuity and exploitation on the big screen.

The Southern filmic identity most frequently presented with the least acumen remains the redneck. The more sensationally deranged or comic redneck caricatures in contemporary films have much more in common with other popular representations of rednecks — filmic and otherwise — than with reality, and they are unapologetically exploitative while making little or no claim to authenticity. However, as critical commentaries in this collection indicate, even the films which no one takes seriously as representative may still have serious cultural and environmental implications. Many contemporary films engaging the redneck image, of course, aspire toward authenticity or at least a popular reception as authentic, and in such films the lines between realism, exploitation, entertainment, and competing cultural functions are frequently blurred. Joel Schumacher's *A Time to Kill* (1996), for example, was a popular film of racial reconciliation in Mississippi, but the reconciliation is predicated primarily on the bifurcation of Southern whites into two opposing filmic identities — educated, genteel, racially sympathetic whites versus violent, ignorant, racist rednecks whose rape of a thirteen-year-old African American girl initiates the conflict of the film. Several essays here demonstrate that the intertwined redneck, hillbilly, and white trash images continue as multifaceted presences in contemporary film and that the images, rather than becoming standardized in their cultural implications, continue to evolve and resist reductive interpretations of their cultural relevance. In addition to essays that consider the South in transition and the redneck image, others address a variety of aspects of the cinematic South, ranging from unique engagements with some traditional Southern studies areas (race, Southern gothic, and the Civil War) to reconsiderations of Southern gender constructs and evaluations of the South from transnational perspectives.

The first two essays of the collection engage Hollywood's representations of the South as reluctant to embrace multicultural change. In her essay, Amy Corbin considers the filmic South of the long 1980s decade in terms of the region's resistance to burgeoning multiculturalism in America, and she argues that Alan Parker's *Mississippi Burning* (1988) prioritizes the suffering of white women over racial oppression as part of her larger argument that working class women in films such as Martin Ritt's *Norma Rae* (1979) and Jon Avnet's *Fried Green Tomatoes* (1991) provide audiences with the points of moral identification in films of multicultural reconciliation. Likewise, Oliver Gruner's essay on Boaz Yakin's *Remember the Titans* (2000) addresses Hollywood's engagement with the contentious changes of the civil rights era and argues that *Titans* elides different stages of the civil rights movements to challenge standardized cinematic depictions of the civil rights struggle.

The next three essays emphasize the interdependent nature of music and various (racial, geographical, and temporal) Southern identities as suggested in contemporary films. Courtney George's study of three Southern-based hip hop films, Craig Brewer's *Hustle & Flow* (2005), Chris Robinson's *ATL* (2006), and Bryan Barber's *Idlewild* (2006), repositions the urban South as central to African American male identity and contends that a connection to Southern African American roots strengthens the seemingly urban-oriented hip hop artists. My essay examines *O Brother, Where Art Thou?* in relation to the redneck and romanticized Souths of Mark Twain's *Adventures of Huckleberry Finn* (1884) and Selznick's production of *Gone with the Wind* respectively, and I contend that the folk music in the film acts as a nostalgic agent alleviating the comic brutality with which the Coens treat Depression-era Mississippi in the midst of social and economic change. Hugh Ruppersburg's essay considers country music in Robert Altman's *Nashville* (1975) and Daryl Duke's *Payday* (1972) and contends that the political and musical focus of *Nashville* embodies the tensions of a region and nation in transition from traditional and agrarian values to modern commercial and industrial values in the early 1970s.

The two subsequent essays consider the filmic construction of Southern gender and class identities relative to the national constructions of the same. Landon Palmer examines Andy Tennant's *Sweet Home Alabama* and Phil Morrison's *Junebug* as films that engage the same regional ideological delineations of feminine identity. Although these films juxtapose northern, materialistic, career-oriented notions of femininity with "traditional" concepts of Southern femininity as shaped through the prisms of family, race, and the Civil War, they reach contradictory valuations of those gender roles. C. Scott Combs argues in his essay that class scapegoating is a standard aspect not only of America's displacement of guilt over racial tensions but also of the Vietnam War. Combs examines the tensions in contemporary filmic representations of "white trash" (Sam Peckinpah's *The Wild Bunch* (1969), Walter Hill's *Southern Comfort* (1981), and *Deliverance* among others) in which the cinematic exploitation of poor whites as America's scapegoat has been overshadowed by the popularization of a white trash identity detached from its origin in rural poverty.

Phillip Lamarr Cunningham and Stephen Broomer address filmic considerations of the continued relevance of the South for individual and familial identities of Southerners who have left the region. Cunningham contends that Charles Burnett's *To Sleep with Anger* (1990) features conjure as the source of family conflict in Los Angeles that extends from the tensions between Southern African American traditions and contemporary African American life outside the South. Stephen Broomer's essay analyzes the films of Ross McElwee — *Backyard* (1984), *Sherman's March* (1986), and *Bright Leaves* (2003) — as studies in the personal identity of a filmmaker who has left the South but returns to investigate Southern history relative to his sense of family and self.

Both Bryan Giemza's essay and Thomas R. Britt and Usame Tunagur's co-authored essay consider the South through a transnational lens. Giemza compares *Junebug* to James Joyce's literary Ireland as similar artistic engagements with regional identity, arguing that *Junebug* provides an authentic depiction of the cultural tension between transition and paralysis. Britt and Tunagur examine the cultural implications of Maggie Greenwald's *Songcatcher* (2001), a movie that, on the surface, celebrates Appalachian identity through the region's music. They provide a comparative study of Appalachian stereotypes in the film with Muslim stereotypes in George Melford's *The Sheik* (1921) as reflective of the cultural other and focus on the commodification of music in *Songcatcher* as a means by which cultural misconceptions are promulgated.

Marlisa Santos and Maria Hebert-Leiter consider changes in the environmental landscape in relation to film and ethnicity. Santos examines filmic representations of multicultural Florida in relation to the natural environment in *Adaptation* and John Sayles's *Sunshine State* (2002) and concludes that nostalgia for an Edenic environmental past displaces and transcends ethnic divides. Hebert-Leiter studies such films as *Southern Comfort*, Frank Coraci's *The Waterboy* (1998), and Iain Softley's *The Skeleton Key* (2005) to argue that Hollywood's depictions of Louisiana swamps and their Cajun inhabitants as threatening entities may contribute to the national disregard for disappearing Louisiana wetlands.

The collection closes with two critical assessments of recent popular movies that embrace traditions of the gothic and comic South on film. James A. Crank contends that recent "South-sploitation" films such as Craig Brewer's *Black Snake Moan* (2007), *The Skeleton Key*, and Stephen Hopkins' *The Reaping* (2007) present self-conscious engagements of the Southern gothic tradition and feature the South as an exotic idea that provides cultural juxtapositions for mainstream America. Tara Powell considers Adam McKay's *Talladega Nights* (2006) as a self-conscious parody of the popular images of the modernizing South through the prism of Southern masculinity and NASCAR. Through her comparison of the film to *Deliverance*, she argues that *Talladega Nights* demonstrates that the cultural transition of the South becoming more American is matched by America becoming more Southern in the new millennium.

Considered together the essays of this collection offer new critical possibilities for a variety of Southern and film studies subjects including gender, class, race, ethnicity, music, environmental criticism, civil rights, the Civil War, comedy, gothic, and melodrama. Yet, while the collection emphasizes plurality and diversification in terms of filmic representations and critical approaches, the essays demonstrate a cohesiveness found in their attention to the nature of Southern identities on individual and regional levels. They collectively address what it means to be Southern on film, and while some contributors suggest a correlation between representation and reality with regard to individual identity as Southern and African American, or as Southern and female, and so on, other contributors are more concerned with the implications that extend from the disconnection between the realities of various Southern identities and their representations on film. The basic scholarly parameters guiding this collection, then, lie in the triangulation of a multi-faceted Southern reality, the filmic representations of the region, and the critical evaluation of authenticity and significance.

Works Cited

Bachofner, Simone. *Hollywood Film and the Cultural Memory of the Civil War South: How America's Memory of the Civil War Is Reflected in Films Like "Gone with the Wind" and "Cold Mountain."* Saarbrücken: VDM Verlag, 2008.
Bogle, Donald. *Toms, Coons, Mulattoes, Mammies, and Bucks: An Interpretive History of Blacks in American Films.* New York: Viking, 1973.
Campbell, Edward D. C., Jr. *The Celluloid South: Hollywood and the Southern Myth.* Knoxville: University of Tennessee Press, 1981.
_____, consultant. "Media." *Encyclopedia of Southern Culture.* Ed. Charles Reagan Wilson and William Ferris. Chapel Hill: University of North Carolina Press, 1989. 905–980.
Chadwick, Bruce. *The Reel Civil War: Mythmaking in American Film.* New York: Knopf, 2001.
Diawara, Manthia, ed. *Black American Cinema.* New York: Routledge, 1993.
French, Warren, ed. *The South and Film.* Jackson: University Press Mississippi, 1981.
Graham, Allison. *Framing the South: Hollywood, Television, and Race during the Civil Rights Struggle.* Baltimore: Johns Hopkins University Press, 2003.
Harkins, Anthony. *Hillbilly: A Cultural History of an American Icon.* New York: Oxford University Press, 2004.
Heider, Karl G., ed. *Images of the South: Constructing a Regional Culture on Film and Video.* Athens: University of Georgia Press, 1993.
Kirby, Jack Temple. *Media-Made Dixie: The South in the American Imagination.* Baton Rouge: Louisiana State University Press, 1978.
Langman, Larry and David Ebner. *Hollywood's Image of the South: A Century of Southern Films.* Westport: Greenwood, 2001.
Lhamon, W. T. *Jump Jim Crow: Lost Plays, Lyrics, and Street Prose of the First Atlantic Popular Culture.* Cambridge: Harvard University Press, 2003.
McPherson, Tara. *Reconstructing Dixie: Race, Gender, and Nostalgia in the Imagined South.* Durham: Duke University Press, 2003.
Meer, Sarah. *Uncle Tom Mania: Slavery, Minstrelsy and Transatlantic Culture in the 1850s.* Athens: University of Georgia Press, 2005.
Oliver, Lawrence J. and Terri L. Walker. "James Weldon Johnson's *New York Age* Essays on *The Birth of a Nation* and the 'Southern Oligarchy.'" *South Central Review* 10 (1993): 1–17.
Reid, Mark A. *Redefining Black Film.* Berkeley: University of California Press, 1993.
Richardson, Riché. *Black Masculinity and the U.S. South: From Uncle Tom to Gangsta.* Athens: University of Georgia Press, 2007.
Rocchio, Vincent F. *Reel Racism: Confronting Hollywood's Construction of Afro-American Culture.* Boulder: Westview, 2000.
Taylor, Helen. "*Gone With the Wind*: The Mammy of Them All." *The Progress of Romance: The Politics of Popular Fiction.* Ed. Jean Radford. London: Routledge, 1986. 113–36.
Von Doviak, Scott. *Hick Flicks: The Rise and Fall of Redneck Cinema.* Jefferson: McFarland, 2005.
Willett, Ralph. "Dixie's Land: Cinema of the American South." *American Film and Politics from Reagan to Bush Jr.* Ed. Philip John Davies and Paul Wells. Manchester: Manchester University Press, 2002. 105–120.
Williamson, J. W. *Hillbillyland: What the Movies Did to the Mountains & What the Mountains Did to the Movies.* Chapel Hill: University of North Carolina Press, 1995.
Wray, Matt and Annalee Newitz, ed. *White Trash: Race and Class in America.* New York: Routledge, 1997.

I.

Multiculturalism and Melodrama: Southern White Heroines of the 1980s

AMY CORBIN

Following the civil rights era, the image of the American South in popular culture needed recuperation: images of white brutality against peaceful civil rights protestors were imprinted on the national consciousness. In the mid-to-late 1970s, such recuperation began to show through the growing national popularity of country music, "homespun" Southern dramas such as the TV show *The Waltons* (1972–1981), a cycle of movies known as "Southern action" or "redneck and car" (exemplified by Burt Reynolds in the *Smokey and the Bandit* series), the use of Southern authenticity as a symbol in the Jimmy Carter presidential campaign, and the growth of the fast food chain Kentucky Fried Chicken using "down-home" style marketing and other similar advertising campaigns.[1] While stereotypes of ignorant rural or mountain "rednecks" did not disappear, the above-mentioned cultural products promoted an alternate strand of imagery that saw the lower-class white (often male) as the holder of simple, family-based, anti-authority values at a time when anti-government sentiment was moving from the political left to the political right — years that Philip Jenkins calls the "anti-sixties" (5).

In the 1980s and early 1990s, however, a further evolution in Southern imagery can be found in popular film's use of white *female* heroines to offer a politically-moderate compromise position based on the new mainstreaming of multiculturalism. These heroines combined working-class white Southern authenticity and humble backgrounds with a new assumption of moral authority that came from identifying with abused white women and people of color — the victims of multiculturalist melodramas. The Manichean moral dichotomies in films like *Norma Rae* (1979), *Mississippi Burning* (1988), and

Fried Green Tomatoes (1991) incorporate but transcend civil rights imagery by using the white male racist to menace white women, with African Americans as their secondary victims. The popularity of these films, along with others with strong female protagonists like *Coal Miner's Daughter* (1980), *Steel Magnolias* (1989) and *Driving Miss Daisy* (1989), supplanted the largely masculine portrait of the white South in the mid-to-late 1970s with a woman-centered cultural landscape[2] that ranged from the victim-focused end of the melodramatic spectrum in *Mississippi Burning* to the empowered victim-heroes of *Norma Rae* and *Fried Green Tomatoes*.[3] The latter two films, bookending the 1980s, illustrate the way the female victim-to-be-rescued by a male hero in *Mississippi Burning* was often replaced by a hybrid victim-hero (a term borrowed from Carol Clover's study of the slasher film in which a female "final girl" suffers through endless violence, finally becoming tough enough to save herself at the end). In this way, the traditional melodramatic gendered triangle of male villain, female victim, and male hero is condensed into a white male villain threatening a white female victim-hero who saves herself— and being Southern, she thus demonstrates that redemption may come from within that landscape.

Melodrama and Multiculturalism

Melodramatic narratives rely on the undeserved suffering of their heroes and heroines, which in turn encourages spectatorial sympathy and establishes their characters' morality through their unjust punishment (Brooks; Williams; Gledhill). Such suffering is caused by other characters who are either purposely cruel or who "misrecognize" the virtue of the protagonists. In these melodramas, white female protagonists create sympathetic white Southern characters, thus attempting to situate the cinematic spectator emotionally within the Southern landscape, while simultaneously criticizing its "backwards" and racist values. Because the protagonists are white, they are perceived as more marketable in mainstream films, but because they are women, they also have the moral weight of victimhood, as opposed to the white Southern man, who is often associated with the white racist. The aristocratic young woman found its most popular expression in *Gone with the Wind* (1939); Scarlett O'Hara continues to resonate with readers and viewers because of her ability to survive against the odds, upsetting social convention when necessary (Taylor). But after the midcentury, it was more difficult to see an aristocratic white Southern woman as heroic; John Cawelti notes that the literary sequel to *Gone with the Wind* published in 1994 had to take Scarlett out of the South because by then there was no way to write about an aristocratic character in the South as both mythic and politically correct (Cawelti, "Searching for Scarlett"). The older aristocratic woman and, more often, the younger working class woman take the suffering-yet-feisty quality of Scarlett and place an additional social handicap on the protagonist, making her a more "deserving" heroine.[4] The heroines of films like *Norma Rae*, *Steel Magnolias*, *Driving Miss Daisy*, and *Fried Green Tomatoes* embody qualities such as familial love and successful struggle against adversity that fit melodramatic patterns and resonate with views of the South as underdog. Their triumphs, using compassion and individual bonds with "others," establish them as multicultural leaders of post-sixties America. They blend their compassionate liberalism with respect for roots and tradition (often associated with conservatism) to form an exemplar for American identity in the 1980s — and here, I expand on John Cawelti's reading of *The Prince of Tides* (1991), with its white male Southern protagonist embodying the South's status as a "flawed exemplar" vis-à-vis the rest of America (Cawelti, "'That's What I Like'" 11–12).

In *Mississippi Burning* (Alan Parker, 1988), the main characters are two male white FBI agents who come to a small Southern town to investigate the deaths of three civil rights workers; a subplot includes a quasi-romantic friendship between one of them, Anderson, and Mrs. Pell, the white wife of the sadistic deputy sheriff Frank. While the film's ostensible subject is Klan violence against African Americans, it spends most of its emotional energy on the suffering of the two FBI agents and Mrs. Pell, so that their pain is what the spectator feels in a much more visceral way than that of the African American community or the civil rights workers specifically. After its release, Parker said that it probably would not have been made if it had black heroes (Kempley). This defensiveness seems in response to immediate criticisms of the film for its relegation of the African American characters to passive background, almost literally part of the physical landscape. The result is that the primary historical victims of the Klan are narratively displaced by Mrs. Pell, whom the spectator gets to know as a character and whose abusive husband turns out to be a Klan member. Hers is the suffering that one sees up close, through Frank's beatings and her timid expressions of emotion to Anderson, the only man who treats her with respect. Because her oppression comes from her racist husband, who is simultaneously constructed as the most villainous character in the murder investigation, his sexism and racism is conflated and her gendered victimization at his hands also comes to stand for African American victimization, which the film keeps more generalized.

This displacement is made clearest when Mrs. Pell is visually linked to the black community through a scene in which she sits with her black maid and admires her baby. The film demonstrates the genuine affection and bonding between the two women, which is broken up when Deputy Pell comes up from behind his wife and chases off the black woman. This alliance goes beyond the feminization of black victimhood that Linda Williams demonstrates is a central aspect in racial melodrama. Here, the victimization of the black community is *transferred* to the white woman, and it is her suffering the film follows. The effect is similar to one that Allison Graham notes in her discussion of *The Long Hot Summer* (1958): "Within the socially conscious portrait of the contemporary Deep South, the white misfit *stands in* for the victimized black man" (Graham 140). Through the time spent at the Pell household and the sympathetic representation of another younger, poor white girl who is oppressed by the white patriarchal establishment of the town, the spectator is meant to gain empathy for the white victims of the white South.

And while superficially the heroes come from "outside"—FBI agents whose professionalism contrasts with the anarchy of the South ("The rest of America don't mean jackshit—you're in Mississippi now," the sheriff informs them when they arrive)—the film is in part the story of a savvy, undercover "insider." Anderson is from the South and his methods involve talking to the residents in a folksy, approachable manner, and sometimes behaving in violent ways that match the savagery of the corrupt sheriff's force they are fighting. His informal, rough-around-the-edges character is portrayed as far more appealing than Ward's stiff, by-the-books government man. Thus the seeds for the South's redemption are found within the landscape, not from outside it—both in the informal, common-man persona of Anderson and in the moral authority of Mrs. Pell's victimhood. And it is the redemption of Southern whiteness, not the exploration of the African American experience, that becomes the film's priority (a quality it shares with other films ostensibly about racial injustice from *To Kill a Mockingbird* [1962] to *A Time to Kill* [1996]). So *Mississippi Burning* includes some of the ingredients for the redeemed white South that we will find more developed in the other films— and in this film most overtly, the good and evil white South fight with each other over the wrongs done to African Americans, who stand passively on the sidelines. The moral clarity of this fight, while keeping whites in both active roles of the melodramatic triangle of villain/hero/victim, makes the film fit perfectly a popular multiculturalist worldview of the 1980s.

Such multiculturalism had its roots during and after World War II, due to desires to promote America's image of inclusiveness abroad, but it developed its modern form and widespread recognition through changes in primary and secondary school curricula in the 1970s and 1980s, innovations that were joined in the 1990s by other phenomena like diversity training in the corporate world and local festivals that exhibited different ethnic and racial cultures (Newfield and Gordon; Singh 473–476, 498–499; Lowe 415). As used in this essay, the phrase "popular multiculturalism" refers to the notion that ethnic-racial (though usually called "cultural" and potentially referring to other populations) diversity is a social good, a distinctive quality of America, and should be "sampled" for entertainment or educational purposes without a significant change to political or economic power structures. This combination of visible diversity and integration into an American national identity represents a middle road between extremes in the post-sixties era. The attacks on the civil rights agenda in the 1970s and 1980s (against school busing and affirmative action, for example) were under the banner of color-blindness; multiculturalism made color visible, but in the arena of personal identity and culture (in one of its more limited definitions: the production of art, music, clothing, food, etc.). It thus offered creative power to groups of people who lacked political and economic power. Advocates of multiculturalism could appear less threatening than Black Power and other separatist movements, but more enlightened than those who thought race no longer mattered. In fictional narratives, multiculturalism often manifests itself in the casting of people of color without transforming the narratives themselves into non–Eurocentric stories. As we saw with Alan Parker's defense of his choice of protagonists, there remained in Hollywood at this time a strong sense that only white lead characters were bankable — but with a race-conscious subject matter or person of color in a secondary or "buddy" role, the film could be a "cross-over" hit (Willis 27–59; Guerrero 127–134; Jordan 77–98; Ames).

Female Victim-Heroes as White Multiculturalist Leaders

Idgie and Ruth of *Fried Green Tomatoes* (Jon Avnet, 1991) are more fully developed versions of Mrs. Pell: Southern white women who also suffer from domestic violence, racism, and personal loss. Instead of playing secondary roles to male heroes, however, they are the protagonists of the film and become empowered by forming a female-centered community that protects their own devoted friendship (a toned-down version of the lesbian relationship that was depicted in the source novel) and other marginalized people. Female bonding transcends time in the film through a narrative structure in which Evelyn, a contemporary Southern suburban housewife, listens to the memories of Ninny, an elderly woman who tells Idgie and Ruth's story. Ruth and Idgie's trauma begins in adolescence as they witness Idgie's brother being run over by a train, and continues with Idgie's status as a social misfit, Ruth's abusive marriage to an alcoholic Klan member, both women's harassment for running a racially integrated restaurant, and Ruth's death from cancer. Although Evelyn's life has many fewer dramatic trials than Ruth and Idgie, she lives with an insensitive husband and suffers from low self-esteem. Many of the women's trials can be broadly blamed on white male Southern patriarchy, again consolidated into the single villainous character of Ruth's husband.

Norma Rae, of *Norma Rae* (Martin Ritt, 1979), works in a cotton mill that wears down the health and spirits of her family. Her experience of this suffering and the guidance of an out-of-town union organizer lead to her transformation from victim to union leader. The mill leadership easily fits into the roles of melodramatic villain, through such moments as their refusal to allow Norma's father a rest when he is ill and their misogynist taunting of Norma. The odds stack up against Norma when her husband expresses his exasperation at her all-consuming work and fearful workers hesitate to join the union—and here the melodramatic villain is more truly seen as systemic. While the film could easily have used the male northern union organizer Reuben as the active hero and the mill workers as the passive recipients of his leadership, it portrays Reuben and Norma Rae's partnership as quite equal. As important, Norma Rae's personal growth and independence are not "gifts" from him but earned on her own, and techniques ranging from camera point of view to range of knowledge encourage the spectator to ground his or her identification with Norma Rae and her working-class Southern community, not with the northern outsider as in *Mississippi Burning*.

So in *Norma Rae* and *Fried Green Tomatoes*, the narrative center has shifted entirely to the South (away from the idea that outsiders must "fix" the region) and the melodramatic trope of suffering lines up with the old sense of the South as an underdog that stems from Reconstruction. But since this notion was then discredited in the minds of Americans horrified by the white South's response to civil rights, these films resurrected it in a new context of white women who share the victimhood of African Americans but whose racial identity made them more bankable protagonists in 1980s Hollywood films.

Like Mrs. Pell, the heroines of *Norma Rae* and *Fried Green Tomatoes* link the moral authority they claim through their own suffering with their association with African Americans. The difference is, as empowered victim-heroes, these protagonists become the active shapers of multicultural communities that serve as moral exemplars to the films' audiences. Doing so while maintaining a white center *and* endowing that whiteness with the specificity of Southern "underdog" culture gives rise to one manifestation of what I call "white multiculturalism." White multiculturalism is a sympathetic expression of white culture that seeks distinctiveness alongside other ethnic and racial groups, claims innocence from the dynamics of power, and allies itself with the marginalized.[5] White multiculturalism finds its perfect expression in communities led by working-class white Southern women because they possess the cultural authenticity of the white South without any inherited moral taint. The melodramatic qualities of a landscape that revolves around white, Southern, working-class female characters are used to suggest that their values are the ones that must be resurrected in order to confront contemporary social inequalities. Instead of attributing such inequalities to individual weakness, as pure conservatism does, this worldview acknowledges systemic discrimination and the articulation of civil rights. It then proposes to solve these problems by employing values that are often associated with the South, particularly resilience in the face of adversity, independence from institutions, a sense of community beyond the nuclear family, and an attachment to place.

Norma Rae is from the beginning portrayed as a "feisty" woman — only her feistiness is initially channeled towards sexual promiscuity. Once she is introduced to the ideals of the union, her natural fighting instincts kick in, and she urges those around her, who are portrayed as more meek and fearful, to stand up for themselves. Norma Rae's best remembered action is a literal enactment of standing up: she stops working and stands on a machine holding a sign that simply says "union." The camera tracks around her in a circle from a low angle and emphasizes her refusal to move, though the mill bosses are trying to throw her out. Here, her height and stasis represents the strength that comes from staying in place; the potentially disempowering quality of immobility is turned on its head to instead signify the power of having roots.

One reason *Norma Rae* appears to have been so popular despite its social realist subject matter is its ability to make its Southern landscape and protagonist seem both Southern and American at the same time — that is, both relatable to a national audience and distinctive at a time when whites were searching for a cultural identity (Jacobson; Frankenberg; Newitz and Wray 172–176). The intimate details with which the film renders Norma Rae's milieu (extended scenes of her taking care of her children, her work at the factory and at home, and her gradually unfolding romance with a fellow factory worker) makes her cultural landscape familiar and universal to diverse viewers; thus, they can identify her behavior and values as typically American. As one professional reviewer wrote, "*Norma Rae* is real people with real faces... You come out saying 'I know that woman.' And if you don't, you wish you did" (O'Toole 51). The spectator's locus of identification is grounded with her when Reuben enters the Southern town, the opposite of *Mississippi Burning*'s use of the outsider-traveling-in narrative.

For instance, the camera is inside Norma's house when Reuben, a union organizer from New York, knocks on the door. So the audience sees him through the window just as Norma and her family do. We know only what they know about him; thus we are both spatially positioned to view him from the family's point of view, and we share their range of knowledge. Further, Reuben only slowly becomes a casual agent of the plot — for a while after he arrives, Norma's life goes on unchanged. The slow buildup to the organizing campaign and the fact that the audience only sees Reuben when Norma does ensure that spectatorial alignment stays with Norma and her community. By seeing Norma's private life but not Reuben's, the spectator knows how much Reuben is missing and has much greater insight into Norma's psyche and motivations — including the important intra-community conflict between Norma and her family and neighbors, who disapprove of her organizing. This information has the function of increasing sympathy with Norma, highlighting the obstacles she has to overcome in order to become the victim-hero, and putting the film's agency more fully in her corner.

At the same time, Norma's distinctive culture is marked in opposition to Reuben's; as she tells him, he is "like a fish out of water down here." In one sequence, he falls in cow dung, cuts himself whittling a stick, and proves ignorant of how to change a tire. He must repeatedly get Norma to show him the ways of the community in order to successfully relate to the people he is trying to organize. Norma even takes to calling him "New York," a nickname that reflects how significant his geographical outside-ness is to the film's discourse; Reuben is importantly also Jewish. (*The Prince of Tides* also uses a New York Jewish character to show the most culturally opposite "white" character possible to the rural white Southerner.) So while reviewers described the film with phrases like "a superb look at American life" (Pollack 20) and "Miss Field has a quality of Americanness that pervades the film" (Gilliatt 128), the film is also very distinctively regional. How do we understand this contradiction? Norma is in fact using traits that are categorized as Southern to fulfill American ideals. Norma's stubbornness, her digging in her heels to bring about change from within her home-place, the way she has no need to shed her culture in order to learn about union organizing — these traits all point to her faith in her small-town, working-class, white roots. Further pursuing Norma's overlapping cultural identities, Vincent Canby in the *New York Times* attributed the film's success to Norma's embodiment of "much of what we like to think is best about our national character... her relationship with Reuben... represents the happiest kind of conjunction of different American cultures" (24), thus linking multiculturalism with American values.

Canby notices this intercultural bonding through her relationship with Reuben, but the film also emphasizes Norma's insistence on including African American mill workers in the union. When the local church where Norma plans to hold a union meeting refuses to allow blacks, she questions its status as a "house of God" and moves the meeting to her own home. Her husband then protests, and Norma counters that she has never had any trouble with black men, only with white men. Norma's liberal-ness is presented as common sense, rooted in day-to-day interactions instead of abstract, radical ideals.

Norma Rae (Sally Field, right) and Reuben (Ron Leibman, center) organize a biracial union in *Norma Rae* (1979, 20th Century–Fox): a coalition of different ethnicities and geographies empowers the marginalized.

Thus she is an acceptable figure to viewers who think of themselves as moderate and not radical—even though the multiracial coalition she is building is a significant challenge to the power structure. She uses this strength in order to bring about greater democracy in her town via union organizing and to bring together white and black workers, learning from a New York Jew. This is the discourse of multiculturalism as a particularly American strength—one with which different cultures can enhance rather than threaten democracy.

Spaces of Multicultural Innocence

The multiculturalist ethos of the 1980s and early 1990s is projected historically onto the 1930s in *Fried Green Tomatoes* to suggest how female victim-heroes could have used their moral authority to triumph over prejudice even in a pre-multicultural age. Unlike pre–civil rights era romanticizations of the antebellum South or the light-hearted all-white settings of *Smokey and the Bandit* and *Steel Magnolias*, *Fried Green Tomatoes* romanticizes the South not by denying its oppressive qualities, but by modeling insider characters that fight against those qualities. This optimism led some professional reviewers to call it overly sentimental, but it is why many ordinary viewers loved it. Industry insiders and observers suggested that the film struck a chord with viewers, who saw in it examples of friendship and community that felt deeper than what they had in their own lives. Producer Norman Lear reported: "I'm getting mail and calls and the message is always the same: In this very alienated time, it's invoking the longing for friendships and connections" (Fox F1). A *New York Times* essayist was told by acquaintances that they appreciated the film's demonstration of people who are willing to "take chances for each other" (Brown, "Why Audiences Hunger" H22).

The film constructs Idgie and Ruth as exemplary human beings who create an alternative space within the South by binding together individuals who represent different marginalized populations. While Idgie rebels against Southern gender roles on her own behalf, she rebels against racial and class oppression on behalf of those around her. As a young woman, she takes Ruth onto a train from which she tosses food out to poor families as they pass by. Ruth is scandalized by what she perceives as stealing, but Idgie retorts that such behavior exemplifies true Christianity (and here is another example of the racial transference of moral authority I have been observing, as in the source novel it was an African American man who threw the food off the train [Willett 116]). As the film cuts to close-ups of the grateful faces of black and white children, it positions the spectator as an observer of inequality, alongside the empowered heroines, who are part of this landscape but also above it. On the train, Idgie and Ruth are spatially higher, looking down at people on the ground, and they are in motion in contrast to the families' stasis, symbolic of their roles as active heroines to the victims' passivity.

Idgie's role as champion of the underclass continues when she and Ruth open their restaurant, at which they serve African Americans despite threats from law enforcement and eventually the Klan, and Idgie makes sure to feed and care for a white alcoholic hobo. Her insistence that African Americans are part of the community is similar to Norma Rae's inclusion of African American workers in the union. Throughout her life, Idgie is consistently identified with Sipsey and Big George, her family's African American servants — as a teenager she goes to stay in their cabin when she wants to escape her family, and later they work by her side at the restaurant. Sipsey and Big George's devotion to her and Ruth is emphasized repeatedly through their defense of the women against Ruth's abusive husband and close-ups of them crying at Ruth's death, among other moments. So, with Ruth like the victimized Mrs. Pell in *Mississippi Burning* and Idgie like the empowered Norma Rae, the Southern female victim-hero continues to be associated with the moral virtue of helping African Americans and the impoverished, all while

Idgie (Mary Stuart Masterson) and Big George (Stan Shaw) work together to cover up the murder of Ruth's abusive ex-husband in *Fried Green Tomatoes* (1991, Universal): African Americans come to the aid of victimized white women in the South.

her suffering is more individualized than theirs. The lower middle-class white man again represents Southern evil. His opposite, the ordinary white woman, becomes the moral center of a landscape that would otherwise be viewed with suspicion and disdain.

While contemporary commentators understood the film's cultural politics in terms of its feminism, when we read the film through the lens of cinematic geography, we see how it also heralds the positive qualities of staying in place — attachment to place being one value commonly attributed to the South. If one result of multiculturalist discourse was that whites began to feel they had no culture — as Annalee Newitz and Matthew Wray put it: "whiteness has suddenly come to seem like the only identity not associated with a rich and specific historical tradition or like some type of separatist space sanctioned as authentically white" (172–3) — then *Norma Rae* and *Fried Green Tomatoes* are examples of the way films of this era offer portraits of the South as a place where whites possess a strong sense of identity and community that is not tainted by Jim Crow or racist brutality. These alternative communities where people from different backgrounds can bond are importantly created as oases *within* the South and do not require departure from it.

These communities also exhibit popular multiculturalism's faith in personal interaction as a way to heal social division. Viewers of *Fried Green Tomatoes*, in particular, are offered the chance to identify with Southern characters who rebel against their own oppressive cultural landscape, thereby offering a spectatorial experience of moral fantasizing. The characters' actions were perceived as *"learnable"* (Brown, "Why Audiences Hunger" H22) to modern viewers; the overtly didactic discourse is created through the film's story-within-a-story, in which the elderly Ninny tells the stories of Ruth and Idgie to suburban housewife Evelyn. Evelyn's character functions as a stand-in for the modern spectator; while she lives geographically in the South, she could live anywhere in the US, for this is the new "Sunbelt" South, full of the same office parks and suburban sprawl as the rest of the country. It is a South that has lost its quintessential (mythological) Southernness. As the modern-day Southern woman, Evelyn is portrayed as a generic American housewife who attends self-help classes, is fixated on junk food because of the emptiness in her life, and lives in a cookie-cutter subdivision — details meant to connect her to a majority of female viewers.

Toward the film's end, Ninny takes Evelyn to an African American gospel church service, where the elderly woman nods her head to the music, looking entirely at home. It is new territory to Evelyn, who looks around uncomfortably as they walk in, but eventually relaxes and connects to the experience. This moment marks her completed transformation into a modern version of Ruth, whom the Idgie/Ninny figure has guided into an understanding of the true, moral South. The church is a joyous locale that combines roots and religion, representing a culture more authentic than the modern Southern suburban one in which Evelyn actually lives. So in addition to connecting Evelyn to the traditional victims of the Southern landscape (African Americans), the scene also gives Evelyn a cultural place, something the film codes as more "real" than the "no-place" where she has been living a consumption-heavy generic American life with her husband. Her healing by finding roots in the authentic and compassionate multicultural South can be seen as a metaphor for the contemporary white spectator finding a symbolic ethnic identity and moral center in a cinematic white South.

Both the restaurant and the church of *Fried Green Tomatoes* are more complex versions of melodrama's spaces of innocence. In traditional melodramas, the space of innocence is the nexus of time and place that represents the way things are supposed to be, before the impending threat, and to which the hero and victim return after defeating the villain, thus giving the melodramatic narrative a cyclical pattern and conservative function of returning things to a prior, idealized past (Brooks; Williams). A socially conscious, post-sixties melodrama like *Fried Green Tomatoes* does not employ the concept so purely: Idgie and Ruth can never regain the innocence they lost through the suffering inflicted by the Southern patriarchal system. That suffering is represented by Southern homes, both the upper-class manor of Idgie's youth and the humble rural home of Ruth's married life; thus the film critiques both dwellings that symbolize the Janus-faced demons of the South: the plantation system and the "white trash" lifestyle. Both homes are then doubly burdened with the sins of white patriarchy and racism. Instead of restoring those forever-tarnished spaces of innocence, Idgie and Ruth create their own utopian space in the form of the Whistlestop Café, where two women can have an unconventional relationship and welcome in African Americans. In the film's contemporary time, this space of interracial friendship is briefly echoed in the church scene.

Conclusion

The South of *Norma Rae* and *Fried Green Tomatoes* offers an imagined white, woman-centered landscape that feels more specific than the generalized white culture of America and recuperates the South through melodramatic narratives of victimization, updated for the post-sixties era through the politically-moderate discourse of white multiculturalism. *Norma Rae* stands as a transitional film at the end of the era of the comic male redneck anti-authority hero and moves cinematic imagery of the South towards the socially conscious and woman-centered. It must also be recognized that it lies further on the social realist end of the spectrum than most similar films that followed. *Fried Green Tomatoes* came at the end of a cluster of films in the late 1980s that sought in the South a remedy against 1980s white malaise. As a *New York Times* essayist wrote, speculating about the spate of popular Southern films from 1988–90, "It's no surprise that we would turn to this geographically identifiable territory that seems, as we all tumble together in the relentless blender of American culture, to have kept its own texture and flavor more than most" (Brown, "Why, in the Movies" H22). Such films offered a specifically geographical remedy, for this particular gendered, regional identity could function as a cultural category with the moral currency to (apparently) stand amongst people of color. The South became a cinematic destination where white viewers of other places could imaginatively travel to experience a simplicity that was authentic and moral, not regressive, that opposed northeastern "urban elitism" and "suburban blandness" in its sense of roots and community.

All three films, to differing degrees, distill social problems into Manichean binaries within the South and provide spectatorial pleasure at witnessing particular native Southern values employed to defeat evil. Independence from institutions, the bonds of community (especially one of "misfits"), a strong sense of place and history, and even Christianity (not often referenced in mainstream Hollywood films) are proposed as the ways that social injustice can be defeated in America, making the South a moral exemplar for multicultural America. The films therefore give the South a prominent place in a moderate-liberal worldview that was developing as an alternative to the post-sixties white backlash. Through the sympathetic female victim-hero, the spectator is encouraged to identify with an insider to Southern culture, and thus feel it is familiar; yet the culture retains a sense of particularity that secures its place in multicultural America, where moral authority is awarded to groups of people that have distinct customs and histories.

In these films, the woman-centered community becomes the new Southern space of innocence. It is not innocence in the sense of lack of knowledge of sin, but in the lack of guilt — for these are women who have experienced suffering, and to varying degrees, are flawed, real individuals themselves. But they are foremost victims of a white patriarchal system, and through their victimhood, they have earned the moral credentials to separate them from any of the blemishes that tarnish other popular imagery of the white South. Then, they have risen above their victim status to become leaders of a community that includes African Americans and other marginalized people, those white poor who are even more disenfranchised than themselves. They carve out utopian places that, in the 1980s, served to redeem a previously condemned or mocked landscape. These imagined places seduced viewers from throughout America with a vision of a place that both holds onto its roots and accepts others, is white-centered and yet morally-authoritative for a multicultural age.

Notes

1. See Graham; Kirby; Cawelti, "'That's What I Like About the South.'" "Redneck and car" movies include *Thunder Road* (1958) (the forerunner of the genre), *White Lightning* (1973) and its sequel *Gator* (1976), *The Last American Hero* (1973), *Dirty Mary Crazy Larry* (1974), *W.W. and the Dixie Dancekings* (1975), *Smokey and the Bandit* (1977) and its two sequels in 1980 and 1983, *Thunder and Lightning* (1977) and the TV show *The Dukes of Hazzard* (1979-85).

2. "Cultural landscape" refers to the combination of a physical setting and its inhabitants as a social group, as well as implying an awareness of representation: that there is an inextricable combination of a real place that is experienced and the image of it held either by insiders or outsiders. See W. J. T. Mitchell and D. Mitchell.

3. Popularity can be assessed through a combination in box office rankings, Academy Award nominations, and the amount of "buzz" in popular media. Ranking within the top 50 out of the hundreds of films released per year can be considered relatively popular for "social issue" films that must compete with the sorts of films that usually top the charts: action films, comedies, and children's films. The years 1988-1991 were prominent ones for Southern films: *Driving Miss Daisy* was number nine in domestic grossers released in 1989 and *Steel Magnolias* was 14th ("Worldwide Box Office"). While *Steel Magnolias* was largely

dismissed by the critics, *Driving Miss Daisy* was a critical hit as well, scoring Oscar wins for Best Picture, Best Adapted Screenplay, Best Actress, as well as five other nominations (Academy of Motion Picture Arts and Sciences). *Mississippi Burning*, released in December 1988, ranked 40th on *Variety*'s 1989 domestic box office rankings ("Big Rental Films of 1989" 24) and now ranks 33rd among movies released in 1988 ("Worldwide Box Office"). *Mississippi Burning* was nominated for Best Director, Best Picture, Best Actor, Best Supporting Actress, Best Editing, and Best Sound, and it won for Best Cinematography ("The Official Academy Awards Database"). It also generated an unusual amount of discussion in the popular press. The *New York Times* editorial pages hosted a lively debate about its historical distortions and lack of African American characters (Staples 1; Zellner A30; Steele H3; Nelson H3). *Fried Green Tomatoes* was 14th in 1992's box office rankings ("Top Rental Films for 1992" 22) and received Oscar nominations for Best Adapted Screenplay and Best Supporting Actress (Academy of Motion Picture Arts and Sciences). The film started out with a limited release, classified as a "little film," but picked up steam through word of mouth (Fox F1; King B1). Going back a decade, *Norma Rae*, 53rd in box office receipts in 1979 ("Big Rental Films of 1979" 21), was successful as a modest-budgeted social problem film that made more money than expected and garnered Academy Award nominations for Best Picture and Best Adapted Screenplay, and a Best Actress Award for Field (Academy of Motion Picture Arts and Sciences). It led to the very popular *Coal Miner's Daughter* (sixth highest grossing in 1980 ["Big Rental Films of 1980" 29]), which told the life story of country singer Loretta Lynn, *Places in the Heart* (1984), the most popular of three "farm films" in 1984-5 and also starring Sally Field, and another country music biopic *Sweet Dreams* (1985). While *Coal Miner's Daughter* was a greater box office success, I have chosen *Norma Rae* for in-depth analysis because it paved the way for a spate of films about working-class white Southern women and because of the central role of actress Sally Field in creating a Southern female character for the nation.

4. For examples other than those I discuss here, see the country singers from humble backgrounds in *Coal Miner's Daughter* (1980) and *Sweet Dreams* (1985), the poor widow struggling to keep her farm afloat in *Places in the Heart* (1984), and the female lawyer in *The Client* (1994) whose low-status is signaled by her tiny office and her colleague's condescension towards her practice of family law.

5. The term is similar to that Hudson uses in talking about recent vampire films in which a few people of color are present amongst white performers; the "good" ones behave like whites while the "bad" ones represent racial otherness. However, my emphasis is more on whiteness being given a "culture" that has enough ethnographic interest to make it worthy of being placed side by side with those cultures that have been historically exoticized, usually because they are non-white.

Works Cited

Ames, Christopher. "Restoring the Black Man's Lethal Weapon: Race and Sexuality in Contemporary Cop Films." *Journal of Popular Film and Television* 20.3 (Fall 1992): 52-60.
"Big Rental Films of 1979." *Variety* 9 Jan. 1980: 21.
"Big Rental Films of 1980." *Variety* 14 Jan. 1981: 29.
"Big Rental Films of 1989." *Variety* 24 Jan. 1990: 24.
Brooks, Peter. *The Melodramatic Imagination: Balzac, Henry James, Melodrama, and the Mode of Excess*. New Haven: Yale University Press, 1976.
Brown, Rosellen. "Why Audiences Hunger for 'Fried Green Tomatoes.'" *New York Times* 19 Apr. 1992: H22.

———. "Why, in the Movies, the South Rises Again." *New York Times* 11 Feb. 1990: H22.
Canby, Vincent. "Sally Field's 'Norma Rae' Is a Triumph." *New York Times* 11 Mar. 1979: D19, 24.
Cawelti, John. "Searching for Scarlett: The Quest for Southern Identity in the 1980s and 90s." *Studies in Popular Culture* 19.2 (Oct. 1996): 91-104.
———. "'That's What I Like About the South:' Changing Images of the South in the 1970s." *The Lost Decade: America in the Seventies.* Ed. Elsebeth Hurup. Aarhus, Denmark: Aarhus University Press, 1996. 11-40.
Clover, Carol. *Men, Women, and Chain Saws: Gender in the Modern Horror Film.* Princeton: Princeton University Press, 1993.
Fox, David J. "'Green Tomatoes': Why a Little Film Bloomed." *Los Angeles Times* 10 Feb. 1992: F1.
Frankenberg, Ruth. *White Women, Race Matters: The Social Construction of Whiteness.* Minneapolis: University of Minnesota Press, 1993.
Fried Green Tomatoes. Dir. Jon Avnet. Perf. Kathy Bates, Mary Stuart Masterson, Mary-Louise Parker, and Jessica Tandy. Universal Pictures, 1991. Film.
Gilliatt, Penelope. "The Current Cinema." *New Yorker* 19 Mar. 1979: 126-8.
Gledhill, Christine. "The Melodramatic Field: An Investigation." *Home is Where the Heart is: Studies in Melodrama and the Woman's Film.* Ed. Christine Gledhill. London: BFI, 1987. 5-39.
Graham, Allison. *Framing the South: Hollywood, Television, and Race During the Civil Rights Struggle.* Baltimore: Johns Hopkins University Press, 2001.
Guerrero, Ed. *Framing Blackness: the African American Image in Film.* Philadelphia: Temple University Press, 1993.
Hudson, Dale. "Vampires of Color and the Performance of Multicultural Whiteness." *The Persistence of Whiteness: Race and Contemporary Hollywood Cinema.* Ed. Daniel Bernardi. London: Routledge, 2008. 127-156.
Jacobson, Matthew Frye. *Roots Too: White Ethnic Revival in Post-Civil Rights America.* Cambridge: Harvard University Press, 2006.
Jenkins, Philip. *Decade of Nightmares: The End of the Sixties and the Making of Eighties America.* Oxford: Oxford University Press, 2006.
Jordan, Chris. *Movies and the Reagan Presidency.* Westport, CT: Praeger, 2003.
Kempley, Rita. "'Burning': Potent but Problematic." *The Washington Post* 9 Dec. 1988: C1.
King, Thomas R. "Little Film Shifts Its Aim to Big Audience." *Wall Street Journal* 31 Jan. 1992: B1.
Kirby, Jack Temple. *Media-Made Dixie: The South in the American Imagination.* Baton Rouge: Louisiana State University Press, 1986.
Lowe, Lisa. "Imagining Los Angeles in the Production of Multiculturalism." *Mapping Multiculturalism.* Ed. Avery F. Gordon and Christopher Newfield. Minneapolis: University of Minnesota Press, 1996. 413-23.
Mississippi Burning. Dir. Alan Parker. Perf. Gene Hackman, Willem Dafoe, and Frances McDormand. Orion Pictures, 1988. Film.
Mitchell, Don. *Cultural Geography.* Oxford: Blackwell, 2000.
Mitchell, W. J. T. "Imperial Landscape." *Landscape and Power.* Ed. W. J. T. Mitchell. Chicago: University of Chicago Press, 2002. 5-34.
Nelson, George. Letter. "After Silence, Too Much Noise." *New York Times* 22 Jan. 1989: H3.
Newfield, Christopher, and Avery F. Gordon. "Multiculturalism's Unfinished Business." *Mapping Multiculturalism.* Ed. Avery F. Gordon and Christopher Newfield. Minneapolis: University of Minnesota Press, 1996. 76-115.
Newitz, Annalee, and Matthew Wray. "What is 'White Trash'? Stereotypes and Economic

Conditions of Poor Whites in the United States." *Whiteness: A Critical Reader*. Ed. Mike Hill. New York: New York University Press, 1997. 168-186.
Official Academy Awards Database. Academy of Motion Picture Arts and Sciences. Web. 11 Jan. 2010.
O'Toole, Lawrence. "A Working-Class Woman is Something to See." *Maclean's* 5 Mar. 1979: 51.
Pollack, D. "Norma Rae." *Variety* 28 Feb. 1979: 20.
Singh, Nikhil Pal. "Culture/Wars: Recoding Empire in an Age of Democracy." *American Quarterly* 50.3 (1998): 471-522.
Staples, Brent. "Cinematic Segregation in a Story About Civil Rights." *New York Times* 8 Jan. 1989: Section 2, 1.
Steel Magnolias. Dir. Herbert Ross. Perf. Sally Field, Dolly Parton, and Julia Roberts. TriStar Pictures, 1989. Film.
Steele, Pamela. Letter. "Blacks and the Box Office." *New York Times* 5 Feb. 1989: H3.
Taylor, Helen. *Scarlett's Women: Gone With the Wind and Its Female Fans*. New Brunswick: Rutgers University Press, 1989.
"Top Rental Films for 1992." *Variety* 11 Jan. 1993: 22.
Willett, Ralph. "Dixie's Land: Cinema of the American South." *American Film and Politics from Reagan to Bush Jr.* Ed. Philip John Davies and Paul Wells. Manchester: Manchester University Press, 2002. 105-120.
Williams, Linda. *Playing the Race Card: Melodramas of Black and White from Uncle Tom to O. J. Simpson*. Princeton: Princeton University Press, 2001.
Willis, Sharon. *High Contrast: Race and Gender in Contemporary Hollywood Film*. Durham: Duke University Press, 1997.
Worldwide Box Office. Web. 11 Jan. 2010.
Zellner, Dorothy M. Letter. "F.B.I. is a Strange Hero for 'Mississippi Burning.'" *New York Times* 13 Jan. 1989: A30.

II.

You're Only as Good as Your Last Game: *Remember the Titans* Remembers Civil Rights

OLIVER GRUNER

"Alexandrians have been mightily celebrating this week's opening of the film *Remember the Titans*," reported the *Washington Times*: "Galas, rallies and fund raisers culminated in Mayor Kerry Donley declaring today [September 29, 2000] as 'Remember the Titans Day'" (Washington C2). A grand accolade indeed, but perhaps such civic pride was understandable given the film's subject matter. Director Boaz Yakin's *Remember the Titans* (2000) had immortalised the city of Alexandria, Virginia, in an uplifting tale of triumph over adversity, and it was all based on a true story. Set in 1971, against the backdrop of federal government sponsored civil rights legislation — affirmative action policies and the desegregation program of public school "busing"— *Titans* chronicles how a successful championship football season helped assuage the racial conflicts ignited by these forced integration programs.

This essay locates *Remember the Titans* within a broader political and popular culture that had, throughout the 1980s and the 1990s, frequently revisited or "remembered" the struggle for civil rights in the U.S. South. Providing a close textual analysis, I argue that *Titans* offered a challenge to popular representations of the civil rights movement that had appeared throughout the 1980s and 1990s. Since the mid–1980s, the civil rights movement of the 1950s and 1960s has gained a prominent place in public memory (Marcus; Monteith 120–143; Hall 1233–1263; Romano and Raiford). Politicians, filmmakers and journalists have returned to and commemorated this era. The focus of this remembrance has, however, tended to be the early years, roughly 1954–65, rightly celebrated as a time when civil rights movements fought to overturn government sanctioned segregation and discrimination. *Titans* moves beyond these years to an era that has been the subject of less positive commemoration. The period from the mid–1960s to the mid–1970s has been negatively associated, particularly by conservative commentators, with riots in northern cities, the emergence of radical groups such as the Black Panthers and "unfair" government sponsored civil rights quota systems and legislations.

I argue that *Titans* transposes the "spirit" of early Southern civil rights remembrance onto an arguably far more controversial period in American history. The film, I suggest, depicts the struggle for civil rights in the South as an ongoing process, one which is not isolated to a single narrow historical epoch. Furthermore, this struggle is shown to require the active involvement of both African American and white characters, and thus avoids the singular tales of "white redemption" that are said to have been common to the "civil rights cinema" of the 1980s and 1990s (Monteith 137). I conclude with reference to a range of reception materials, which highlight the manner in which *Titans* offered a lesson in cross-racial cooperation that resonated in the public sphere.

Hollywood and the Civil Rights Movement

Issues pertaining to the Southern civil rights movement have been explored in the visual media since the 1950s. Allison Graham charts the "framing of the South" in film and television through the 1950s and 1960s. Examining a range of representations of Southern race relations and civil rights, from television news coverage to cinematic productions such as *To Kill a Mockingbird* (1962) and *In the Heat of the Night* (1967), Graham identifies several themes and characterizations that were featured consistently in the visual media at this time and which continue to inflect more contemporaneous revisiting of the movement. Firstly, the South is constructed as "an arena of white — not black — heroism." Secondly, white society is often split simplistically between "good" characters who are either pro–civil rights to begin with, or whose racism will evaporate by the film's conclusion, and evil, ignorant, racist, (usually) working class "redneck" or "cracker" Southerners. Thirdly, many of the fictional representations contain narratives that focus upon white characters as opposed to exploring seriously African American participation in the freedom struggle (Graham 13–17).

Borrowing heavily from these earlier representations, films of the late 1980s have nevertheless been suggested to mark a historically distinct period in Hollywood's representation of the civil rights movement. Sharon Monteith argues that films such as *Mississippi Burning* (1988), *Heart of Dixie* (1989) and

The Long Walk Home (1990) constitute an emerging "sub-genre" that she calls "civil rights cinema." While 1960s and 1970s films may have referenced civil rights, it was during the late 1980s that a group of high-profile films self-consciously commemorated key events and personages of the late 1950s and 1960s civil rights movement: the Montgomery bus boycott (*Long Walk Home*), the Mississippi Freedom Summer (*Mississippi Burning*) and the integration of southern universities (*Heart of Dixie*), for example (Monteith 121; Graham 148). Appearing just after the establishment of Martin Luther King Day as a public holiday in 1986 and the successful documentary series on civil rights *Eyes on the Prize* in 1987, these films intersected with an explosion of public memorials of the movement. By the time that *Remember the Titans* had reached cinema screens in late 2000, popular 1980s and 1990s representations had consecrated a very particular narrative of the civil rights movement, one defined by a set of prominent motifs and iconography.

Civil rights commemoration was part of a broader revisiting of this period of American history (the 1960s) that was taking place in politics and culture during the 1980s and 1990s (Marcus). As Daniel Marcus has demonstrated, Sixties[1] commemoration was more than mere nostalgia. The very term "the Sixties" became a discursive battleground, an appellative armory loaded with political significance (2–4). In terms of civil rights commemoration, it led to a distinct periodizing of the movement that celebrated what has been termed its "classical" phase in the U.S. South (roughly 1954–1965) while simultaneously demonizing, or at least forgetting, the continued struggle that took place in the southern and *northern* states during the late 1960s and into the early 1970s (Hall 1234).

By the mid–1990s, museums dedicated to the movement proliferated across the South. The *New York Times* provided the following account of Memphis's National Civil Rights Museum which was built in 1991: "As visitors wend their way down a chronological path through the movement, walking past the burned-out hull of a freedom riders bus ... many are moved to tears as they come upon the culmination of the tour and, in the minds of many, the movement itself" (Sack TR12). The climax of the tour is the assassination of Martin Luther King. In 2000, proposals to immortalise King with a gigantic "stone of hope" statue in Washington's National Mall were received (Molotsky A24). Easily the most celebrated of civil rights figures, King was ever-present in political and cultural representations of the 1980s and 1990s. Memory of the civil rights leader provides an entrance point into the discrepancies that existed between memories of the 1950s and early 1960s movement and those of the later 1960s and early 1970s. As several historians point out, King in public memory "is a perennial dreamer frozen in time at his most famous address [the "I have a dream" speech] during the 1963 March on Washington"

(Lawson 460). The later Martin Luther King has been largely forgotten in popular memorialization. Jacquelyn Dowd Hall notes the erasure of "the King who attacked segregation in the urban North ... who opposed the Vietnam War and linked racism at home to militarism and imperialism abroad ... [and] who advocated unionization, planned the Poor People's Campaign, and was assassinated in 1968 while supporting a sanitation workers' strike" (1234). King's evolving politics and philosophies were forgotten; his anti-war beliefs, his activism on behalf of poor people in northern cities and his turn from attacking government sanctioned segregation to de facto economic segregation were all lost. This selective remembering of the civil rights leader runs hand in hand with a selective remembering of the movement itself. It confines the civil rights struggle to the South. Economic segregation in the North — which King and the movement fought throughout the 1960s — does not receive the same amount of attention. As a result, the South is depicted as the "nation's 'opposite other,'" and ignores the "patterns of exploitation, segregation, and discrimination in other regions of the country" (Hall 1239).

Titans is significant for the very reason that it appears after a long line of civil rights films that had played a central role in promulgating this "declension" version of history. In many ways it offers an alternative to late 1980s and 1990s films such as *Mississippi Burning, Heart of Dixie, The Long Walk Home, Love Field* (1992), and *Ghosts of Mississippi* (1996). These earlier films were set in the early 1960s (*Burning, Dixie, Long Walk*) or looked back to this historical period (*Ghosts*). With their evil rednecks and noble white protagonists these films tend, as Monteith notes, to foreground the white characters, their journeys from ignorance to activism and, the shedding of prejudice in favor of tolerance. They are "stories set in the 'bad old days'"; films in which "morally charged action heroes succeed against evil racists by deploying the requisite quotient of violence" (137). By focusing on the pre–Civil Rights Act and pre–Voting Rights Act South, they commemorate much positive activism and heroic action in the name of equality, but they also seem to be beholden to the message "look how far we've come." In true 1940s social problem film style,[2] the films confine their "illness" (racism) within a fixed geographic area, in this case the South. With the problem identified and isolated it can then be dealt with or cured. The struggle for civil rights beyond the early 1960s is therefore rendered unnecessary or ineffectual.

Titans, on the other hand, re-imagines civil rights as an ongoing battle. It uses a Southern setting and much of the iconography of "civil rights cinema" as a backdrop against which it promotes a temporally and spatially extended civil rights narrative. Touchstones of popular representations — Martin Luther King, white on black violence, racism and integration — are combined with issues of the late 1960s and 1970s and in particular government sponsored civil rights legislations such as affirmative action and busing. This thematic content is incorporated into a formal framework that allows the film to reshape the boundaries of civil rights remembrance and, at times, to provide an interpretation of these issues that transcends regional, Southern, specificity. Rather than being America's "opposite other"—a racist backwater in which prejudice is contained and resolved—*Titans*' Southern setting might almost be seen as a synecdoche for the nation. The issues explored in the film are not regionally but nationally resonant, and of relevance to the present as much as to the past.

Titans Frames the Civil Rights South

In a contemporaneous review of *Titans*, *Washington Post* journalist Stephen Hunter complained that the film's "chief failing is its reinvention of that city [Alexandria], a sophisticated, multicultural suburb with an actual French restaurant or two, as a small, isolated Southern town somewhere between Selma, Ala., and Meridian, Miss." (Hunter C1). Quite how "multicultural"—in terms of positive race relations—the city was at this time was disputed by others ("Remembering" A21). Nevertheless, it is true that the filmmakers went to great lengths to remake a suburb of Washington, DC in the image of a Deep South enclave or, at least, a Deep South enclave as it has been commonly represented in civil rights cinema, for many of the stock characters and motifs that were present in *Mississippi Burning* and its contemporaries find their way into *Titans*: the rednecks, the white on black violence, the desperate attempts (on the part of some) to protect an archaic, unequal way of life. Yet the manner in which this material is mediated receives a new spin. Visuals, dialog, editing and cinematography contribute to the overriding tone of the film's political and historical representation. *Titans* does not seek to tell a white redemption tale, nor does it attempt to leave racism and racial discord in the distant past. Progress is not linear, but comes about through negotiation of conflict. Every political statement has its counter-statement; every perspective its opposite; every scene its double.

Titans begins in 1981. A funeral is in progress. A procession of smartly clad black and white characters makes its way to the cemetery. It is fall and reddish leaves flutter from trees, scattering on the ground. A voiceover begins: "In Virginia, high-school football is a way of life: it's bigger than Christmas Day ... Up until 1971 in Alexandria, there was no race mixing." The characters gather together—blacks and whites, men and women, side by side. Next appears the film's title, "Remember the Titans," suggesting, at this early stage, that the "Titans" are everyone present at this funeral. The integrated society is the Titans as emphasized by the voiceover: "Then the school board forced us to integrate ... the city was on the verge of exploding."

The film then flashes back to the summer of 1971. Autumnal mellowness is replaced by intense summer conflict. This emphasis upon seasons is the first of many devices used throughout that promote history as a cyclical process rather than a linear narrative. The juxtaposing of fall and summer offers a means to transcend chronology and view the fight for equality as an endless struggle, seasonal rather than linear. A crowd of blacks stand shouting and waving placards. A slow pan reveals a police car, on the other side of which stand a group of whites shouting abuse. This sequence is a stark contrast to the previous scene of racial harmony; it re-segregates blacks and whites, igniting the battle that will be the film's central concern throughout. Racial conflict is then explicitly associated with what will become eventually its palliative — football. An object thrown through a shop window instigates a cut. The next image on screen is a close-up of a football helmet. The visual link is obvious: battles on the streets will become battles on the sports field.

Football serves as the crucible within which social and political ruptures are reconciled. This places *Titans* in a long line of films that use sports to mediate broader public concerns. Indeed, the sports film, and sporting activity in general, has long been associated with pressing political, social and cultural exigencies. According to the historian Harvey Green, the post–American Civil War era saw sports such as baseball and, especially, football adopted by top colleges in the hope that, as well as improving a young man's fitness level they would promote "the desire and will to win." Green contends that "winning was a critically important result in the preparation of the social, economic, and political leaders of the new age." Success on the sports field was preparation for success in the modern age, i.e. the 20th century. Thus did "sports and culture become more and more intertwined" (Green 204, 208).

It is also worth considering the close and turbulent relationship between football and the civil rights movement. Events in Alexandria were not a unique phenomenon. Throughout the 1960s and 1970s the sport was inextricably linked to broader political exigencies such as Southern race relations and, in particular, desegregation. College football in the South was largely segregated until the 1960s when — facing enormous amounts of physical and verbal intimidation — a small number of black players turned out for previously all-white teams (Wolff). It has since been argued that the demonstrated abilities and courage of these players helped in no small part to bring about a change in Southern racial mores, leading to a rapid desegregation of football teams throughout the region. Those colleges that fielded black players tended to be far more successful than their all-white counterparts. Not only did a winning streak temper the furious criticisms of local whites angry at their team's deseg-

Coach Boone (Denzel Washington) integrates and inspires the team in Disney's *Remember the Titans* (2000, Disney Enterprises; credit Tracy Bennett).

regation, it also encouraged others to follow suit. Jerry Claiborne, assistant to the legendary coach Paul "Bear" Bryant, at the University of Alabama, has claimed that losing to a desegregated team pushed Alabama toward integration. According to Claiborne, Sam Cunningham, a black fullback for the University of Southern California who helped them destroy Alabama 42–21 in 1970, "did more to integrate Alabama in 60 minutes than Martin Luther King had done in 20 years" (Harwell). A bold statement, perhaps, but there is nevertheless a general consensus that sports, and in particular football, helped win hearts and minds during the civil rights struggles of this era.

It is no coincidence, then, that the "sports film," as Aaron Baker argues, has consistently offered an ideal forum for the overcoming of obstacles and resolution of conflicts: "once the contest begins, success depends primarily on one's determination and effort." He does, however, state that individual achievement is privileged over communal action and social unity. In this sense "the team operates as a social structure to foster the development of self-reliant individuals" (12). Since the silent era, contends Baker, the sports film has played a part in promoting normative versions of masculinity, white racial superiority and the mythic American Dream whereby individualism, hard work and self-reliance is a pathway to riches (49–50, 141–42). Baker's brief reference to *Titans* suggests that he views it as a slight deviation from the norm. It is "dialogic in how it portrays the successful integration of blacks and whites as requiring something from both sides" (147). Whilst *Titans* certainly has prominent individual characters, it is the way in which they function as a team that guarantees their success. In its wake, other civil rights themed sports films including *Coach Carter* (2005) and *Glory Road* (2006) offered something similar. In many ways, they exhibit similarities to another genre that is based on team action and communal effort: the war film. Discussing the characteristic traits of the war film, Steve Neale highlights the genre's "regular stress on cooperative goals, [and] its frequent critiques of extreme individualism" (133). *Titans* refuses to allow us to view the story from the perspective of any single individual. Nor does it place complete moral legitimacy in the hands of any one character.

The divisions between black and white characters are, at least on the surface, pronounced. Head football coach Herman Boone (Denzel Washington) is introduced from the perspective of white football player Gerry Bertier (Ryan Hurst). Bertier at first seems to be fulfilling the role of the redneck: "I don't want to play with any of those black animals," he declares as, from his point of view, Boone comes into frame. We view Boone and his family moving into their suburban residence from the perspective of bigoted white characters. Perhaps the most malicious characters are those in the upper echelons of society — the white members of the school board. They are the ones who possess the power to maintain the status quo. They bribe referees and threaten assistant coach Yoast (Will Patton) in the hope of ruining any chance of racial reconciliation. On the other hand, black characters initially express no great desire to cooperate with their white counterparts. African American football players declare that they will not need their white counterparts. "This team is soul powered now!" they proclaim.

Certain visual and editing techniques, however, undermine the characters' attempts to separate themselves from each other along racial lines. One scene, for example, makes use of an ellipsis to bring blacks and whites together. Coach Yoast sits pondering over whether to remain with the Titans as assistant coach or to quit in protest at not being offered the head coach job. His young daughter Sheryl (Hayden Panettiere) asks him: "so, coach, what you gonna do?" Of course he does not answer. Instead, the film cuts to the gymnasium and one of the black players answers for him: "we're gonna play some ball, ya'll." Similarly, scenes of the players dressed in the same outfits and exercising in unison counteract the racial conflicts that are raging around them. The linking of white and black characters through cinematic form and style becomes particularly pronounced when *Titans* engages with federal government programs of affirmative action and busing.

Titans and Social Policy

Affirmative action was a nationwide program started in the late 1960s. It dictated that the preferential hiring of minorities and women was a way of offsetting years of unequal hiring practices that favored white men. In *Titans*, Boone is offered the job of high school football coach at the expense of the more experienced white coach, Yoast. After initially hearing the disgruntlement of the latter, the film cuts to a parallel scene featuring Boone and school board chairman Dr. Day. We then see the issue of affirmative action depicted from the black character's perspective. Boone is hesitant to accept this preferential treatment. "I left North Carolina because I was passed over for a job that I had rightfully earned," he informs the chairman. "Now you are asking me to do the same thing to this man," he continues, "I can't do that." In response to this, the following dialog ensues:

> DR. DAY: Folks down in North Carolina said you marched with Dr. King, said you stood toe-to-toe with the Klan. They said you were a *race* man.
>
> BOONE: That's right, I'm also a *family* man.

Taken at face value, a rather bizarre dichotomy — "race" man and "family" man — has just been bestowed upon Boone. Need his race and his family allegiances be mutually exclusive? In the context of this conversation, Boone uses the term "family" not simply to denote his own kin, but as a sign of empathy for his white counterpart. A "race man" he may be but, when it comes to preferential hiring and its perceived "unfairness" toward whites, Boone initially opts for the color-blind social category: family. That *Titans* could have Boone march with Dr. King whilst simultaneously be dubious of affirmative action was not an unusual concept. Throughout the 1990s, political conservatives had sought to separate the civil rights leader from government sponsored civil rights programs.

For example, in his 1995 book *The End of Racism* Dinesh D'Souza declared: "We are confronted with a new civil rights program that is substantively different from that of Martin Luther King, Jr." D'Souza argued that "a demand for race consciousness in private and public hiring [and] public school assignments" were a "repudiation" of King's vision (205). In 1996, the California Republican Party proposed a television advertisement to demand the end to affirmative action. It closed with the following quotation: "Martin Luther King was right; Bill Clinton was wrong, end affirmative action now" (Bennet B11). Though King had spoken favorably of affirmative action as an acceptable remedy to years of inequality, a snippet from his "I have a dream" speech, where he looked forward to his children being judged "not on the color of their skin, but the content of their character," supposedly proved he was against such policies (Dyson 12–29). Thus another affirmative action critic, Shelby Steele, referentially titled his book that attacks the policy *The Content of Our Character* (Steele 114).

One might conclude, on this evidence, that *Titans* was mediating conservative discourse by having Boone display his reticence in accepting the job. Through his marching with King and adversity to affirmative action, he might be seen to be privileging early 1960s civil rights ideals over later civil rights legislation. However, the remainder of the scene re-aligns Boone and, by extension, King, with the positive value of these programs. Dr. Day encourages Boone to accept the post because all the "black folks have never had anything in this city to call their own, except humiliation and despair." Eventually, it is the sight of hundreds of black citizens cheering outside his house that spurs Boone to take the job. But, in keeping with the film's dialogic approach to politics, affirmative action is once again re-negotiated when the football season begins in earnest. Dr. Day reports to coach Boone. This time the news is not so good. Day tells the coach that one losing game will cost him his job; the board has decided to renege on his preferential hiring. He must win every game to maintain his post and, fortunately for him, Boone manages to do just that. Here is an attempt to reconcile the position of both pro and anti-affirmative action advocates. Regardless of the reasons for which he was hired, Boone turns out to be, as coach Yoast puts it at the film's conclusion, "the right man for the job."

The road to Alexandria's integration begins by way of another civil rights program: busing. *Titans*' representation of busing, the transportation of children to unfamiliar neighborhood schools in order to ensure racial diversity, came at a time when its continued relevance was the subject of much debate amongst American thinkers and policy makers. In what was described by Glenn C. Loury, director of the Institute on Race and Social Division at Boston University, as "the end of an era in American social policy," September of 1999 saw a judge order an end to busing in the city where it had begun, Charlotte, North Carolina (Yellin and Firestone A1). When, in 1969, the authorities implemented busing there, it was hailed as a pioneering move for public school integration and, when the Charlotte plan was upheld by the U.S. Supreme Court in 1971, numerous other state authorities started their own busing systems — Virginia, in *Titans*' case. By 1999, however, a federal judge had ruled that "forced integration was no longer necessary because all vestiges of intentional discrimination had disappeared" (Yellin and Firestone A1).

With regards to busing, *Titans* once again goes about negotiating the political controversy with a great deal of care. On the one hand, this legislation forces blacks and whites together and thus integrates Alexandria; on the other hand, it is almost undercut by the slightly dubious suggestion that it was not really necessary in the first place. The fall semester has yet to begin, and the football team is about to embark on a pre-season training camp. Before the first integrated school bus arrives at T. C. Williams High School, *Titans* provides an allegorical representation of this program. Two buses arrive; black and white players board separate vehicles. "Listen up!" barks coach Boone: "I don't care if you're black, blue, green, white or orange; I want all of my defensive players on this side, and all of my players going out for offense over here." The players are reassigned to integrated buses. This symbolic integration of school buses begins what the training camp completes. By the end of the camp the team is a paragon of racial harmony, their shared love of football overcoming any of the prejudices that they may once have held. And, it is the team, not busing, behind which the city of Alexandria rally when school begins. As the story unfolds, citizens progress from waving placards and banners reading "we love our kids, we hate busing" to cheering on the football team from an integrated sideline. It is not the policy, but the football team — integrated before this unpopular program begins — that ends up being the deciding factor in Alexandria's passage from racial conflict to comity.

Like its treatment of affirmative action, *Titans* veers from approval of the principles of busing to a celebration of the people's own agency in integrating their city. Boone received the job through affirmative action but proved himself to have been the best man for the job anyway. The schools were forced to integrate by busing, yet it was the football team that "really" did the integrating. When shots of the team's championship success and the players' integrated celebrations appear toward the end of the film, one might wonder whether the filmmakers behind *Titans* are, like much conservative rhetoric of the 1990s and 2000s, dismissing the need for these legislations in the present. Such a question is, however, complicated by the final scene. We return to the funeral that pre-empted the main action. We know now that the deceased is Titans hero Gerry Bertier. The voiceover provides the closing commentary: "People say it can't work black and white, well here we make it work every day. We have our disagreements of course, but before we reach for hate, always, always we remember the Titans." The story has finished, yet it ends at the place where it started. This circular narrative suggests that race relations is an issue that requires ongoing vigilance and care. The film began in fall, ends in fall, and was released in fall (September 2000): like the changing of the seasons, there is no foreseeable end. This voiceover provides an example of looking back in order to look forward. "Always, always we remember the Titans," she says, a call, perhaps, for the audience to do the same and to take these lessons into their own lives. Based on reception materials, it would seem that some individuals and groups attempted to do just this.

Conclusion: *Titans* in the Public Sphere

Joining the *Titans*' cast and crew at its Washington, DC premiere was a notable guest: President Bill Clinton. Afterwards, the President made a brief congratulatory speech in which he declared that the 1971 Titans were "a model for the whole country." He continued: "if only we could learn over again every day the lesson these young men ... learned from each other" (Clinton 2222). Clinton's sentiments were echoed time and again by cultural commentators. For, in extending the civil rights narrative beyond the early 1960s and into the more controversial territory of early 1970s government legislation, *Titans* was also representing issues that remained pertinent in late 20th and early 21st century America. The actual coaches Boone and Yoast upon whom the fictional characters were based were propelled into the spotlight. They became spokespeople for cross-racial cooperation and were invited to schools, conventions, business meetings, even professional football teams to speak on the value of teamwork and tolerance (El-Bashir D3; Keating A1).

The film itself was also used as a motivational tool. At T. C. Williams High, the school at which *Titans* is set, students were encouraged to view it as a way of stimulating cross cultural relations amongst the student body. Teachers and student leaders waxed rhapsodic over this cinematic tale of triumph against-the-odds. At a time when there were complaints that the school — one of the most racially diverse schools in the country — was becoming "balkanized," it was hoped that *Titans* would spur some students toward a greater understanding of other races and cultures (Wax B2). Looking back to 1971, remembering the Titans, was not, like previous civil rights films set in the South, a case of remembering a time long gone, the dark days of Jim Crow. The film's engagement with issues that were still resonating in contemporary society gave it an endless quality, like the changing of the seasons (or the start of a new football season).

Within weeks of its release, millions of Americans had seen this movie. Exit polls and anecdotal evidence indicated that it had crossed age, gender, and racial demographics, appealing to a wide range of theatergoers.[3] After watching the film in Washington's Uptown Theater, one reviewer observed that the crowd gave *Titans* a "standing ovation" and commented, "I can't recall a time when I've witnessed so many blacks and whites having similarly positive responses to anything racial, even if it was only a movie" (Milloy B1). Such responses suggest that, for some, *Titans* acted as what Alison Landsberg calls a "prosthetic memory." Landsberg argues that mainstream cultural institutions, including Hollywood, are capable of providing memories that an individual may not have physically experienced. When a film represents political or social injustices of the past, it can "produce empathy and social responsibility as well as political alliances that transcend race, class, and gender" (Landsberg 21). They can positively alter the ways in which one interacts with other people, groups and institutions. Given the impact *Titans* was reported to have had upon some, it might at least be said that the film was promoted as a "prosthetic memory" of sorts.

Admittedly, critical reaction to *Titans* veered from the laudatory to the hostile. Perhaps the most surprising aspect of its reception was the fact that most negative reviews appeared in mainstream newspapers and magazines, while the African American press, virtually without exception, praised it for both its dramatic impact and its treatment of race relations. Reviews in the *Washington Post* and *Los Angeles Times* described it as "formulaic," "predictable" and "ham-fisted" (O'Sullivan N43; Turan 1). *The New Pittsburgh Courier* on the other hand wrote that "[t]he production never gets too light or too sappy to trivialize its profound message. The payoff is huge when a movie can so convincingly convey a transition from intolerance to acceptance" (Williams B4). "If you're an African American," wrote the *Los Angeles Sentinel*, "you'll probably love this movie" (Dungee B6).

Reviews aside, it would seem that *Titans* managed to cross demographics and enjoy a universal appeal. Its themes, its form and its style all contribute toward a re-imagining of the civil rights South in which the struggle for equality is ongoing and predicated upon black and white agency. It takes its fight beyond the years of government sanctioned segregation into a period of history which spawned several conflicts not yet resolved at the turn of the 21st century. Black and white relations, affirmative action, busing: wherever one turns in *Titans*, one does not find a definite answer but, rather, both sides of the argument. Here is a film that provides no simple answers, nor does it consign its conflicts to the dustbin of history. Rather, its cyclical narrative and dialogic address calls for constant debate, cooperation and vigilance with regards to the civil rights struggle. In her book *Reconstructing Dixie,* Tara McPherson argues that "in the South's legacies, one might also find productive terrains for envisioning solidarity" (30). McPherson criticizes a number of visual representations such as Ken Burns' *Civil War* and Ross McElwee's *Sherman's March*, that "attempt to bring black and white together [for] their inability to sustain a true double vision to see a joining that respects both commonality and difference" (30). However, one might consider her more positive suggestion in the light of *Remember the Titans*. "You don't have to like each other, but you have to respect each other," says Boone. He and *Titans* present a vision of solidarity that is reliant on constant dialog, debate and even conflict. It is a solidarity whereby — to use a well-worn football phrase — you're only as good as your last game.

Acknowledgments

I would like to thank Peter Kramer, Richard Nowell, Andy Leiter and Maggie Gruner for their helpful comments and advice on various drafts of this essay.

Notes

1. By this term he means the long Sixties, less a strict chronological entity than a conceptual category encompassing a wealth of political and cultural phenomena such as the civil rights, feminist and counterculture movements as well as the Vietnam War.
2. Monteith suggests that these films are very much influenced by earlier social problem films such as *Pinky* (1949), *Intruder in the Dust* (1949), and *To Kill a Mockingbird* (1962) (125).
3. The film notched an impressive $21.2 million in its opening weekend alone. Statistics offered by Buena Vista Distribution, the company charged with distributing *Remember the Titans*, found the film's opening weekend audiences to be composed of 30% teens, 55% men and 45% women (Welkos 8; Natale 2).

Works Cited

Baker, Aaron. *Contesting Identities: Sports in American Film.* Chicago: University of Illinois Press, 2003.
Bennet, Jamie. "Dole Plans $4 million in California Ads." *New York Times* 24 Oct. 1996: B11.
Clinton, Bill. "Remarks Following the Premiere of 'Remember the Titans.'" *Collected Presidential Documents: Administration of William J. Clinton.* 26 Sept. 2000: 2222.
D'Souza, Dinesh. *The End of Racism: Principles for a Multiracial Society.* New York: The Free Press, 1995.
Dungee, Ron. "At the Movies: *Remember the Titans.*" *Sentinel* 4 Oct. 2000: B6.
Dyson, Michael-Eric. *I May Not Get There with You: The True Martin Luther King, Jr.* New York: The Free Press, 2000.
El-Bashir, Tariq. "Boone to Address All-Met Athletes." *Washington Post* 1 June 2001: D3.
Graham, Allison. *Framing the South: Hollywood, Television, and Race During the Civil Rights Struggle.* Baltimore: Johns Hopkins University Press, 2001.
Green, Harvey. *Fit for America: Health, Fitness, Sport and American Society.* Baltimore: Johns Hopkins University Press, 1986.
Hall, Jacquelyn Dowd. "The Long Civil Rights Movement and the Political Uses of the Past." *The Journal of American History* 91.4 (2005): 1233–1263.
Harwell, Hoyt. "Bryant and Blacks: Both had to Wait." *Huntsville Times* June 6 1983. Web. 20 Dec. 2009. <http://www.al.com/alabamafootball/bear/story6.html>.
Hunter, Stephen. "Fumbled Opportunity: *Remember the Titans* Falls Short of Reality." *Washington Post* 29 Sept. 2000: C1.
Keating, Patrick. "Students Find Belafonte, Other Speakers Inspirational." *Michigan Chronicle* 4 Apr. 2001: A1.
Landsberg, Alison. *Prosthetic Memory: The Transformation of American Remembrance in the Age of Mass Culture.* New York: Colombia University Press, 2004.

Lawson, Stephen. "Freedom Then/Freedom Now: The Historiography of the Civil Rights Movement." *The American Historical Review* 96.2 (1991): 456–471.
Marcus, Daniel. *Happy Days and Wonder Years: The Fifties and the Sixties in Contemporary Cultural Politics.* New Brunswick: Rutgers University Press, 2003.
McPherson, Tara. *Reconstructing Dixie: Race, Gender, and Nostalgia in the Imagined South.* Durham: Duke University Press, 2003.
Milloy, Courtland. "*Titans* Creators Went Extra Yard to Forge Unity." *Washington Post* 11 Oct. 2000: B1.
Molotsky, Irvin. "Design Chosen for Memorial to Dr. King." *New York Times* 14 Sept. 2000: A24.
Monteith, Sharon. "The Movie-Made Movement: Civil Rites of Passage." *Memory and Popular Film*, ed. Paul Grainge. Manchester: Manchester University Press, 2003. 120–143.
Natale, Richard. "*Titans* Dominates Over a Nearly Abandoned Field." *Los Angeles Times* 2 Oct. 2000: Calendar, p. 2.
Neale, Steve. *Genre and Hollywood.* London: Routledge, 2000.
O' Sullivan, Michael. "Ham-Fisted 'Titans.'" *Washington Post* 29 Sept. 2000: N43.
Remember the Titans. Dir. Boaz Yakin. Perf. Denzel Washington, Will Patton, Ryan Hurst, Wood Harris, Hayden Panettiere. Disney, 2000. DVD.
"Remembering the *Titans'* Reality." *Washington Post* 7 Oct. 2000: A21.
Romano, Renee C., and Leigh Raiford, eds. *The Civil Rights Movement in American Memory.* Athens: University of Georgia Press, 2006.
Sack, Kevin. "Museums of a Movement." *New York Times* 28 June 1998: TR12.
Steele, Shelby. *The Content of Our Character.* New York: St. Martin's, 1990.
Turan, Kenneth. "Running a Tight Pattern." *Los Angeles Times* 29 Sept. 2000: Calendar, 1.
Washington, Adrienne T. "In Hollywood Spotlight, Schoolmates Remember the Titans." *Washington Times* 29 Sept. 2000: C2.
Wax, Emily. "Alexandria Revels in 'Titans' Glory." *Washington Post* 27 Sept. 2000: B2.
Welkos, Robert W. "Weekend Box Office; Wide-Range Audience Roots for 'Titans.'" *Los Angeles Times* 3 Oct. 2000: Calendar, p. 8.
Williams, Kam. "Denzel Sensational in '70s Desegregation Saga: *Remember the Titans* Opens This Weekend." *New Pittsburgh Courier* 27 Sept. 2000: B4.
Wolff, Alexander. "SI Flashback: Groundbreakers." *Sports Illustrated* 7 Nov. 2005. Web. 20 Dec. 2009. <http://sportsillustrated.cnn.com>.
Yellin, Emily, and David Firestone. "By Court Order, Busing Ends Where It Began." *New York Times* 11 Sept. 1999: A1.

III.

"Every Man Has the Right to Contribute a Verse": Representin' Black Masculinity and the South in Three Popular Hip Hop Films

COURTNEY GEORGE

Film scholars and historians have traced the origins of black male character representations to the cinema of the South, for instance the stereotype of the "black brute" in D. W. Griffith's *Birth of a Nation* or the "Uncle Tom" in film versions of Harriet Beecher Stowe's novel or even *Gone with the Wind*. In these early films, black men were portrayed as polar opposites on the spectrum of stereotypes — either the terrifying and animalistic rapist or the desexed and subservient Uncle Tom; the South itself was represented as a place where white patriarchs tried to reign over the chaos of the collapsing race and class hierarchies.[1] More recent scholarship discusses the growth of realistic and non-stereotypical black representation in American film; scholars have charted the progress of independent black cinema set in the South, particularly in films like Julie Dash's 1991 independent film, *Daughters of Dust*, about the Gullah community and culture of South Carolina.

Outside of the region, the 1990s also saw the advent of popular and critically successful "hood" films associated with "gangsta" rap, such as *New Jack City*, *Boyz n the Hood*, *Juice*, and *Menace II Society* which created superstars out of rappers Ice Cube, Ice T, and Tupac Shakur. In these films, which typically end in violence and then flight, representations of black men were made richly complex through themes of racial and socio-economic-spurred violence associated with coming-of-age as a young black man in an inner city hood in urban centers like Los Angeles or New York.[2] In the new millennium, "hood" films have morphed into films about hip hop artists struggling with their talent, as in 2002's *8 Mile* starring rapper Eminem and 2005's *Get Rich or Die Tryin'* with rapper 50 Cent, or biopics like 2009's *Notorious* about rapper Notorious B.I.G. These films treat the rise-to-fame of real-life male rap stars in a fictional vein, showing how each rapper's musical ability helps them sometimes overcome a violent lower-class urban lifestyle.

In the three popular films discussed here, *Hustle & Flow* (2005), *Idlewild* (2006), and *ATL* (2006), themes of the 1990s "hood" films are blended with themes from the more recent hip hop films to directly counter-attack stereotypes about Southern black men and the region they inherit and inhabit. With the recent trend in Southern-produced rap music, the hip hop culture of the South and its subsequent influence on black masculinity has created nuanced portrayals of black men that seriously challenge and question the "black brute" or the "Uncle Tom;" the Southern hip hop films discussed here ask viewers not only to rethink negative stereotypes of black masculinity in the South but also to reconsider how the black community reclaims the region as a creative, uplifting space for positive growth.

Due to the novelty of the Southern trend in rap music, scholars have not yet thoroughly discussed the possible effects of the music and culture on film. In fact, because hip hop culture is constantly changing, popular music scholar Nelson George argues that hip hop films in the past have not contributed much insight: "Because hip hop moves so rapidly, any aspect of the culture ... can make a film seem a bit behind the times.... The dictates of plot or perhaps more accurately the formulas of Hollywood storytelling have rarely enhanced viewer understanding of any subculture, much less one with this many layers" (108). George argues that hip hop is too complex to be clearly defined, listing the many elements that make up the culture: the art of verbal battling, dance, literature, crime, sex, politics — "too many to simply say that hip hop means any one or even two things" (viii). While George carefully engages the flexibilities of hip hop, he also specifically places the culture's birthplace and influences: "at its most elemental level hip hop is a product of post–civil rights era America, a set of cultural forms originally nurtured by African American, Caribbean American, and Latin American youth in and around New York in the 70s" (viii). Nearly all hip hop scholars would agree with Nelson; as Riché Richardson writes, "when rap emerged in the mid–1970s, the East Coast was its undisputed epicenter" (197). Rap music originated in New York City as both a political statement against and a jovial reprieve from the increasing drug and gang violence, racism, and poverty in inner city communities.

As rap music grew in popularity, its center shifted to the West Coast city of Los Angeles, where the "gangsta" rap of the 1980s and 1990s challenged the political beats of the East Coast; just as hip hop shows flexibility in genre and definition, the culture's center also presents a flexible — and sometimes highly contested — regional movement and distribution. As Tricia Rose explains, hip hop and rap identity "is deeply rooted in the specific, the local experience, and one's attachment to and status in a local group or alternative family" (34). However, while local identity remains in flux as hip hop and rap music transforms itself from one crew to the next (as in the example of East v. West Coast), one aspect of the culture seemingly remains uncontested: hip hop and rap music are clearly urban expressions, whether originating in East or West Coast urban centers. Rose's definition of rap suggests this urban focus: "rap is a black idiom that prioritizes black culture and that articulates the problems of black urban life" (4). Because of the way artists and scholars have centralized urban plights in hip hop culture, historically the South (considered anything but an urban landscape) produced very few successful rap artists.

However, in recent years, hip hop's most popular players have originated in the South. Richardson celebrates this trend but also implies that it is surprising:

> The idea of the South as a legitimate base and space for artists to produce rap, which has often been viewed as an inherently urban (and masculine) verbal art, had been virtually unthinkable until recent years ... there was a time not too long ago when the very idea of an MC or DJ from the South, if ever it crossed the minds of major producers or celebrated artists in the rap industry, was more likely to come across as amusing [197–9].

In the past decade and a half, the increasing popularity of figures and groups like Lil Wayne, Outkast, Ludacris, and T.I. has led Southern metropolitan areas like New Orleans, Houston, Memphis, and Atlanta to become the new meccas for hip hop expression. Following this trend, writer/historian Charlie Braxton attributes this rise to Southern roots music like the blues: "there is no style of music in America that didn't originate in the south ... hip-hop is the only one that didn't. But so much of the music hip-hop was built off — James Brown drum breaks, old school soul — is Southern. So in a lot of ways, hip-hop is returning to its roots" (qtd. in Green). Although Braxton agrees that hip hop's beginnings can be traced to the East Coast, he argues that rap is greatly influenced by regional Southern music. James "FLX" Smith, who directed and produced a documentary chronicling Southern hip hop (*Dirty States of America*), argues that "getting hip-hop to acknowledge those roots has always taken some effort" (Green). Tony Green, a reviewer of *Dirty States*, concurs:

> Hip-hop was born in New York, which is where nearly all the music media in the country are concentrated (*Vibe, Spin, XXL, Rolling Stone* and *The Source* are all based in Manhattan). Given that situation, it was easy to see how tunnel vision developed. Even today, some northeastern hip-hop heads still don't see the South as a legitimate inheritor of the hip-hop cultural heritage [par. 4].

Some rap artists and listeners might dismiss Southern rap as too rural or "country" because Southern rap often draws on specifically Southern locations, expressions, experiences, and traditions foreign to northern audiences. Yet the representations of the black Southern experience as rooted in the history of slavery, civil rights, poverty, and racial oppression — most notably in songs like Field Mob's "Georgia" and Outkast's "Rosa Parks" — offer a historical credibility distinct from East and West Coast urban centers.[3]

Just as hip hop culture and gangsta rap bled into the "hood" films of the 1990s, Southern rap music has influenced three recent popular films, *Hustle & Flow*, *Idlewild*, and *ATL*. Hip hop scholars might agree that the culture originated in northern urban centers, but these films suggest that hip hop grew out of the Southern experience. Particularly for the black male protagonists of each film, this experience is riddled not only with conflict, pain, and violence but also filled with community, love, and resolution through artistic and communal expression. These three films attempt to reclaim the South's hip hop origins, positing that the region can offer a space for artistic growth and accomplishment for the black male and the black community in general.

Of the three films discussed here, white Memphis-native Craig Brewer's 2005 film *Hustle & Flow* was strongly embraced by both critics and the popular audience, earning the Sundance Audience Award, both Academy Award and Golden Globe nominations for the film's actor Terrence Howard, and an Academy Award for Best Original Song for Three 6 Mafia's "It's Hard Out Here for a Pimp." While Craig Brewer wrote and directed the film, legendary producer of *Boyz n the Hood* John Singleton funded the movie, which grossed around $22 million on an $18 million budget. Although the film received mostly favorable reviews, some critics were quick to attack Brewer's depiction of pimp DJay as a negative reinforcement of the "black brute" character presented in early films like *Birth of a Nation*; however, the film actually attempts to represent Southern black men and their homes as sympathetic and deserving of respect.

Hustle & Flow focuses on main character DJay, a poor Southern pimp and drug dealer, who conquers a mid-life crisis with fantasies of rap stardom. DJay's story is not a typical American rags-to-riches tale, and DJay is certainly not the sympathetic hero. Neither is DJay a glamorized gangster with fast cars, flashy women, gold jewelry, and big guns (like *Scarface*'s Tony Montana or *American Gangster*'s Frank Lucas). In fact, Michael Eric Dyson has argued

Opposite: Director Craig Brewer's *Hustle & Flow* (2005, Paramount) features the down-and-out pimp DJay (Terrence Howard), who pursues a fresh start as a hip hop artist.

III. "Every Man Has the Right to Contribute a Verse" (George)

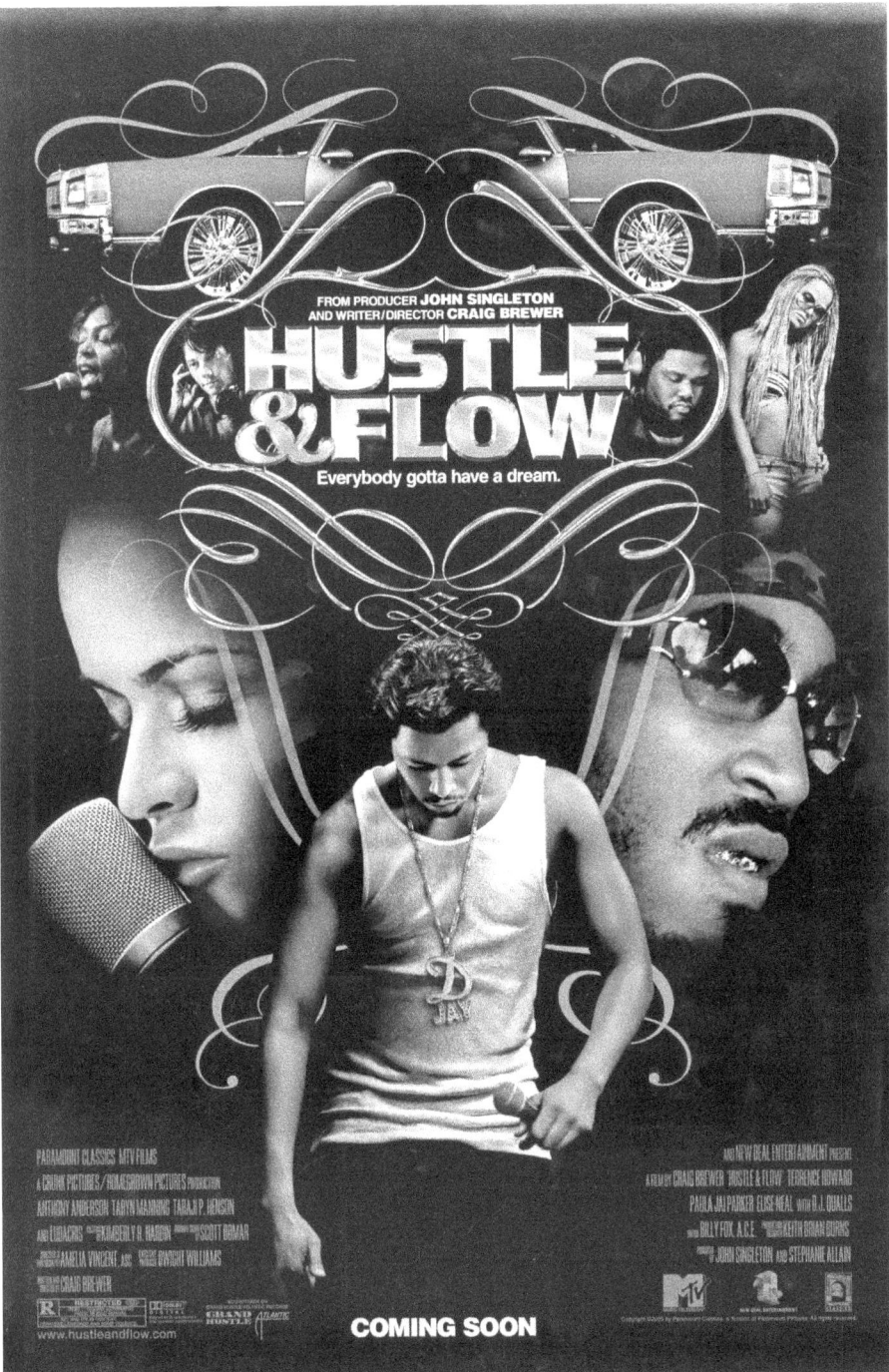

that the movie "demythologizes the pimp narrative and mythology" where the pimp typically represents "notions of upward mobility, especially when the pimp is viewed as providing an escape hatch for the economically degraded working-class man" (25–6). The film's opening attests to DJay's impoverished and pathetic status; he sits in his un-air conditioned car in the middle of the Memphis summer heat and lectures to his white prostitute Nola about why they have to do what they do. DJay's life metaphor explores the difference between mankind and dogs:

> Because men, well, we a lot like a dog. You know, we like to piss on things. Sniff a bitch when we can. Even get a little pink hard-on the way they do. We territorial as shit, you know, we gonna protect our own. But man, he know about death. Got him a sense of history. Got religion. See ... a dog, man, a dog don't know shit about no birthdays or Christmas or Easter bunny, none of that shit. And one day God gonna come calling, so you know, they going through life carefree. But people like you and me, man, we always guessing. Wondering, "What if?" You know what I mean? So when you say to me, "Hey, I don't think we should be doing this." I gotta say, baby, I don't think we should be doing this neither, but we ain't gonna get no move on in this world, lying around in the sun, licking our ass all day.

DJay and Nola sell themselves in order to survive; DJay's philosophical sense of history and religion as driving forces of mankind might seem misplaced in a poor pimp's mouth, but these words underscore DJay's position as the poor hustler who struggles to make ends meet and honestly wishes for a more fulfilling existence (as does Nola).

In a later conversation with his pregnant prostitute (and love interest) Shug, DJay reveals that his mid-life crisis is somehow directly related to his family history. His father — a dedicated bus mechanic for the Memphis school systems who was rewarded for his services with a gold watch — died from a heart attack when he was DJay's age. DJay forges a connection between his own life and his father's recognizing that no matter the job — pimp or mechanic — Southern black men slave away to die young unfulfilled and unrewarded. As DJay suggests to Nola, what separates man from the dogs is the historical knowledge of struggle and impending death; in *Hustle & Flow* this struggle is specifically rooted in the Southern experience of race and class discrimination.

DJay's chance to make more out of his life comes when he reunites with his old high school friend, producer and mixer, Key. The film suggests an almost revelational religious experience during a poignant scene where DJay visits Key's church and listens to gospel music that moves him to tears. Later the two launch a home recording studio, with the help of white piano player Shelby, in order to lay down DJay's rap music, which is directly inspired by his experiences as a poor black pimp living in Memphis. Unlike earlier "hood" films that often portray poverty and street life as motivation to kill or be killed, DJay's Southern environment and community become an inspiration for his art, his music.

While the viewer quickly recognizes DJay will use rap to reclaim the decaying Memphis hood as a space for growth and success, the film also presents the subtle idea that hip hop culture should more generally recognize and reclaim its Southern roots. The background music in the film tells the musical history of the South — from opening with the blues of Buddy Guy moving to the bluegrass of Jason Freeman to the gospel solo in Key's church to the R&B of Arnell's club to the award-winning hip hop songs. DJay also tells viewers that his "mode" — the inner rap that flows through his mind at all times — draws inspiration from both Memphis rappers 8Ball and Georgia bluesman Otis Redding. In these subtle instances, the film communicates how the diverse musical history of the South directly contributes to American hip hop culture and rap music. The most notable moment comes when, after DJay, Key, and Shelby lay down their first track together, Shelby — the white piano player — makes an astute comment which supports the film's soundtrack:

> Rap is coming back home to the South cause this is where it all began. Heavy percussion, repetitive hooks, sexually suggestive lyrics — it's all blues, brother. "Back door man" to "Back dat ass up." It's all about pain and pussy ... and making music with simple tools by any means necessary. You've got to get what you've got to say out because you've got to — every man has the right — the goddamned right — to contribute a verse.

Shelby's words remind viewers of the Memphis blues tradition that has historically given the black community the power to express themselves through music; here the film suggests that Southern rap acts as the new blues which unites and gives life to the contemporary black community. When Three 6 Mafia won the Oscar for Best Original Song, the band's Jordan Houston argued something similar about the power of Southern rap: "This is big for hip-hop, but we're also representing for the black community, letting kids know you can do something positive and make it bigger than life" (qtd. in Donalson 131).

While the film's music, along with Shelby's speech, subtly attest to the film's view of the South as the region which engendered hip hop, the scenes with Skinny Black (played by rapper Ludacris) further emphasize the links between Southern community and hip hop. To make his dream rap of stardom come true, DJay must establish a connection with Skinny, Memphis's popular rap celebrity. When DJay gets the opportunity to sell drugs to Skinny, DJay forges a plan to give Skinny the demo tape the group has slaved over all summer in the Memphis hood. The scene takes place at Arnell's club during a

July 4th celebration; unlike DJay, Skinny supports an entourage of gun-toting guards and beautiful women. Skinny has achieved the glamorous pimp position, but the fame and money come at the price of his connection to his hometown community. Skinny tells DJay that he holds no appreciation, loyalty, or even respect for Memphis: "Got all these folks telling me I been gone too long — like I'm coming back or something — like y'all are a back to get back to. I say fuck — the best place to keep Memphis is in my rear view." When DJay produces Skinny's first bootleg tape and Skinny balks at the old-school technology, DJay ably reminds Skinny that Memphis is his home and that the community sales and representation of Skinny's tapes are what brought his fame. After he convinces Skinny that Skinny's underground bootleg tape speaks for the Memphis experience, DJay passes his own tape to Skinny, who replies with the film's tagline, "Everybody gotta have a dream, boy."

However, DJay later finds Skinny passed out in the bathroom while his demo tape sits in the bottom of a dirty toilet; DJay violently reacts by attacking Skinny and ends up with a jail sentence for assault. Even while DJay is in jail, the group (Key, Nola, Shug, and Shelby) still succeeds in getting DJay's music on the radio, and the film ends as DJay — unlike Skinny Black — readily accepts a demo from his fellow Memphis rappers with a sincere delivery of the line "Everybody gotta have a dream." The stereotype of the "black brute" or, in this case, the brutal pimp, is transformed. The themes in *Hustle & Flow* show the South as a subversively creative space where black men overcome the forces of poverty that have historically held them back; the South also becomes a region that boasts the origins of hip hop. Brewer's film warns against straying too far from home (as Skinny does), ultimately suggesting DJay's dependence on and respect for his community contributes to his success as much — or possibly even more — than his talent.

Released one year after *Hustle & Flow*, the story-line of the 2006 film *Idlewild* literally positions hip hop's origins in the South of the 1930s, implying that hip hop is a direct descendent of the blues and jazz of Prohibition-era speakeasies. Produced on a smaller budget of $10 million, *Idlewild* was written and directed by music video guru Bryan Barber. While the film was not as successfully received as *Hustle & Flow*, most reviewers admired the unique story-line and musical numbers, even if the plot was overwhelming at times. The film stars Outkast members André Benjamin and Antwan Patton respectively as Percival and Rooster, two childhood friends coming of age in the small rural town of Idlewild, Georgia. As the narrator, Percival is an introspective young man who works and lives at his father's funeral home by day and plays piano at the Church, a local juke joint, by night. His best friend, Rooster, is a full-time gangster who sings at and manages the Church, but who also struggles daily to please his fundamentalist Christian wife and their

III. "Every Man Has the Right to Contribute a Verse" (George)

six daughters. As Percy tells the audience, even though the boys come from different sides of the tracks, their common ground is found in music.

Different from the poor pimp-life of DJay and the women represented in *Hustle & Flow*, *Idlewild* glamorizes the gangster lifestyle in scenes at the Church. Although the viewers see the constant familial struggles of Percival and Rooster during the daylight hours, most of the film's action takes place at night in the Church where "hooch" is easily accessible and cabaret-style music and dance roar on every night. The décor and costumes in the Church are true to visions of a 1930s speakeasy; the rims on modern cars, baggy clothes, graffiti art, and other elements often associated with hip hop culture are clearly absent. However, unlike the music in *The Cotton Club*, *Harlem Nights* or other popular jazz films, the music at the Church is infused with rap and hip hop beats, including songs from Outkast's 2003 Grammy-winning cd, *Speakerboxxx/The Love Below*. Percival plays variations on jazz piano, and when Rooster takes the stage to sing, he raps instead, and the Church's audience breaks into hip hop dance styles uncharacteristic of the film's time period. While this blurring of hip hop and 1930s jazz styles caused some confusion for reviewers and might appear anachronistic to viewers, *Idlewild* makes a clear point about the rise of Southern hip hop. While Shelby in *Hustle & Flow* suggests that hip hop is returning home to the South, Percival and Rooster's musical acts suggest that hip hop's home has *always* been the South.

The Southern hip hop aspects are not the only similarities between the films; although Percival is not a pimp, his struggle to find himself through music is akin to DJay's struggle. Percival signifies on William Shakespeare as he repeats throughout the film, "All the world is a stage. We have our roles to play. All the men and women merely players. They all have their specific exits and entrances." Percy searches for a musical role to play, but much like DJay, Percival cannot escape the traumas and responsibilities of his family history. While Percy struggles with his conservative father and his work with the (literal) dead, Rooster fights with his church-going wife about his lack of responsibility; both men appear restricted by the conventionality of their families, so both men seek out a different type of "church"— the nightclub wherein they can perform without boundaries. While DJay allows the gospel music at Key's church to inspire his rap ambitions, Percy and Rooster rebel against the traditional Southern church community to create a new place (ironically named the Church) where they can openly express themselves.[4]

When Angel Davenport, a fictional jazz diva, appears to sing at the Church, she and Percy fall in love, and like an angel, she begins to watch over him and change his views on life. Angel questions Percy about why he will not leave the conservative Southern town and father that will not allow him to play piano in his own style; Angel wants to take Percy with her to see the world, particularly the 1930s evolutions of black culture in cities like Chicago and New York. Percy responds by showing Angel pictures of his dead mother (also a singer) and aunt (a piano player) and tells Angel that his whole life is wrapped up in taking care of his father in Idlewild. While visions of his aunt and mother might inspire his musical creativity, this family history also keeps him from achieving his dream — his role on the stage. Like DJay, Percival connects his family history with his own dissatisfaction; the early deaths of Percy's mother and aunt combined with the current misery of his father lead him to believe that his dreams will not be fulfilled in the stifling Southern environment of Idlewild.

At the film's conclusion, a violent revolution at the Church leaves Angel dead and Percival heartbroken. After a religious revelation with a strange abandoned woman on a lonely road, Rooster faithfully recommits to his wife and children. Telling Percy that "God don't make no mistakes," Rooster saves him from suicide and convinces him to finally leave Idlewild for Chicago, where Percy records his own music and becomes a successful jazz and hip hop musician. In these moments, the film suggests that, even if hip hop originates from Southern music and community, this early community could not nourish the culture and combat oppression like the urban centers of the North, which supports hip hop's designated northern birthplace. However, even though Percival must exit his home town, *Idlewild* clearly establishes the roots of hip hop and rap as Southern, suggesting that with the migration of Southern musicians like Percival, the music and the community spread throughout the country (as did the blues). While giving credit to the northern development of hip hop, *Idlewild* also subversively represents how the Southern black community — tied together not only through violence but also music, friendship, family, and even religion — influenced hip hop culture.

Like *Idlewild*, music video creator Chris Robinson's 2006 film *ATL* is set in Georgia and also stars Antwan Patton of Outkast. Based on a screenplay by Antwone Fisher, the movie received favorable reviews and grossed $21 million on a $20 million budget. In *ATL* the setting shifts to the contemporary era in the metropolis of Atlanta, where Patton plays supporting actor to the film's star, Atlanta-native and rapper Tip "T.I." Harris. T.I. plays Rashad, a young high school senior in Mechanicsville — the inner city south side hood of Atlanta, Georgia and what Rashad terms the "center of our universe." Like *Idlewild*'s Percival, Rashad narrates the story of his best friends and their coming of age, which takes place mostly at a roller skating rink called Cascade. The orphaned Rashad and his little brother Ant live with their uncle, a broken man who complains about how he sacrificed his own happiness to care for the boys after their parents' tragic death. Like *Hustle & Flow*, *ATL* explores the unfulfilled dreams of black men living in the impoverished South.

III. *"Every Man Has the Right to Contribute a Verse"* (George)

Just as hip hop culture expresses itself in varied aspects, Rashad and his friends all have different dreams and different means of achieving them: Rashad is an aspiring artist who wants to see his comic in the Atlanta papers; Ant wants the easy gangster life that impresses girls and brings him money; Esquire attends a private (mostly white) school and works at a country club

Director Chris Robinson's *ATL* (2006) sets the story of young men coming of age against the backdrop of the Cascade skating rink and the Mechanicsville hood.

in order to bolster his chances of attending an Ivy League college; Teddy's artistry lies in his ability to apply custom grills and gold teeth for the Mechanicsville hood; Brooklyn, who is originally from New York, is trying to find his place in the South. While none of the characters are aspiring rappers or musicians like DJay or Percival, the crew is brought together when they compete as a rollerblading team to the hip hop beats on Sunday nights at Cascade. Rashad tells his viewers that Cascade "was the only place where we all felt like we could be free ... nothing matters ... you can be whatever you want to be ... no lies, no pain, no worries about what tomorrow might bring." The act of rollerblading offers the same creative outlet and community power previously established by music in the other two films; the Cascade community allows the young friends to transcend their day-to-day struggles with poverty, racism, and street violence.

However, Cascade is not the only setting where hip hop booms in the background. Even though the New York character Brooklyn jokingly calls the South too "country," the film's opening scenes counter this northern stereotype. *ATL* makes clear that contemporary hip hop culture — much like blues culture — originates from the still-present oppression and segregation of African Americans in the South. While the Field Mob/Ludacris rap hit "Georgia" blares in the background, the audience sees a montage of images: a confederate flag waving in the breeze, a white plantation-style home with a manicured lawn, cotton in the fields, kudzu covering the landscape, a black-owned barber shop, Martin Luther King, Jr., walking with Coretta Scott King, a barbeque restaurant, the city skyline of Atlanta, Georgia. While these images appear as stereotypical representations of the South, when juxtaposed and flashed across the screen, they also show a stark contrast between the poor and rich, the black and white Souths. However, the song "Georgia" heard in the background is not a song about sadness, poverty, or oppression; the song's lyrics confess a pride at Georgia heritage and an ability to transform oppression into motivation. Combined with such images, the rap anthem sets the tone for *ATL*—a film that shows how hip hop culture engendered in the South can rise above the oppressive strictures of Southern culture.

While all of the young men in the film fight to achieve their dreams, Rashad focuses on his responsibilities as a man and neglects his own dreams. He begins his story by telling the audience that "My pop always used to say, 'Dreaming is the luxury of children' ... when you got responsibilities, you ain't got time to dream. That's the difference between a boy and a man ... and down South, we grow up quick." Rashad cites himself as "the man of the house" and insults his guardian, Uncle George, by telling the audience that "responsibility was not really his strong point." While Rashad attends school by day and works as a janitor by night, in his free time he sketches comics about the lives of his friends, but, as he tells his girlfriend New New, he views this artistic expression as "nothing" but "fooling around." Though he has managed to save a good bit of money, Rashad plans to use his savings to fulfill his responsibilities and send his brother Ant out of the hood; although he is a talented artist, Rashad envisions no success for himself and resigns to watching over Ant.

Throughout the course of the movie, Rashad faces many conflicts that test his manhood, and his sense of community falls apart around him. His girlfriend, New New, lies to him about her wealthy background when she pretends to be "ghetto," and to make matters worse, his best friend Esquire (a stereotypical "Uncle Tom") hides New New's identity from him in order to advance his own goals in the upper-class black community. When Ant is arrested for selling marijuana, Rashad seems haunted by the same sense of familial history (particularly the absent father) that haunts Percy and DJay, as he tells himself, "I keep trying to think of what my Pops would do but I can't think of nothing." Rashad's struggles with poverty and the lack of opportunity it brings come to a head when Ant is shot over a drug deal gone wrong. However, this moment also brings Rashad's community back together. New New apologizes repeatedly for her actions, and Esquire recognizes the importance of Mechanicsville as he shakes off his "Uncle Tom" role. As everyone stands together, Rashad understands that manhood is not about responsibility but more about mutual acceptance within one's community. As he sits by Ant's hospital bed, Rashad begins to let go of his sense of responsibility: "I could teach you everything under the sun, but I can't be a man for you. You got to figure out the best way to do that for yourself." Rashad can now focus on his own dreams.

Rashad tells the audience, "I didn't even know I was dreaming all along cause I was always drawing." His comics — vibrant visual interpretations of the hip hop world of Cascade and Mechanicsville splashed across the screen towards the film's conclusion — keep his dreams alive, and they are later published in a top Atlanta newspaper. As with DJay and Percy, the encouragement and support of Rashad's extended network in Mechanicsville directly inspires his art and his success. In fact, at *ATL*'s somewhat fairytale ending, everyone achieves their dreams. Unlike DJay who must use violence to gain attention or Percival who must leave his family and hometown, the crew remains in and around Mechanicsville and reaches its goal without violence. *ATL* offers an alternative from the earlier East and West Coast "hood" films of the 1990s; young black men are able to achieve their dreams without violence or the necessary escape from violence.[5] As the lights fade at film's end, Rashad puts his skates away and tells viewers, "This is the beginning," underscoring the continuing recognition of and flourishing success of Southern hip hop culture.

ATL, like *Hustle & Flow* and *Idlewild*, suggests that the Southern black community will continue to nurture hip hop culture and artistic achievement, despite the racism and poverty that might still exist in the South.

These three popular films each contribute a "new verse" in the evolution of Southern film and hip hop studies. After scorning most earlier "hood" films, Nelson George writes that a successful hip hop film should contain "nuance, humanity, and [a] refusal to perpetuate stereotypes" (109). These films are nuanced in their attention to the "Southern" hip hop experience, and each film depicts complex black male characters who challenge earlier stereotypes of the "brute" or "Uncle Tom." Unlike the 1990s "hood" films (or even more recent hip hop biopics), these films move away from East or West Coast urban environments filled with inescapable violence to reveal a less "country" South that overcomes violence through artistic achievement. *Hustle & Flow*, *Idlewild*, and *ATL* portray the South as a region where the black community triumphs and the days of the conquering white patriarchs diminish; the artistic desires and dreams of black Southern men can reach fruition with the faith and love that emanates from both the historical and the contemporary Southern black community. As *Hustle & Flow*'s Shelby reminds viewers, hip hop, rap, and in this case film, are "coming back home to the South cause this is where it all began."

Notes

1. For more on the history of black cinema, see the following: Thomas Cripp's *Black Film as Genre*, Manthia Diawara's *Black American Cinema*, Valerie Smith's *Representing Blackness*, and Donald Bogle's "Black Beginnings."

2. For more on the hip hop influence in film, see Melvin Donalson's *Hip Hop in American Cinema* and Celeste A. Fischer's *Black on Black: Urban Youth Films and the Multicultural Audience*.

3. For an enlightening analysis on the nuances of Southern hip hop lyrics, see Richardson's chapter "Gangstas and Playas in the Dirty South" in *Black Masculinity and the U.S. South: From Uncle Tom to Gangsta*. Richardson argues that Southern rap can disrupt certain country or even gangster stereotypes of Southern black men, but she also suggests that Southern rap reinforces a reliance on "folk" stereotypes of the Southern black experience.

4. Both films point to the importance of Southern religion and gospel music as it influences (and challenges) secular music culture. I am reminded of earlier historical conflicts between blues and gospel music in the Southern black community where the blues was often referred to as "The Devil's Music"; one could argue that hip hop culture and rap music is sometimes represented similarly in contemporary society. However, in their conclusions, the three films discussed here vaguely imply that religious faith, along with a strong sense of family, is a key component in achieving one's dreams. While I do not specifically mention this in my discussion of *ATL*, it should be noted that the film subtly hints toward the importance of faith; a portrait of *The Last Supper* is focused on during a time when Rashad is experiencing a loss of faith in his family, and at the film's end, Uncle George finally finds a good "church woman" with whom to spend his life (*ATL*).

5. Specifically, I am thinking of Tre and Brandi's exit at the end of *Boyz n the Hood;* the couple leaves the violence of South Central Los Angeles to attend college in Atlanta. Their destination seems particularly significant because, especially in the film *ATL,* Atlanta becomes a positive space for artistic and communal growth.

Works Cited

ATL. Dir. Chris Robinson. Perf. Tip Harris, Lauren London, Antwan Andre Patton. 2006. Warner Home Video, 2006. DVD.
Bogle, Donald. "Black Beginnings: From *Uncle Tom's Cabin* to *The Birth of a Nation.*" *Representing Blackness: Issues in Film and Video.* Ed. Valerie Smith. New Brunswick: Rutgers University Press, 1997. 13–24.
Cripps, Thomas. *Black Film as Genre.* Bloomington: Indiana University Press, 1978.
Diawara, Manthia, ed. *Black American Cinema.* New York: Routledge, 1993.
Donalson, Melvin. *Hip Hop in American Cinema.* New York: Peter Lang, 2007.
Dyson, Michael Eric. *Know What I Mean? Reflections on Hip Hop.* New York: Basic Civitas Books, 2007.
Fischer, Celeste A. *Black on Black: Urban Youth Films and the Multicultural Audience.* Lanham, MD: The Scarecrow Press, 2006.
George, Nelson. *Hip Hop America.* New York: Penguin, 1998.
Green, Tony. "South on the Rise in Hip-Hop World: Southern Artists Bringing New Style, Experiences to Rap World." *MSNBC.* 23 June 2004. MSNBC, Web. 15 Mar. 2009. <http://www.msnbc.msn.com/id/5270870/>.
Hustle & Flow. Dir. Craig Brewer. Perf. Chris "Ludacris" Bridges, Taraji P. Henson, Terrence Howard, Taryn Manning. 2005. MTV Films, 2005. DVD.
Idlewild. Dir. Bryan Barber. Perf. Andre Benjamin, Terrence Howard, Antwan Andre Patton. 2006. Universal Studios and HBO Films, 2006. DVD.
Richardson, Riché. *Black Masculinity and the U.S. South: From Uncle Tom to Gangsta.* Athens: University of Georgia Press, 2007.
Rose, Tricia. *Black Noise: Rap Music and Black Culture in Contemporary America.* Hanover: Wesleyan University Press, 1994.
Smith, Valerie, ed. *Representing Blackness: Issues in Film and Video.* New Brunswick: Rutgers University Press, 1997.

IV.

"That Old-Timey Music": Nostalgia and the Southern Tradition in *O Brother, Where Art Thou?*

ANDREW B. LEITER

Joel and Ethan Coen's popular 2000 film *O Brother, Where Art Thou?* is a redneck comedy set in Depression-era Mississippi that embraces a slack-jawed hilarity belying its heartfelt soundtrack and its frequently sophisticated engagement with Southern history as well as cinematic and literary traditions. The film establishes its literary roots and its mock epic tenor by opening with a translation of Homer's invocation of the muse from the beginning of *The Odyssey*: "O muse sing in me and through me tell the story...." The Homeric analogs have been well-documented by such scholars as Barbara P. Weinlich and Janice Siegel, and they include a blind African American prophet, John Goodman as a bible salesman Cyclops, seductive creek sirens who appear to turn Pete into a horny toad, and George Clooney as a Ulysses figure who is attempting to return home and reclaim his wife. Other scholars such as R. Barton Palmer and Hugh Ruppersburg have demonstrated that the Coens engage various cinematic predecessors such as *Sullivan's Travels* (1941) in the film's title, *Cool Hand Luke* (1967) in the film's representation of hard-nosed law enforcement, and the *Wizard of Oz* (1939) in a hilarious parody of a Ku Klux Klan rally featuring a synchronized dance routine and infiltration that mimics the Wicked Witch of the East's guards and castle (Palmer 132–34; Ruppersburg 12, 18). From classical literature to classic Hollywood, *O Brother* is hardly coy in many of its allusions to its cinematic and literary antecedents, yet for a film steeped in Southern history and culture to the extent of *O Brother*, it has received little attention for the manner in which the Coens engage classic literary and filmic representations of the South.

This essay considers *O Brother, Where Art Thou?* as a comic discourse on the modernizing South that prioritizes folk music in a self-conscious engagement of Southern literary and film traditions. More specifically, I argue that the yokelism of *O Brother* embraces Mark Twain's comic realism in a celebration of the endurance of "redneck" cinema while dismissing the nostalgic impulses of Depression-era romanticized plantation cinema embodied by *Gone with the Wind* (1939). Set in 1937, *O Brother* engages in its own form of nostalgia, however, and expresses ambivalence about Southern progress, instead, through its veneration of the popular "old-timey music" featured on the radio broadcast of the Pappy O'Daniel Flour Hour. The music mitigates the more brutally Twainish ridicule of the South by offering its audience a point of identification in a manner consistent with the strong cinematic tendency to distinguish between acceptable and deviant Souths. Furthermore, I contend that the music invites nostalgic considerations of Southern distinctiveness at a time of increasingly homogenized regional identities and that it does so in a guiltless fashion of sorts by distancing that nostalgia from less savory aspects of Southern distinctiveness.

In two brief scenes from *O Brother*, the lead characters — three escaped convicts named Everett, Delmar, and Pete (played respectively by Clooney, Tim Blake Nelson, and John Turturro) — sit around campfires on consecutive evenings. In the first of the paired scenes, their African American companion, Tommy Johnson (Chris Thomas King), plays "Hard Time Killing Floor Blues," while the convicts discuss what they intend to do with their shares of the treasure that Everett is supposedly leading them to recover. Delmar explains that he intends to buy back the family farm from the bank which foreclosed on it, because "You ain't no kind of man if you ain't got land." In the second scene, the convicts are seated on the fallen and vegetation-covered columns of an antebellum mansion, while Pete plays an instrumental version of Tommy's song and their latest companion, George "Baby Face" Nelson (Michael Badalucco), wanders off in bipolar depression. Aspects of these two scenes, specifically Delmar's response and the ruined mansion, resonate strongly with the most famous film about the South, *Gone with the Wind*. Delmar's identification with the land resembles Gerald O'Hara's passionate plea with Scarlett to remember that "Land is the only thing in the world worth working for, worth fighting for, worth dying for, because it's the only thing that lasts"— a claim that echoes through the closing scenes of the movie and revitalizes Scarlett enough to declare, "Tomorrow is another day." The movie concludes with Scarlett returning to her beloved Tara, a classically columned plantation home thoroughly emblematic of the disappearing Old South.

Delmar's intention to buy back the family farm can be understood as a minor thematic engagement with the Southern love of land and, as such, one

John Turturro (Pete), Tim Blake Nelson (Delmar), and George Clooney (Everett) star as escaped convicts in Joel and Ethan Coen's redneck comedy *O Brother, Where Art Thou?* (2000 Blind Bard Productions) set in Depression-era Mississippi (credit Melinda Sue Gordon).

of the many forays that the film makes into various thematic staples of Southern-oriented films, including among others, folk life and music, religion and salvation, hard-nosed law enforcement, demagogic politics, racism, lynching, and the Klan. Likewise, the convicts' perches among the ruins might be understood as the juxtaposition of the wealthy antebellum plantation South with the poverty of Depression-era Mississippi, although nothing in the film suggests that the Coens look wistfully toward the Old South as does *Gone with the Wind*. Two critical possibilities arise from the scenes, however, that strike me as particularly intriguing. First, the Coen brothers invoke a parallel between the Civil War and the Great Depression as times of significant change for the South, and in doing so, they indicate both an interest in the transitory nature of Southern society as well as a sense of the history of cinematic engagement with Southern regional identity relative to that change. The second consideration extends from the first: the poor white convicts among the ruins represent an apropos metaphor for the decline in the popular image of the romanticized Old South and the continued strength of the redneck South in popular culture.

The two most influential films about the South, *Gone with the Wind* and its infamous predecessor D. W. Griffith's *The Birth of a Nation* (1915), set the bar in terms of cinematic mythmaking for the South. Both films engage the South in its transition from the antebellum world through the devastation of the Civil War and the turmoil of Reconstruction, and they construct an image of the South as a once gallant and benign patriarchy struggling to maintain (white) civilization against the depredations of freedmen and carpetbaggers. Griffith's notoriously racist defense of white supremacist violence was the cinematic sensation of its generation and reportedly led President Woodrow Wilson to declare, "It is like writing history with lightning. And my only regret is that it is all so terribly true" (Oliver and Walker 4). Written and produced during the Depression, David Selznick's film version of Margaret Mitchell's novel looks away from its contemporary South of the 1930s and emphasizes a nostalgic antebellum world of hoopskirted Southern belles and faithful slaves before turning to the convulsions of the Civil War and Reconstruction. The film's suggestions of economic modernization and shifts in traditional gender roles as symbolized in Scarlett's business ventures at the mill are ultimately overshadowed by social unrest and vigilante violence against freedmen and carpetbaggers. While less vitriolic than *The Birth of a Nation*, *Gone with the Wind* represents an extension of the same Southern mythology that sought to reconcile Southern history as integral to a white national identity, and Tara McPherson contends that Scarlett's iconic status remains incongruously dissociated from American racial history as part of "our cultural schizophrenia about the South" (3). Nonetheless, the film's enduring popularity is such that journalist Tony Horwitz, who traveled through the South in search of pop cultural remnants of the antebellum world, found that "*Gone with the Wind* had done more to keep the Civil War alive, and to mold its memory, than any history book or event since Appomattox" (296).

The slack-jawed yokelism of *O Brother* does not, of course, engage in this sort of romanticized mythmaking that Edward D. C. Campbell, Jr., has shown to be a staple of early Hollywood representations of the South; rather, the film embraces the other extreme of the South in popular imagination, the poverty-ridden and ignorant redneck South. Indeed, in its celebration of redneck comedy, *O Brother* invites snickering comparisons to *Gone with the Wind* as the embodiment of the plantation South. Critics have noted, for example, that George Clooney's character — from his mannerisms to his moustache — parodies Clark Gable (Taylor; Scott). When the Coens parody a 1930s heartthrob playing a roguish nineteenth century Southern gentleman with a new millennium heartthrob playing a 1930s bumpkin conman, it suggests that they are keenly interested in the relationship between such contradictory representations of the South, and it is from this perspective that I consider the convicts among the plantation ruins in *O Brother*. Again, one might interpret this scene as the juxtaposition of a once wealthy plantation South with the poverty of the Depression, but I prefer to understand the scene more abstractly as a sort of declaration of cinematic supremacy. More specifically, I view it as emblematic of the endurance of "redneck" cinema that has outlived romanticized plantation cinema — a relationship somewhat analogous to the scene from Mark Twain's *Adventures of Huckleberry Finn* (1884) in which Twain suggests the ascendency of literary realism and the decline of romantic literature in the form of the sinking *Walter Scott*, a steamboat named after the author of chivalric romances that Twain despised. Such a comparison emerges in part because the contradictory images of the redneck South and the romanticized South, in all their variations, have been the most pervasive popular images of the region since the antebellum period; it emerges in part because of the Coens' expressed interest in Southern literature; and it emerges most fully because the movie bears so many other similarities to Twain's classic including the down-and-out interracial solidarity, the attention to the vernacular traditions, the style of comic caricature, the picaresque structure, the emphasis on superstition, and the displays of mob mentality.

In a review of *O Brother* for *Salon.com*, Charles Taylor suggested that "If Mad magazine had attempted to do 'Let Us Now Praise Famous Men' the result might be 'O Brother, Where Art Thou?,'" and such a suggestion — the film as a zany reimagining of a Southern literary classic — is not as whimsical as it perhaps sounds. The Coens have expressed their appreciation of Southern literature with Ethan acknowledging in an interview: "A film like *Raising Arizona* should make you suspect, I suppose, our admiration for Southern writers like William Faulkner and Flannery O'Connor" (Palmer 161). W. P. Mayhew, the alcoholic author and screenwriter in *Barton Fink* (1991), was inspired by Faulkner's stints in Hollywood, and Joel has noted that Vernon T. Waldrip of *O Brother* is a name borrowed from *The Wild Palms*, one of his favorite Faulkner novels (Coen 180). From a scholarly perspective, Thomas Ærvold Bjerre has noted allusions to Faulkner's works in the names of various other characters in *O Brother* and to O'Connor in the representation of the corrupt and cyclopean bible salesman Big Dan Teague (59). With regard to *Adventures of Huckleberry Finn*, however, I find *O Brother*'s relationship less overtly allusive than conceptual in nature — something similar to the brothers' description of Sam Elliott's character and voiceover in *The Big Lebowski* (1998) as "rediscovering the old earthiness of a Mark Twain" (Coen 103).

I find Twain to be a most fitting model for the Coens' grimly comic version of Mississippi as Twain was the greatest literary assailant against Southern pretensions and illusions. As interracial picaresques set in the South, *Adventures of Huckleberry Finn* and *O Brother* share an episodic structure that lends itself to the satirical portrait of various aspects of Southern life. In his portrayal of the senseless and brutal Shepherdson and Grangerford feud and in his depiction of the morally corrupt Duke and King, Twain directs his satirical ire toward Southern claims of aristocracy, honor, and chivalry. It is this same idea of a noble South that *Gone with the Wind* reifies in its cinematic yearning toward a notion of a better South than existed in the 1930s, and while *O Brother* pays scant attention to any grandiose claims of Southern gentility, it engages those aspects of the Depression-era South that lent to the region's miserable reputation and which *Gone with the Wind* avoids: poverty, brutality, fundamentalism, political demagoguery, ignorance, and racism. With the exception of politics, Twain addresses all of these issues, and in his approach to this seedier South, Twain shares a style of comic caricature with the Coens that often relies on the disjuncture between the con artists' wit and general human stupidity. Likewise, the mobbish town mentality that Twain emphasizes at various stops along the river and that culminates with the tar and feathering of the Duke and King has analogs in *O Brother* such as the gubernatorial candidate who is ridden on a rail or the charivari accompanying Baby Face Nelson to the electric chair. Similarly, one might point to Delmar's belief that Pete has been turned into a toad as reminiscent of Twain's heavy emphasis on his characters' superstitious natures, or one might point to Everett's lies and cons as reminiscent of Huck's handiness with a lie.

Such similarities might simply arise from like-minded humorists targeting ignorance in its familiar Southern forms, but when they are coupled with the similarities in the depiction of interracial solidarity, the Coens appear to have Twain's classic in mind. The parallels permeate various aspects of the respective interracial flights from authority and society. The symbiotic relationship that Jim and Huck enjoy is repeated in the manner that Tommy contributes to the convicts' musical success and eventual pardon and in the convicts rescuing Tommy from the Klan. Such interracial sympathy presumably extends from the white characters' outcast status. Huck and the convicts are products of a racist society as clear from seemingly innocuous vernacular comments suggesting their racially defined concepts of behavior. When Jim risks his freedom to save Tom Sawyer, Huck proudly relates, "I knowed he was white inside" (230). Likewise, when Everett forgives Pete for having revealed the secret of the supposed treasure, Pete responds, "It's awful white of ya to take it like that, Everett." Despite such ingrained cultural racism, Huck and the convicts maintain an antithetical racial innocence that allows interracial camaraderie and serves as the benchmark of common human decency in terms of race in both novel and film.

The parallels between *O Brother* and *Huckleberry Finn* are not absolute of course, and most significantly for my essay, it should be noted that Twain's distaste for romantic literature was a distaste for the most popular literature of the day, whereas, while *Gone with the Wind* may continue to inform popular perceptions of the antebellum South as Horwitz argues, *O Brother*'s parodic jabs at Selznick's film mock a cinematic tradition that has been outmoded for some time. As a film deeply engaged with the popular conceptions of Southern identity explored through a historical prism, however, *O Brother* exists in the same continuum as *Huckleberry Finn* and *Gone with the Wind* and exhibits a similar interplay between contemporaneous audience and the representation of the Southern past. Twain's novel addresses, among other topics, Reconstruction-era racial anxieties through its withering portraiture of the antebellum world, and he offers very little that might reconcile his audience to the region. If Twain indulges in any nostalgia, it is not directed toward the region's history but rather toward a notion of childhood innocence that serves to endear readers to Huck while further damning the Southern society from which he flees. *Gone with the Wind*, on the other hand, makes every effort to reconcile its audience with the Southern past through its nostalgic fantasy that turns fully away from the South's Depression-era problems. *O Brother*'s depiction of the South is comically brutal in Twain fashion, but unlike Twain, the Coens invite reconciliation between their audience and their filmic South. Less grand than *Gone with the Wind*'s epic focus on the Civil War and Reconstruction, *O Brother*, nevertheless, exhibits similar — albeit mock epic — tensions extending from changes in Southern society that surface in nostalgia for better times, the promise of progress, and attendant anxiety about the social, cultural, and economic transitions. Set in 1937, the film's nostalgia is not oriented toward the Old South but rather toward the better economic times prior to the Depression. Delmar's comments on redeeming the family farm from foreclosure suggest as much as does the primary vehicle for nostalgia and reconciliation in the film, the popular "old-timey music" featured on the Pappy O'Daniel Flour Hour.

The soundtrack to the film was a resounding commercial success as a multi-platinum bestseller and a Grammy award winner. Not everyone, however, was enamored with its popular success, and Julie Koehler declared it to be the worst thing to happen to bluegrass music since *Deliverance* (14). Others viewed it more positively as ushering in a folk revival (Michaels 50; Goldmark 33). I will leave the debates about the merits of the album, questions about its folk authenticity, and its impact on popular perceptions of bluegrass to those with a vested interest in such questions.[1] I am more interested in how music functions as a multi-layered agent of nostalgia and as the predominant cultural capital of the Depression-era representations within the film. Throughout *O Brother*, the "old-timey" music moderates hard times with its musical glance backward toward better days or, at least, the notion of such, and offers the characters both figurative and literal returns to innocence. From an audience perspective, the music serves a similar moderating function by softening the depictions of an otherwise miserable Southern world. Likewise, when the music restores the main characters to legal innocence, it also restores mainstream Southern society to innocence and moral authority by vanquishing the most reactionary and racist figure of the film. This restoration of the South to an innocence of sorts is a thematic culmination of the musical effect throughout the film, namely the prioritizing of Southern folk cultural history over less palatable Southern socio-political history.

The music structures the film from the opening scene featuring a chain gang singing "Po' Lazarus" to the final scene featuring a rendition of "Angel Band." Performances are integral to various scenes, such as the Klan leader and gubernatorial candidate singing "O Death" or the sirens singing "Didn't Leave Nobody but the Baby." For the characters of the film, the music acts as the salve to the misery of hard times. "Hard Time Killing Floor Blues" in accompaniment to Delmar's desire to reclaim the family farm is only one of many such instances. Pete's cousin has been reduced to eating horse which he believes is "beginning to turn," and the radio plays the Pappy O'Daniel Flour Hour in the background as he relates the brutal impact of the Depression on Pete's extended family. The film presents an over-alled farmer behind a span of mules against a faded and dreary farmscape in juxtaposition to a rendition of "Keep on the Sunny Side." When a group of revivalists sing "Down to the River to Pray" in procession to a river baptism, Everett declares: "Yes sir, hard times have flushed the chumps." His cynical assessment in no way deters Delmar and Pete who, enticed by the music and the promise of salvation, plunge into the river for an easy spiritual restoration. It is the radio station manager who records the convicts' version of "I Am a Man of Constant Sorrow" that propels them to fame, however, who phrases the music's allure most succinctly: "Yes sir, folks just can't get enough of this old-timey stuff." In this sense the prominence of the music in *O Brother* celebrates the power of music to transform and transcend that is central to so much of folk, bluegrass, country, and blues or, to borrow Ralph Ellison's famous definition of the blues, the music fulfills "an impulse to keep the painful details and episodes of a brutal experience alive in one's aching consciousness, to finger its jagged grain, and to transcend it, not by the consolation of philosophy but by squeezing from it a near-tragic, near-comic lyricism" (78).

In another sense, however, the music performs an oddly similar function to the nostalgic impulse within *Gone with the Wind*. If *Gone with the Wind* asks its audience to look away from the hardship and racism of the 1930s, *O Brother*, it might be argued, asks us to listen away those same issues. This occurs throughout the film as various songs and performances transcend the action in terms of focal points such as when gubernatorial candidate Homer

Stokes (in Klan attire) sings "O Death" at a Ku Klux Klan rally. The prioritization of folk music in this scene overshadows and softens the grimmest aspects of Southern reactionary sentiments during the 1930s. This is not to say that *Gone with the Wind* and *O Brother* share perspectives on these sentiments. Whereas *Gone with the Wind* validates vigilante violence as a defense of Southern (white) civilization, *O Brother* ridicules the Klan, their veneration of the rebel flag, and the Grand Wizard's intention to lynch Tommy in order to "preserve our hallowed culture and heritage from intrusions, inclusions and dilutions of color, of creed, of our old-time religion!" The hollow rhetoric appears as nonsensical resistance to the perceived threat of cultural and social change and, while the violent reaction to the threat is focused on Tommy's black body, Stokes extends the so-called intrusions to include "papists," "Jews," and "all those smart-ass folks say we come descended from monkeys." The ridicule of such sentiments notwithstanding, the manner in which the music upstages the demagoguery serves to moderate such racism as a social factor just as it does poverty at various other points.

The tendency of the music to overshadow the unpleasant staples of Southern image culminates in an outright musical triumph over the reactionary voices in the movie's climactic scene. The convicts and Tommy perform as the Soggy Bottom Boys at a political rally in a last attempt to win back Everett's wife. In a scene that brings together the gubernatorial candidates, the convicts, and the general Mississippi public, the Soggy Bottom Boys vanquish the Klan candidate Stokes, earn pardons from the incumbent governor Pappy O'Daniel, and re-unite Everett with his family. Described by one critic as a "utopian musical fantasy" (Chadwell 7), this all results from the group's performance of "I Am a Man of Constant Sorrow," the popularity of which has grown so fast that the crowd dismisses Stokes's litany of the group's offenses that include not only being escaped convicts, but also integration, miscegenation, interfering with a Klan ritual, and Tommy selling his soul to the devil. Stokes, in essence, calls on the crowd to be "good" Southerners and reject the threats to religion and racial purity that the group represents. None of the offenses, however, register with the crowd which wants to hear the song, and in a clear statement that such social fears pale in comparison to the joy brought by a song of woe, Stokes is pelted with refuse and ridden out on a rail. The music in this scene not only restores the convicts to legal innocence and to mainstream Southern society, it also expurgates that society by leading it to renounce the Klan and all it represents in the figure of Stokes. In a final reconciliation of the convicts — and by extension the audience — with a newly avowed non-racist Southern society, the Soggy Bottom Boys lead the crowd and Governor O'Daniel in a rendition of the folk classic "You Are My Sunshine."

One hesitates to critique a film as exquisitely ridiculous as *O Brother* for its treatment of social issues; however, the film is so smart in so many of its approaches to the Depression-era South that the convenient musical dismissal of historical racism warrants at least some consideration for its implications. Critics have differed in their opinions as to the extent that the Coens engage social issues in *O Brother*. John-Paul Spiro, for example, argues that the film succeeds in "resolving the dilemma of the artist's social obligations by making a film that is enjoyable without being empty, morally significant without being didactic or simplistic" (65). Palmer, on the other hand, contends: "*O Brother* is witty and sophisticated, but ... dedicated to uncomplicated emotional uplift, it avoids serious questions of any kind" (133). For their part, the Coens have rejected social conscience as a necessary aspect of their filmmaking in comments such as Joel's claim that "We're not trying to educate the masses," and Ethan's successive question: "Does that make us bad people" (Pooley 47). One can imagine them relishing Twain's famous warning at the beginning of *Adventures of Huckleberry Finn* that "persons attempting to find a moral in it will be banished." I tend to agree with the Coens that a film need not "educate the masses" but, as Douglas McFarland has noted, their titular allusion to *Sullivan's Travels*— a film that considers the suitability of comedy and social realism for representing the Depression — suggests a self-conscious awareness of the tensions between social ills and comedy that belies any flippant disregard of the social politics (42). What I find interesting in the simultaneous restoration of the convicts and the purification of Southern society is not that, at its worst, this might be construed as a comic dismissal of segregation-era racial violence as insignificant, but rather that the scene embraces a musical nostalgia that masks a rather standardized process of reconciliation between the film's audience and the historical South.

While the filmic South has frequently provided an easy focal point for the entertaining displacement of many stigmatic deviancies — racial, religious, sexual, economic, or otherwise — in American culture, a tendency in contemporary films about the South is to offset any national displacement with an internal regional displacement. This internal displacement proffers two white Souths, one deviant and another, however identifiably Southern, that shares what are perceived to be normative American values from an audience perspective. As Allison Graham has argued, this division is commonplace in race and civil rights films which displace Southern racism onto the redneck South (13). Such division might range from the obvious split between good whites and "white trash" racists in films like *A Time to Kill* (1996) to more complicated and astute presentations such as the suffering white females in multicultural films of the 1980s that Amy Corbin discusses in her essay for this collection. This two-Souths filmic divide is not limited to race films, and while some films portray the American-normative South as a minority within the region, in other films the deviant South exists at the fringes of mainstream society. As Maria Hebert-Leiter notes in her essay in this collection, Bobby Boucher of *The Waterboy* (1998) triumphs by escaping the ignorance of his bayou roots and entering normal Louisiana society. Likewise, while the hillbillies of *Deliverance* (1972) remain an enduring popular image of the South, the weekend wilderness adventurers who battle that hillbilly terror are, after all, Sunny South suburbanites from Atlanta.

Catering to an audience's desire to identify with some characters and reject their antagonists in a simplified and frequently emotionally generic fashion is standard fare for movies and television, but representations of the South follow a uniquely regionalized pattern within this broader tendency by emphasizing Southern distinctiveness as the antagonistic or deviant elements. *O Brother* follows suit with its presentation of mainstream Mississippians rejecting demagoguery and the Klan; however, the film also breaks with this pattern by celebrating the folk music as a more important aspect of Southern distinctiveness. In an article for *Southern Cultures*, the cultural historian Benjamin Filene described his discomfort with the resurgent popular interest in folk music at the start of the new millennium: "The idea of folk culture as geographically isolated, chronologically removed, and socially deviant remains instrumental to the current folk vogue. People are drawn to the notion of the 'old, weird America'" (Filene 61). Filene's remarks are directed at the folk fad in general with an emphasis on the audience's fascination with the content of the songs rather than *O Brother* specifically, but his sense of folk music as a voyeuristic window into a grittier past resonates with the function of music in the film. The music of *O Brother*, however, extends beyond mere historical voyeurism and offers a purified regional voyeurism, in which the audience can enjoy the comedy and brutality widely associated with the South on screen but can do so relieved of their own social sensibilities. The soundtrack of *O Brother*, taken as a whole, does not feature a particularly deviant South, rather it provides the emotional antidote that turns the poverty, racism, and demagoguery of Depression Mississippi into palatable comic fare.

The manner in which *O Brother* reprioritizes standard filmic notions of Southern distinctiveness accounts, I believe, for much of its popularity in a period of ever-increasing homogenization of region and nation. Grits and barbecue, y'all and ma'am, fishing and football — these, and the aggregate of any other number of Southern delineators, still suggest a region with its own personality, but the expanding suburbanization, ubiquitous strip malls, and growing multinational presence, not to mention the general sense of harmonious regional reconciliation with the nation in the wake of the civil rights era, suggest that remaining points of Southern distinctiveness amount to little more than modest variations within a predominantly homogenous national identity. Such transition in regional identity has been accompanied by a contemporary quandary for many Southerners, a quandary that is marked by a tension between a desire for a sense of continuity with a distinctive past and the knowledge that Southern distinctiveness in a historical perspective is marred, and overwhelmingly so, by images of racism, poverty, and ignorance. *O Brother* navigates that quandary by embracing a Twainish South in all of its comic brutality and by simultaneously offering its audience a positive and — in the film — a more powerful manifestation of Southern culture in the celebration of folk music. Despite being a film that dismisses the nostalgic erasures of plantation cinema, *O Brother* replaces that erasure with a less offensive nostalgia in the form of folk music.

In the scene following the political rally, Everett and the gang return to Everett's family home to recover Penny's wedding ring, and they are caught first by the law which refuses to acknowledge the pardons and then liberated by inundation as the Tennessee Valley Authority floods the valley in order to bring electricity to the region. In this flood of biblical proportions, various items float by including a banjo, a picture of a Civil War soldier, and a gramophone. The scene is suggestive of a sea change in Southern identity and reminds the audience of what has been washed away in the intervening years. While floating in the flood waters that have drowned the landscape and his family home, Everett identifies this moment as the South's entrance to modernity:

> Yes sir, the South is gonna change. Everything's gonna be put on electricity and run on a paying basis. Out with the old spiritual mumbo-jumbo, the superstitions and the backward ways. We're gonna see a brave new world where they run everyone a wire and hook us all up to a grid. Yes sir, a veritable age of reason, like the one they had in France, and not a moment too soon.

As Southerners adrift on the tides of change, the convicts are swimming in familiar waters of the cinematic South which provide a rich medium for considering the interplay of nostalgia, change, and resistance in the American South. The biblical cleansing notwithstanding, the film does more than simply suggest that the economic catastrophe of the Depression and segregation-era racial fears could be washed away with a song; it suggests rather that the South in film need not be defined as distinctive exclusively through the region's historical and popular cinematic deviancies.

Notes

1. In addition to Koehler, Michaels, and Goldmark, see among others, David Royko's "O Brother, Where Art Thou?," Randy Pitts's "Traditional Music in Tinseltown in 2002: What Does It All Mean?," Sean Chadwell's "Inventing That 'Old-Timey' Style: Southern

Authenticity in *O Brother, Where Art Thou?*," Benjamin Filene's "*O Brother*, What Next? Making Sense of the Folk Fad," and Martin Harries's "In the Coen Brothers' New Film, the Dark Utopian Music of the American South."

Works Cited

Bjerre, Thomas Ærvold. "Southern Pop Culture and the Literary Tradition in *O Brother, Where Art Thou?*" *American Studies in Scandinavia* 38.2 (2006): 55-65.
Campbell, Edward D. C., Jr. *The Celluloid South: Hollywood and the Southern Myth*. Knoxville: University Tennessee Press, 1981.
Chadwell, Sean. "Inventing That 'Old-Timey' Style: Southern Authenticity in *O Brother, Where Art Thou?*" *Journal of Popular Film and Television* 32.1 (2004): 2-9.
Coen, Joel, and Ethan Coen. *The Coen Brothers: Interviews*. Ed. William Rodney Allen. Jackson: University Press of Mississippi, 2006.
Ellison, Ralph. "Richard Wright's Blues." *Shadow and Act*. 1953. New York: Vintage, 1995. 77-94.
Filene, Benjamin. "*O Brother*, What Next? Making Sense of the Folk Fad." *Southern Cultures* 10.2 (2004): 50-69.
Goldmark, Daniel. "*O Brother, Where Art Thou?* A Musical Appreciation." *Xavier Review* 23.2 (2003): 31-41.
Gone with the Wind. Dir. Victor Fleming. Prod. David Selznick. Perf. Clark Gable and Vivien Leigh. 1939. Warner Home Video, 2000. DVD.
Graham, Allison. *Framing the South: Hollywood, Television, and Race during the Civil Rights Struggle*. Baltimore: Johns Hopkins University Press, 2003.
Harries, Martin. "In the Coen Brothers' New Film, the Dark Utopian Music of the American South." *The Chronicle of Higher Education* 2 Feb. 2002: B14+.
Horwitz, Tony. *Confederates in the Attic: Dispatches from the Unfinished Civil War*. Vintage Departures ed. New York: Vintage, 1999.
Koehler, Julie. "O Brother, Why Did They Make This Movie?" *Bluegrass Unlimited* 35.11 (2001): 14-16.
McFarland, Douglas. "Philosophies of Comedy in *O Brother, Where Art Thou?*" *The Philosophy of the Coen Brothers*. Ed. Mark T. Conard. Lexington: University of Kentucky Press, 2009. 41-54.
McPherson, Tara. *Reconstructing Dixie: Race, Gender, and Nostalgia in the Imagined South*. Durham: Duke University Press, 2003.
Michaels, Bill. "O Brother, Is Bluegrass Music Growing!" *Bluegrass Unlimited* 39.12 (2005): 50-53.
O Brother, Where Art Thou? Dir. Joel Coen and Ethan Coen. Perf. George Clooney, John Turturro, and Tim Blake Nelson. 2000. Touchstone, 2001. DVD.
Oliver, Lawrence J., and Terri L. Walker. "James Weldon Johnson's *New York Age* Essays on *The Birth of a Nation* and the 'Southern Oligarchy.'" *South Central Review* 10 (1993): 1-17.
Palmer, R. Barton. *Joel and Ethan Coen*. Urbana: University of Illinois Press, 2004.
Pitts, Randy. "Traditional Music in Tinseltown in 2002: What Does It All Mean?" *The Old-Time Herald* 8.5 (2002): 28-31, 52.
Pooley, Eric. "Warped in America: The Dark Vision of Moviemakers Joel and Ethan Coen." *New York*. 23 Mar. 1987. 44-48.
Royko, David. "*O Brother, Where Art Thou?*" *Bluegrass Unlimited* 35.8 (2001): 34-36.
Ruppersburg, Hugh. "'Oh, So Many Startlements…': History, Race, and Myth in *O Brother, Where Art Thou?*" *Southern Cultures* 9.4 (2003): 5-26.

Scott, A. O. Rev. of *O Brother, Where Art Thou?*, dir. Joel and Ethan Coen. *New York Times*. New York Times, 22 Dec. 2000. Web. 24 Oct. 2009.
Siegel, Janice. "The Coens' *O Brother, Where Art Thou?* and Homer's *Odyssey*." *Mouseion* 7.3 (2007): 213-45.
Spiro, John-Paul. "'You're Very Beautiful ... Are You in Pictures?': Barton Fink, *O Brother Where Art Thou?* and the Purposes of Art." *Post Script* 27.2 (2008): 62-72.
Taylor, Charles. Rev. of *O Brother, Where Art Thou?*, dir. Joel and Ethan Coen. *Salon.com*. 22 Dec. 2000. Web. 24 Oct. 2009.
Twain, Mark. *Adventures of Huckleberry Finn*. 1884. Boston: Houghton Mifflin, 1958.
Weinlich, Barbara P. "'*Odyssey*, Where Art Thou?' Myth and Mythmaking in the Twenty-First Century." *Classical and Modern Literature* 25.2 (2005): 89-108.

V.

American Dreams and Country Music: *Nashville* and *Payday*

HUGH RUPPERSBURG

When it was released in 1975, Robert Altman's film *Nashville* seemed the culmination of a pattern set in motion in 1970 with *MASH* and *Brewster McCloud* and in 1971 with *McCabe and Mrs. Miller*. These films offered satiric critiques of American popular culture, contemporary history, values, and ideals. Their central interest was the state of the American union. *MASH* used the Korean War to comment on the Vietnamese conflict. *Brewster McCloud*, set in and around the Houston Astrodome, highlighted in absurdist and sometimes surreal fashion the destructive tension between the creative yearnings of the individual and the forces of corporate modern America. Like *MASH*, it placed widely recognized American institutions — the military, law enforcement, professional athletics — in opposition to the humanist values and aspirations of individuals. A young man who wants to escape the corrupting influences of the world by building a flying machine that will carry him to freedom comes up against those who want to foil his dream. (The young man is also a serial killer). Similar tensions are at work in *McCabe and Mrs. Miller*, where 19th century corporate interests destroy a young gambler and his entrepreneurial ambitions in frontier Alaska. In *Nashville*, those who face down corporate America and who are to an extent its witting and unwitting agents are the singers and producers of the country music industry. In *Brewster McCloud* the Astrodome signifies the contemporary environment of America and all that it embodies. In *Nashville* a false Parthenon serves a similar function.

Nashville is deeply marked by issues and controversies of its day: the Watergate crisis, the aftermath of the Vietnam War and the cultural divisions it opened up in the United States, the assassinations of the 1960s, the civil rights movement, the rise of feminism, the American South during the 1970s

Gwen Welles as Sueleen (alongside actors Gailard Sartain and Keenan Wynn), a waitress and an aspiring but untalented singer in Robert Altman's *Nashville* (1975, American Broadcasting Companies).

as an object of pop-culture fetishism, celebrity worship, and a general sense of national malaise — the sickness that Jimmy Carter, in a 1979 speech for which he was much reviled, suggested had infected the nation.[1]

Nashville is a film of many voices and points of view, of conflicting values and judgments. Voices talk against one another, overlap and cancel one another out, blend in harmony and strain in disagreement. They suggest that the nation has lost its national moorings, that consumerism and late capitalism have supplanted its founding values. They suggest we are heading towards self-destruction, that, like Joyce's Ireland, we are the old sow that eats our own farrow. They also suggest that the time is not too late for recovery, that even for someone like the fatuous and hypocritical singer Haven Hamilton, the film's own Bob Hope, there is the final opportunity for redemption.

The city of Nashville is the film's microcosm for the nation at large. As the country music capital of the world, it embodies the American dream of talent, success, and wealth.[2] It is also connected, through its history and the country music industry that insists on this link, to traditional and original American values — family, agriculture, religion, morality, and political conservatism. Yet the city in the film seems marked by ambitious boosterism and a failure of honest self-reflection. It is a city that, seeking to grow and prosper, exploits the vulnerable and unsuspecting. In this sense, the film is about a city of hucksters and exploitationists. A prime example of this exploitation is an aspiring singer and airport diner worker named Sueleen. Her only real friend is an African American counterman, Wade Cooley. In a scene reminiscent of the "Battle Royale" episode in Ralph Ellison's *Invisible Man*, political fundraisers convince Sueleen to do a striptease at a benefit for a political candidate. All the business and political leaders of the town are present to watch her — white men in suits, with cigars and alcohol and leering faces. She doesn't want to take off her clothes, but when she is told that she'll be allowed to sing at a political rally on the steps of the Nashville Parthenon, she agrees. Not especially talented or intelligent, Sueleen never questions herself, even when Wade assures her that she can't sing and that people are going to eat her alive. She's certain of her destiny to be a country music singer. The scene illustrates the power that the desire for celebrity and fame holds over individuals. It also expresses the idea that the men who watch Sueleen are also watching all the other characters in the film, that the power and money they embody are what most of the characters in one way or another desire. Screenwriter Joan Tewkesbury said of this scene: "It was the emotional core of the film. [Sueleen] is every person in that movie. Every person in that movie believes that if they just do that one thing, it won't matter, everybody will forget and they will get famous, or get the job.... Everybody in this movie compromises at some point or another."[3]

The city of Nashville also embodies the American South. The film examines a period of transition when increasing urbanization and accelerating growth of commerce and industry place the modern South in contrast to its traditional origins and the down-home values country music purports to exemplify. This implied tension between the overtly present modern world and the implied past and traditions of country music runs throughout the film. Through various images of nightclubs, the city skyline, tourists, and musicians, and through Hamilton Haven's constant boosterism, the film presents country music as a commodity to be harvested and marketed. (Visitors to Nashville today will find this marketing of the music industry continued in the Country Music Hall of Fame, which enshrines the history and major figures of the industry in the halo of a mythic American Valhalla.)

The changes occurring in Nashville and the rest of the South are evident early in the film in scenes at the airport, where the beloved singer Barbara Jean is returning from a clinic that has treated her for what we are told are burns. The airport is a place of travel, movement, transition. It is the city's portal to the outer world, to modernity. Many of the film's characters arrive in the city through its gates, either literally or figuratively. Expressways are another means by which the modern world has come to Nashville. After Barbara Jean collapses, everyone who had gathered at the airport to greet her leaves at the same time and drives at breakneck speed towards the city. A comic series of crashes and then a pileup and traffic jam result. The film's characters are either constantly in motion, moving from one place to another, or are stuck in traffic. This is the way of contemporary America, Altman is telling us.

Country music typically addresses themes and subjects traditionally associated with the American South. By choosing country music and musicians as his subject, Altman chose an easy target. Who will argue back on their behalf and complain of prejudice, bias, stereotyping, anti-regional arrogance? Because they are people who are, after all (according to the logic of the film), hillbilly hicks and crackers, no group will rise to their defense. But Altman is not as vicious as he could be. There is compassion, empathy, in his portraitures, in some more than others. He finds something to like in most of these characters, even Sueleen, who never gives up on herself. Narcissistic Tom Frank, eager to bed any woman within reach, falls for Linnea, the expressionless mother of two deaf children and wife to the bulbous, soulless Delbert Reese. Tom actually talks with Linnea during their tryst, though he had nothing to say to his other partners. She moves him when all the others are merely objects. His attraction to Linnea humanizes him, despite his narcissism, his sexist exploitation of women and of his own celebrity.

Linnea's deaf children are at the core of one of the film's themes, the need to be heard, the desire for identity and recognition. In several poignant scenes we see her talking with her children through sign language, and we hear her son struggling to speak. Yet with her own husband, Delbert, she has virtually no communication. He can't understand what his children say. In this film set in the American South, it may seem odd to encounter characters struggling to be recognized and heard. The traditional South is supposed to be a place of community and kinship. But this is the modern urban South, afflicted like the rest of the modern world with alienated, isolated, solitary souls struggling to connect. The most obvious example of a character struggling to be heard in *Nashville* is the singer Albuquerque. Genuinely talented, she struggles to gain entry to the country music industry—she tries to be heard throughout the film. When she is given a chance to sing at a stock-car race, revving engines drown her out. Another example is Lady Pearl, business partner and perhaps lover to Haven Hamilton. She tries to explain to the reporter Opal her inchoate ideas about the Kennedys and her anguish over their assassinations—Opal doesn't understand. When Barbara Jean tries to express her feelings about family and tradition to the audience at her Opry

Belle performance, she is so mired in confusion and emotional distress that she can't speak coherently. The audience, angry over her failure to perform, won't listen to what she is trying to say.

The film's concern with media extends this theme. The opening credits are presented in the form of a loud and garish television advertisement for a mail-order collection of the great hits of country music.[4] This initial scene calls attention to the film as a media artifact, a manufactured product, in the same way all the performers and musicians in the film are manufactured products. (*Nashville* is an artifact about artifacts). Immediately following is a scene in which a car with a loudspeaker drives through the streets of the city blaring out the voice and political message of populist political candidate Hal Phillip Walker. Next are scenes in recording studios where Haven Hamilton struggles to record a song, and where Linnea and an African American gospel choir perform. Opal, of course, is a film-maker for BBC, and towards the end of the film Howard K. Smith, an actual news broadcaster for ABC from 1962 to 1979, comments on the Walker campaign. Country music itself is a media-based industry—it communicates with its audience through radio and television shows, through recordings.[5]

Opal, the purported BBC journalist who is making a documentary "about America," is constantly perplexed and confused by everything she sees. She's eager to fabricate and distort meaning—consider her walk through the auto junkyard ("I need something like this for my documentary. I need it. It's ... It's America. Those cars smashing into each other ... and all those mangled corpses"), and later through a group of abandoned school buses ("The buses! The buses are empty and look almost menacing, threatening, as so many yellow dragons watching me with their hollow, vacant eyes. I wonder how many little black and white children have yellow nightmares, their own special brand of fear for the yellow peril."). When she watches a performance by an African American choir, she can talk of nothing but African natives. It is no coincidence that the most uncomprehending and clueless person in the film is a documentary film-maker, a journalist. Ironically, both Altman and screenwriter Tewkesbury conceived of Opal as versions of themselves, wandering through the city and encountering various individuals and scenes in the Nashville and country music landscape.[6]

The heart and center of *Nashville* is Barbara Jean, talented, emotionally ill, and unable to cope without the assistance of her husband/manager and the support of her fans. As Pauline Kael suggests, Barbara Jean lives solely through her music and her memories of her past, which occasionally she struggles to articulate.[7] Everyone admires her and seeks to be associated with her—hoping for a share of her authenticity and talent. Trying to decide whether to appear with Barbara Jean's rival Connie White (they never appear on stage together), Haven Hamilton vows to appear only with Barbara Jean. By associating with her and her songs, he hopes to elevate his own image.

Barbara Jean is the standard by which the film measures all its other characters. No one measures up. Even Connie White, glittery and talented but a calculated clone of sorts, doesn't measure up. She is the most significant threat to Barbara Jean. (Their characters seem loosely based on the singers Loretta Lynn and Tammy Wynette). Connie possesses all the requisite formulaic elements for success. Unlike her rival, she doesn't need the help of advisors to prop her up, and one can imagine her quick rise to first-level stardom should Barbara Jean stumble. Connie may want fame and fortune, but she doesn't need these in the same way Barbara Jean does — they aren't (at least not yet) her soul and identity as they are for Barbara Jean.

Barbara Jean is the sort of singer/songwriter who helps account for the traditions and talent associated with country music and the Nashville name. Her own problems aside, she is a source of stability and gravitas in a time when country music and the city of Nashville are in flux. Country music in the 1970s stood on the verge of obsolescence: too many white people, too homogeneous, too bland. The film shows the arrival in the country music world of different kinds of performers than it has admitted before — Tommy Brown is an African American country singer (similar to Charley Pride); in one scene at the racetrack we see a singer who appears to be Hawaiian; in an uncomfortable scene near the beginning of the film Haven Hamilton dismisses a session player whose long hair and errant keyboard playing enrage him. Nashville and country music stand in the film in danger of losing touch with their roots and, one might argue, their heart and soul. Barbara Jean still retains the authenticity on which the music industry depends.[8]

In her hospital room, where she is recovering from a breakdown, we see a book Barbara Jean is presumably reading. It reappears in several scenes, and it's difficult to make out the title. In one scene the title becomes readable: it's a paperback copy of William Faulkner's novel *Light in August*. Why is Barbara Jean reading this novel? Was this simply a book someone on the movie set was reading, conveniently placed on the bed as a prop — there's significant improvisation in Altman's filmmaking, and it's possible the book found its way onto Barbara Jean's bed in that random way. But the book is there, I am certain, by intention, and even if it is not, its presence works as an intentional statement — associating one of the only authentic characters in the film with the iconic and authentic figure of the traditional literary South.

The final and climactic scene of the film occurs in front of Nashville's Parthenon. The building is a full-size replica of the ruined and famous iconic structure on the Acropolis in Athens, Greece. Originally constructed from plaster and wood for the Nashville bicentennial in 1897, it proved so popular

Ronee Blakley as Barbara Jean, an iconic but emotionally fragile country star in *Nashville* (1975, American Broadcasting Companies).

that a more permanent structure was erected in the 1920s. The Parthenon of Athens, Greece, is a ruin. It remained intact for two thousand years until an explosion in 1687 destroyed much of it. Portions of its marble frieze (the so-called Elgin Marbles) reside in the London Museum. The Parthenon in Greece symbolizes the highest ideals and achievements of Western Civilization. The Parthenon in Nashville is a symbol of all that the film regards as false and artificial about what the city embodies, a symbol of how the country music industry, as presented here, has appropriated, commodified, and commercialized the traditional values and folk life that gave the region and its music a cultural identity.

It is ironically fitting that the film's final scene takes place at this faux Parthenon, a political rally for a populist presidential candidate who promises to create "New Roots" for America. The scene of a political candidate stumping for office, presenting his platform and speaking to potential voters, is fundamentally essential to American democracy. It even recalls the campaign of a famous 19th-century Tennessean, Davy Crockett, who in the 1820s and 1830s used entertaining stump speeches to win over voters in his campaign for Congress. The Hal Phillip Walker campaign organizer, John Triplette, spends much of the film trying to convince the country music stars of the film to appear at the rally. He tells them that it is not important that they agree with Walker's political views, only that they appear. He suggests to Haven Hamilton that Walker has considered him as a possible candidate for governor of Tennessee. All of the characters who appear at the rally are there for reasons unrelated to Walker's campaign — all for various forms of self-interest, self-promotion. The one exception is Barbara Jean, who doesn't know why she's there other than to sing. And she does sing, beautifully, movingly, until the bullet strikes her.[9]

We kill the things we love most. This seems to be one of the film's basic messages. We kill the things that betray our falseness.

What does *Nashville* say about democracy? It expresses little faith in the ability of the electorate to make intelligent decisions. It shows the electorate caught up in worship of material objects, of celebrity, of the vacuous and meaningless present moment. A talented singer is killed on stage. After an instant of panic and chaos, the always bedraggled singer Albuquerque comes to the front of the faux Parthenon and begins to sing. The crowd is caught up in the chorus of her song, "It don't worry me." As if nothing has happened. The mortally wounded Barbara Jean is forgotten. On to the next sensation. Forget the past. A new star is born.

Altman's *Nashville* portrays country music stars as increasingly removed from their country roots and Nashville itself as a modern American city that at best can only simulate its authentic country origins. Despite its encyclopedic, wide-ranging approach, *Nashville* does not offer a realistic portrait of the country music industry. Critics who complain about inaccuracies, about the film's bias against country music singers or the American South, miss the point.[10] Realism is not its purpose. Altman intended *Nashville* as a satirical critique of the American Bicentennial. It is more concerned with America and popular culture and celebrity fetishism than with country music, which is a vehicle for examining these larger issues. Among a few films that give a more realistic view of country music singers, the 1972 film *Payday* stands out as especially interesting, and as a curious analogue to Altman's film. Produced by Ralph Gleason, the co-founder of *Rolling Stone* magazine, directed by Daryl Duke, an obscure director of television dramas, it offers a more conventional and decidedly unromantic account of a country music singer. The only actor of any prominence in the film is Rip Torn, who portrays country music performer Maury Dann. Torn gives one of the best performances of his career.

While *Nashville* revels in the glamour and celebrity of the music industry, *Payday* focuses on the daily grind and routine of a country music singer who has never quite achieved first-level prominence. *Nashville* dwells on how the drive for celebrity and success (or the ambition to possess them) affects the music industry. *Payday* examines the destructive effects of the drive for success from another perspective. While *Nashville* offers a pastiche view of its subject, *Payday* is a character study of a man so caught up in the endless routine of touring and dealing with agents and producers that he has lost track of why he became a singer to begin with. Dann tours nonstop with his band. Together they drive from gig to gig in a pair of Cadillacs. Maury quips, "You only go around once in life. You might as well go in a Cadillac." He's waiting for a big break, hoping for an appearance on the *Johnny Cash Show*, but not counting on it. He's got to keep moving, keep performing, to stay alive and to avoid an ever increasing and threatening burden of debt. The film is structured around his travels from one point to another. Automobiles and travel are a central motif. They signify Dann's uncenteredness, the constant motion and rootlessness that define his life. In *Nashville* the entangled and waylaid cars in the pile-up on the expressway signify the wreckage that the film proposes as its diagnosis of contemporary American culture. In *Payday* they signify the self-destructive lifestyle of the main character, a lifestyle at odds with the traditional values of the music he sings.

The character in *Nashville* most like Dann is Tom Frank. Both are womanizers, and both exploit colleagues and friends in order to move ahead in the entertainment industry. Frank's career is taking off, and he's headed towards prominence and success as a singer. Dann's career is spiraling downwards, and his decline is as much physical and moral as it is artistic, accelerated by alcohol, drugs, and the general disarray of his personal life. It's certainly possible that Tom Frank will one day follow the same path. But the prospect of that decline is not one that Altman imagines for his characters. He's concerned with celebrity and stardom of the present moment, while *Payday* is concerned with personal dissolution resulting from a life poorly lived. Both films explore different dimensions of a failed American dream.

Payday has a flat, documentary style. The cast is composed largely of unknown actors, though a few went on to modest television careers. Their Southern accents are often poor imitations of reality. Only Rip Torn gives the film any life. He seems to base Maury Dann on Merle Haggard, with a trace of Conway Twitty thrown in for good measure. Torn sings a passable imitation of Haggard, though it's a parody too. Although *Payday* is about a country music singer, music itself has a small place in the film. Only once, in the opening scene, does Dann actually perform before an audience. In another scene, in a hotel room late at night, alone, he sings a few bars of a song that he presumably wrote. The song is beautiful and heartfelt. But he sings for only a few moments. These are the only scenes in the film that involve music.

When *Payday* opens Dann is playing a honky-tonk that brings in a box office for the evening of $600—band members are paid $50 each for their efforts. This is part of the title's meaning: struggling to make ends meet, to make it to the next payday. There are other meanings. While *Nashville* shows the glitz and glamour of the music industry, *Payday* shows the grueling routine. We follow Dann from one hotel to another. He stops with his entourage to visit his broken-down mother. He goes bird hunting with friends in the countryside near his childhood home. Later he stops to see his first wife and three children, whose ages and birthdays he cannot remember. Such scenes show how far removed he has grown from the roots and the origins that gave his life and his music meaning. Now, late in his career, country music—which means life in general—is a monotonous routine. Halfway through the film Dann begins to show the debilitating impact of his lifestyle—events and circumstances are piling up on him, closing and hemming him in. He constantly pops pills, often interspersed with shots of whiskey. When a young song writer he has hired complains of fatigue, Dann offers him a pill. When his mother complains that she doesn't have enough energy to get out of bed, he offers her a handful of pills.

As the film moves forward Dann becomes increasingly abusive to those around him. He fires a band member who insists on buying his dog (Maury's mother is neglecting it). When a fan asks for an autograph, he lures her into the backseat of his Cadillac and has sex with her. He tires of the girlfriend he has at the beginning of the film, and has sex with another woman in the backseat of the car where his current girlfriend is sleeping. When she blows up at him, he orders his driver to pull the car to the side of the road and throws her out. He throws a wad of bills at her, drives off, then comes back and retrieves the money, exclaiming "You haven't earned it."

Dann's decline accelerates when he gets into a fight in a restaurant parking lot with the companion of the autograph-seeking girl whom he lured into the Cadillac outside the honkytonk in the opening scene. The man pulls a knife, but Dann manages to deflect the blade, fatally wounding the man, who dies in front of him. Instead of taking responsibility for this accident, Dann orders his manager to "take care of it." The manager pays off the restaurant manager and convinces Dann's driver to "stand in"—that is, to tell the police that he, not Dann, was in the fight. Dann offers a job to the only other witness to this event, a young and untalented singer and songwriter. This is a bribe, in essence, though the young man does not realize it. The film thus makes shockingly clear what Dann has become—a man besotted with his own celebrity (or the hope of it), relying on other people to get him out of trouble, to pay people off, or to "stand in" for him. He consumes people—his girlfriends, his mother, the man who dies on the pavement outside the restaurant.

Late in the film, Dann finds himself back in his hotel room with two policemen, a district attorney, his manager, a promoter, and a songwriter. They all are making demands. He takes the songwriter and leaves the room, driving furiously out of the parking lot. They drive down a country road, sipping whiskey, and Dann talks about what it was like to grow up on a farm. Dann says he hated farm life. They pass a cotton field, and he remembers how he hated to pick cotton. Then without warning he suffers a heart attack and dies. His car runs off the road and comes to rest in a plowed field. The last glimpse of Dann is of his lifeless face, his eyes open, staring into nothing. The scene directly echoes the restaurant parking lot, where the man whom Dann accidentally killed lies dead, his eyes open and empty. This is the real payday towards which the entire film has moved. It is not at all coincidental that Dann comes to his end in the automobile in which he is seen so often throughout the film. Whereas the expressway pile-up in *Nashville* suggests the chaos, confusion, and mayhem that Altman associates with modern America, Maury Dann's final car wreck in *Payday* merely brings to a logical close a life that in effect had already concluded before the film even began.

Dann's career as a singer has demanded a growing series of compromises and concessions that draw him away from his traditional and familial roots. It's possible to view his decline as one created by the world in which he lives — the commercial music world that forces him to attend to his manager and give mindless interviews to disc jockeys and to worry about box office sales and album revenues. He's not in the industry to sing his songs or to share his feelings or to create what in some fashion we might regard as art — he's in it for money, for fame. But the more convincing explanation for Maury is that as an individual he's lost hope, he no longer believes he will get the big break, he rides the highways just to keep going, to avoid the conglomeration of debts, demands, sins, crimes, and failed responsibilities accumulating behind him, to avoid facing reality. In the film's final scene, as he drives down the dirt road deep into the heart of the countryside, the countryside that presumably gave him his values, formed his identity, fueled his songs and his music, we're painfully aware — even before he dies — of how separated he is from those roots. Dann's payday is the day when all these burdens catch up with him in the field where his Cadillac comes to rest.

Payday agrees with *Nashville* on the corrupting force of commercialism. One might compare Dann to Barbara Jean in Altman's film. However, there is a difference that makes Dann more complex than Barbara Jean. She's a true victim of her environment. She's emotionally fragile and unaware of how she is being used. She's not responsible for the act that leads to her death. She knows only that she loves to sing and that she craves the attention of an adoring audience. Dann is complicit in his downfall. His compromises and mistakes and self-indulgences are ones he chooses for himself—his abandonment of his family, his exploitation of women, his indifference to his mother, his abuse of his friends, his personal and artistic compromises, the pills and alcohol that ultimately kill him.

Payday was filmed before Elvis Presley finished eating and drugging himself to death. It appeared in the wake of the deaths of Jimi Hendrix, Janis Joplin, Jim Morrison, Gram Parsons, and others. The popular music industry of the mid-twentieth century in America was well known for alcohol and drug abuse, for self-destructive immolation. Hank Williams' death in 1953 from drugs and alcohol seemed almost to set a pattern. Johnny Cash became notorious for his drug use in the 1960s. Self-destruction and country music—self-destruction and music as a cultural theme in general—are clearly a context in this film.

Although both *Nashville* and *Payday* take different approaches to undermining stereotypical conventions attached to American country music, they reach similar conclusions. Altman's film views the country music industry as a reflection of issues, controversies, and trends that were fundamental to the state of the nation at the moment of its 200th anniversary. His approach is one of satire, comedy, and parody—almost always his approach in his films, in one way or the other. His satire can range from gentle to severe—his film *Cookie's Fortune* (1999), set in a small Mississippi town, is especially mild. But in *Nashville* his satire is sharp and focused. Those who complain about the film's treatment of the South would do well to consider its real targets. *Payday* in comparison at first glance appears to be more directly concerned with the reality of country music through its subject of a singer struggling to find his way after years of failing to make it to the top. Yet *Payday* is not finally a film about country music either. Its subject is the character of a man so driven by the compulsion for wealth and prominence that he forfeits everything of value and meaning in his life.

Notes

1. Carter gave the speech on July 15, 1979. Of particular pertinence is this paragraph from the speech: "In a nation that was proud of hard work, strong families, close-knit communities, and our faith in God, too many of us now tend to worship self-indulgence and consumption. Human identity is no longer defined by what one does, but by what one owns. But we've discovered that owning things and consuming things does not satisfy our longing for meaning. We've learned that piling up material goods cannot fill the emptiness of lives which have no confidence or purpose."
2. In *Framing the South: Hollywood, Television, and Race during the Civil Rights Struggle* (Baltimore: Johns Hopkins University Press, 2001), 183, Allison Graham writes: "Contrary to Hollywood's longstanding tendency to portray Southern crises as distinctly and exotically

regional, *Nashville* (1975) aimed its critique of national political and celebrity culture from a Southern setting; here, the commercialized South became an emblem of Hollywoodized America." See also Jan Stuart, *The Nashville Chronicles: The Making of Robert Altman's Masterpiece* (New York: Simon & Shuster, 2000), 21: "Altman never intended to make a movie 'about' Nashville. . . . Nashville would be, as Altman defended his picture upon its release, his 'metaphor for America.'"

3. As quoted in Mitchell Zuckoff, *Robert Altman: The Oral Biography* (New York: Alfred A. Knopf, 2009), 287. Although Tewkesbury wrote the initial screenplay and is credited as the screenwriter, Altman revised and rewrote much of the script as he shot the film.

4. Such commercials were a common feature of late-night television in the 1970s.

5. The use of country music, of the media in general, as a vehicle for promoting a political candidate was a major theme in Elia Kazan's 1957 film *A Face in the Crowd*. Media and Southern politics are intertwined in such earlier films as *All the King's Men* (dir. Robert Rossen, 1949) and *Sweet Bird of Youth* (dir. Richard Brooks, 1962) and in films as recent as *O Brother, Where Art Thou?* (Joel Coen, 2000).

6. See Jan Stuart, *The Nashville Chronicles*, pp. 64–65, and Geraldine Chaplin's comment in Zuckoff's *Oral Biography* that Altman told her to "Just imitate me. I want you to follow me around and act like me. Do everything I do," 280.

7. "Barbara Jean is the one tragic character [in the film]: her art comes from her beliefs in imaginary roots." Pauline Kael, *Reeling* (NY: Little-Brown, 1977), 449.

8. In *Media-Made Dixie: The South in the American Imagination* (Athens, GA: University of Georgia Press, 1986), Jack Temple Kirby touches on the changes affecting the Nashville music industry during the period the film covers. See 153–160.

9. According to Jan Stuart in *The Nashville Chronicles*, Joan Tewkesbury's screenplay targeted Hal Phillip Walker for assassination, but Altman decided on Barbara Jean instead, 65–66.

10. The reactions of country music singers to the film were especially negative. See *Nashville Chronicles*, 290–94.

Works Cited

Graham, Allison. *Framing the South: Hollywood, Television, and Race during the Civil Rights Struggle*. Baltimore: Johns Hopkins University Press, 2001.
Kael, Pauline. *Reeling*. New York: Little-Brown, 1977.
Kirby, Jack Temple. *Media-Made Dixie: The South in the American Imagination*. Athens, GA: University of Georgia Press, 1986.
Nashville. Dir. Robert Altman. 1975. Paramount, 2000. DVD.
Payday. Dir. Daryl Duke. 1972. Warner Home Video, 2008. DVD.
Stuart, Jan. *The Nashville Chronicles: The Making of Robert Altman's Masterpiece*. New York: Simon & Schuster, 2000.
Zuckoff, Mitchell. *Robert Altman: The Oral Biography*. New York: Alfred A. Knopf, 2009.

VI.

Gender, Regional Identity, and the Civil War: Politics of the North and South in *Sweet Home Alabama* and *Junebug*

LANDON PALMER

The notion of Southern regional identity in America is as wavering as it is continually evolving, yet it remains an idea accepted in the minds of many as identifiable truth. While a term as amorphous as "the South" may be continuously shaky, misleading, indefinite, and contain little correspondence with social reality, the ideas behind the term hold great weight regarding how our national and regional cultures perceive themselves. This essay examines the role that two recent American films—*Sweet Home Alabama* (Andy Tennant, 2002) and *Junebug* (Phil Morrison, 2005)—have played in illustrating, validating, challenging, or perpetuating certain ideas regarding the essentials of "Southernness" in ways both particular to Southern history and reflective of more recent means of articulating the North/South dichotomy within the public sphere in varied and often competing sites of cultural and political discourse. I further contextualize my reading of these films within the history of representations of the South in popular American cinema, assessing to what degree this corresponds with the problematic history of the South and its perceived (and contradictory) regional value systems. Moving from an analysis of the processes perpetuating the idea of a North/South ideological divide through recent cultural dialogue to a brief history detailing the ongoing construction of Southern regional identity in popular American cinema, this essay culminates in an investigation of how these two films reveal processes of regional identification and perceive a regional divide as exercised through their representations and discourses on race, gender, and the legacy of the Civil War.

According to John Shelton Reed's *Southerners: The Social Psychology of Sectionalism*, a sociological study detailing processes of regional identification in North Carolina, Southern regional identity can be predicated upon such factors as political or religious attitudes, geographical affiliation, aspects of one's personality, or accent.[1] In the term's most political usage, Southern identity can be conflated with rural identity or small town identity and with the common, popular perception of a uniform value system existing between such areas, thereby transposing tenets of Southern identity onto other geographic regions despite the fact that the South is hardly homogenously rural. Reed explains that regional identification is vastly different from national identification, and he details two important aspects of determining Southern identity: self identification and identification by others (11). Regional identification is more evidently constructed by what is outside the region. As a result, Reed argues that regional consciousness is most acute amongst those who have the social mobility and economic viability to move out of the region, and are thus able to see the "other" and define themselves in opposition to it (31). For this reason, Reed argues further that, in the region's history, processes of Southern regional identification are more prevalent amongst privileged white males as it was their economic and social status that allowed them to migrate and, therefore, identify themselves with regard to their geography and perceived regional culture. Thus, Reed concludes that to be a Southerner is to be a *white* Southerner (4; 33–36). Reed's frame of examination here inevitably arrives at such a simplistic declaration as the nature of his observations and the questions he asks often come strictly from the perspective of white Southern identity. The author ignores histories of non-white migration such as the Great Migration of poor African Americans who moved to the North for economic opportunity as well as the many visible and influential contributions toward Southern culture and identity from the region's various minority groups. However, Reed's point regarding the determination of regional identification through migration outside of that region can be thoroughly evidenced within American culture. The concept of Northern regional identity is indeed essential to the formative processes of Southern regional identity.

Southern regional identity cannot exist or resonate without Northern regional identity, or the ideological assumptions these terms potentially imply. In fact, some scholars argue that literature and other cultural objects from the North celebrated Southern culture to such an extent that they provided invaluable contributions to the construction of Southern regional identification, myth, and the region's perceived uniform value systems (Gerster 43–59). The term "Northern" is often conflated with "Eastern" or "metropolitan." Metropolitan implies diversity and plurality of politics, ideologies, and cultural backgrounds, all within the close quarters of a city, thus suggesting a variety of cultural value systems in constant dialogue with one another. This diversity stands in contrast to the impression of a homogenous cultural value system intrinsic to the idea of Southernness. What connects the perception of a unity between the Southern and the rural is not exclusive to geography or voting record, but the perception of a common ideology uniting states and the people within them. Southernness is often articulated not on its own terms, but in opposition to perceived northern, eastern, cosmopolitan, or metropolitan value systems.

Although the North is characterized in the social imagination as a place of diversity as well as cultural and ideological plurality, it is paradoxically also alleged to be homogenously liberal and progressive in its politics, from the formation of the Union to the recent shading of the entire west and northeast coasts in blue on electoral maps. States such as California, because of their citizens' voting records, can be thrown into this broad definition of Northern because of its diverse population, handful of large cities, and delineation as liberal, despite the fact that the state has Southern characteristics such as its border with Mexico, its many miles of virtually unpopulated stretches of land, and its sizeable population of conservative and religious voters. Thus, the concept of the North is arguably even more amorphous and unstable than the South, as the map seems to change every election year.

However, this labeling and simplifying of the North is essential for such a powerful ideological tool as the South to exist, despite that neither region is uniformly liberal or conservative, nor rural or metropolitan. In *Reconstructing Dixie*, Tara McPherson argues that the South is in fact looking more and more like the "rest of America":

> The South has changed. Economically and culturally, the South fully participates in a global economy that might easily blunt the registers of difference that once defined the region.... Despite the unevenness of change and the unequal distribution of the region's new resources amongst its population, the South still looks more like the rest of America than it did at the turn of the previous century [14–16].

McPherson argues further that at the very moment in which "globalization blur[red] the boundaries of the nation," the South reinvented itself in its post–civil rights identity crisis as a major competitor in the national — and thus, global — market, whilst retaining its markers of difference (17–18). The South was then commodified into its current form as a site celebrating its alleged culture of authenticity, though this authenticity remains tenuous and evolving, adaptable to the political and economic needs of the given moment. Southern values is a necessarily vague concept remaining in constant flux in order to ensure its terminological flexibility, enabling its easy conflation with other regional value systems like rural values or small-town values.

In the same way, Southern heritage is a concept continually commodified, redefined, and appropriated, thus rendered adaptable to fluctuating definitions of authenticity. According to McPherson, the haunting legacy of slavery must be displaced in order for the celebration of the frontier myth, nostalgia for the agrarian lifestyle, and the broad set of "values" that give Southern heritage its ideological weight to resonate. She argues that this causes a "cultural schizophrenia" regarding the commodification of the region, the South being remembered as both the location that witnessed some of the darkest chapters in America's history of race relations (slavery and Jim Crow laws) and, paradoxically, also the site of core authentic American value systems and frontier culture. Though these conceptions of the South together are clearly problematic if not contradictory, neither version is recounted simultaneously, nor are they perceived as having determined one another:

> In many ways, Americans can't seem to get enough of the horrors of slavery, and yet we remain unable to connect this past to the romanticized history of the plantation, unable or unwilling to process the emotional registers still echoing from the eras of slavery and Jim Crow. The brutalities of those periods remain dissociated from our representations of the material site of those atrocities, the plantation home [3].

Cultural schizophrenia in the South can be witnessed most evidently in debates about the Confederate flag, an emblem allegedly representing Southern heritage by the groups that propagate it. Yet, in order to maintain a viable role for such an emblem in broader American culture, the shadow of slavery and problematic ideological implications of contemporarily appropriating such an image must simultaneously be forgotten, ignored, or simply not articulated.

Though much of the South is far from its rural, agrarian past, what matters is not the immediate relevance of these definitions, but how thoroughly these impressions and prejudices act within our culture. Thus it is the acceptance of the Southern myths that contains value, as opposed to the myths' empirical weight or the social practices they determine. Because of the importance of heritage and tradition in constructing the South's regional mythology, the evolving politics of southern regions have often occurred in clear conjunction with analogous social crises within the region's problematic history.

Cultural myths and narratives — regional, national, or otherwise — are effectively disseminated by a culture's literature, art, or folklore. In the twentieth century, cinema has influenced and echoed cultural myths in profound ways. The accuracy with which a cinematic artifact articulates the value systems of a given region matters not, as the act of articulation alone creates an impression which a culture then decides to accept or reject. Three evident historical factors determining how southern regional identification is expressed, narrativized, and mythologized through cinema include the Civil War, the civil rights movement, and the current North/South political divide. These factors, of course, determine one another and echo and reverberate between each other, and have all held significant prominence throughout American film history.

One of the most iconic foundations of American narrative cinema's visual language was from a film steeped in Southern ideology and myth, D. W. Griffith's *The Birth of a Nation* (1915). While important in establishing dominant formal strategies in American narrative filmmaking, Griffith here utilized the medium to propagandize, reinterpret history, and promote damaging stereotypes if not actively incite racial hatred. This film manifests one of the central myths that structured the institution of racial subordination that has characterized much of Southern history: the fear of the black male as sexual predator through the character of Gus (Walter Long in blackface) threatening white "purity" embodied in the white female, Flora (Mae Marsh). As Glenda Gilmore argues, studies of evolving social politics in the post–Confederacy "New" South, specifically C. Vann Woodward's canonical 1952 text *Origins of the New South*, focus largely on race relations but ignore the critical role gender has played in determining certain processes of racial subordination in the first place. According to Gilmore, it is the myth of the black male as sexual predator and threat to white "purity" echoed in Griffith's film that institutionalized the patriarchal subordination of African American men and white women simultaneously:

> By excluding women in his Southern history, Woodward removed a sticking point in the race "problem"— interracial sex — for his 1950s white Southern readers.... White supremacists had reserved a mythical, monolithic, continuous past, at the same time using sexual terror to portray white women as victims and black men as criminals, in order to keep African Americans and women in their places [226].

Thus, the myths that mobilized white supremacy were built upon a determination of white women and African Americans of both genders as subordinates. Gilmore argues that the South's history of racism is no doubt predicated upon a comparatively less examined history of sexism, as the ethos of white supremacy meant social domination by white males, rather than all whites. It is the fear of the black male imbued in the minds of white women within Southern social structures that enabled white male supremacists to institute subordination of these respective minority groups in the first place, perpetuating a disunity and mutually perceived fear between minorities simultaneously subordinated by the same dominant group. While this myth allowed whites to perceive black males as savage sexual animals, it also allowed white males to perceive white women as fragile property inherited exclusively by them, as white males designated themselves the responsibility to protect white females from a perceived threat of rape and willful miscegenation.

The civil rights movement has taken particular prescience in post–civil rights Hollywood. A few rare but significant independent films tackled the issue of institutionalized or social racism during the civil rights era, such as the independents *Black Like Me* (1964) or John Cassavetes's New York-set *Shadows* (1959) as well as some notable commercial exceptions *To Kill a Mockingbird* (1962) and *In the Heat of the Night* (1967). However, these examples are significantly outnumbered by the volume of civil rights narratives in later Hollywood. Popular Hollywood fare such as *Mississippi Burning* (1988), *Driving Miss Daisy* (1989), *Ghosts of Mississippi* (1996), *The Hurricane* (1999), *Remember the Titans* (2000), *Men of Honor* (2000), *Glory Road* (2006), and *The Great Debaters* (2007) use microcosmic narratives chronicling the overcoming of adversity on a personal scale during the civil rights era (i.e., integrated sports teams or a trial regarding racist violence) to stand in for the civil rights struggle at large. The relationship these films have with contemporary determination or reflection of Southern regional identity is rather tenuous, however, because many of them depict Southern racism as something of the past that has since been overcome through the achievements of civil rights, signified by the victory over adversity within the film's reductive micronarrative diegesis. As a result, many of these films do not seek to comment on the greater sources within Southern ideology that institutionalized racism in the first place (regional myths and narratives), nor do they seek to comment on how such ideas continue to reverberate in contemporary society. Accordingly, Southern sexism is rarely if ever examined or linked to the processes institutionalizing Southern racism in these films.

Contemporary processes of regional identification and delineations between the North and the South are reflected in the narratives and distribution practices of Hollywood and American independent filmmaking. Instead of challenging or questioning dominant value systems, the nature of Hollywood as an industrial force of American capitalism (as all of Hollywood's major movie studios are synergized with other corporations) and as a reflection of the country's principles projected on giant silver screens both domestically and abroad necessitates a consistency of friendly, escapist affirmation in order to achieve the broadest possible audience. The articulation and reflection of such value systems takes many forms and embodies various gradations, whether in the repeated narrative structures conditioning audiences to comfortably anticipate the predictable (three-act structures, narrative closure, happy endings, expectations generated through genre) or through specific details of the stories told on screen (the heroic individual protagonist, affirmations of patriotism, and the value of preserving the heteronormative nuclear family). Marxist film theory of the late 1960s and early 1970s articulated this process of ideological demonstration through illustrating the unconscious means of expression resulting from cinema as a product of industry and culture. As Jean-Luc Comolli and Jean Narboni convey in their essay, "Cinema/Ideology/Criticism," "Because every film is part of the economic system it is also a part of the ideological system, for 'cinema' and 'art' are branches of ideology" (814). The authors go on to categorize films that affirm or challenge dominant ideologies to differing degrees:

> The first and largest category comprises those films which are imbued through and through the dominant ideology in pure and unadulterated form, and give no indication that their makers were even aware of the fact. We are not just talking about so-called "commercial" films. The *majority* of films in all categories are the unconscious instruments of the ideology which produces them [815].

The authors' assertion that each film is reflective of the particular ideology that produces them suggests a connection between how meaning is expressed in a particular film and the nation, region, governance, or industry with which it is directly or indirectly affiliated. From this point we can infer that regions containing different ideologies produce distinctly separate articulations of their respective ideologies on screen and through practices particular to their regional industry.

Though Hollywood itself is often recognized in American culture as a community of outspokenly liberal participants, the repeated ideological affirmations within Hollywood narratives are often manifested through a conservative, traditionalist gaze. Even if the subject matter is politically liberal, the *form* of Hollywood cinema often remains conservative despite any such content (as evidenced by recent Hollywood films championing gay rights within conventional narrative paradigms such as *Milk* (2008) or *Brokeback Mountain* (2005), two films that would fit into a category illustrated by Comolli and Narboni as challenging in content but traditional in form (817)). In an era where traditional value structures are stratified by myths and narratives regarding the moral superiority of small, middle American, or Southern communities and the prominence of regional value systems within those communities, Hollywood generally follows suit in order to ensure wide distribution and mass appeal. By contrast, American independent cinema largely plays exclusively in metropolitan areas, regions generally perceived to contain more liberal value structures, enabling these films to approach their subject matter likewise. But because such films are relegated to limited releases, the value structures embedded within them are inferentially limited to the ideologically progressive confines of the metropolis and not attuned to the larger sociopolitical value structures of mainstream America. Thus, industrial practices such as patterns of limited- and wide-release film distribution are reflective of perceived differences in regional ideology. The industrial paradigm of theatrical exhibition reflects dominant ideas regarding which regions of the United States would be receptive to the particular manifestations of form and content in Hollywood and American independent films.

Inherent to these structures of reception is the myth of rural superiority: the belief that rural areas have a relatively consistent and morally superior value system compared to urban areas of the United States. This myth is, of course, steeped in the South's religious traditions that are threatened by the competing value systems characterizing more densely populated areas of the nation. This particular myth is essential to the respective narratives of *Sweet Home Alabama* (a hit studio film) and *Junebug* (an acclaimed independent film), both of which manifest the North/South schism within their respective diegeses.

Sweet Home Alabama and *Junebug* are particularly important in illustrating differing approaches to the processes of southern regional identification through the conventions of the romantic comedy genre. Both films address gender relations, race relations, and the legacy of the Civil War within narratives that do not obviously intend to define the sociopolitical determinations of the region in any serious way (unlike the civil rights films mentioned before, no courtroom is utilized here to put on trial, without nuance, Southern culture's social myths and problems). That these films seem at first to be harmless comedies allows them to reveal more telling assumptions regarding the processes of southern regional identification and the social politics inherent to it, as the narrative tropes structuring the filmic events rely upon affirmations of automatic presumptions regarding fundamental tendencies of Southern culture that the spectator must possess going into the film. In other words, because these films arguably do not question the Southern character types or value structures presented within, an acceptance by their respective audiences implies an alignment between the way people largely perceive and assume Southern culture to be and the portrayal of said culture within the film.

Sweet Home Alabama concerns the return home of a Southern migrant, Melanie Carmichael (Reese Witherspoon), who has made a life in New York City. In the convention of a fish-out-of-water romantic comedy, the film lightly addresses the perceived differences between North and South as reflected by the song that inspired the film's title chronicling a political clash between Canadian musician Neil Young and Floridian Southern rock band Lynyrd Skynyrd (who often included the icon of the Confederate flag on their album covers). "Sweet Home Alabama" articulates a traditionalist view of

Southern identity, a reactionary counterpoint inspired by the band's negative response to Neil Young's "Southern Man," a song about a white male's racism towards African Americans in the South and his violent reaction to a black man's relationship with a white woman. The film *Sweet Home Alabama* likewise demonstrates, intentionally or not, the expected gender roles inherent to Southern regional identity. The North/South dichotomy is literalized in *Sweet Home Alabama*'s central narrative conflict through Melanie's competing white male love interests. Her hometown sweetheart Jake (Josh Lucas), to whom she is in fact married, stands in for rural value systems through the character's loyal and uninterrupted devotion to his Southern habitat, while Melanie's fiancée Andrew (Patrick Dempsey) stands in stark contrast to Jake as an elite, progressive, Ivy League–educated metropolitan Democrat who possesses emblems of culture, wealth, and intellect, but whose values are portrayed as materialist and inauthentic in comparison to his Southern competitor. As Melanie must decide between the "simple" Southern male she has known her whole life or the wealthy New Yorker, she is also choosing between the gender roles she is expected to embody within each respective region: to further enable her entrepreneurial economic and (relative) social independence by continuing her career as a cosmopolitan working woman in the big city, or to give up her career dreams and become a housemother and caretaker as a necessary sacrifice in affirming the value system of the rural South contextualized by its unaddressed but still-resonant history of white male supremacy.

The narrative up to this point sets up Jake's refusal to divorce Melanie in order for her to marry a New Yorker to be an act of mere spite in return for Melanie's rejection of her Southern roots, a desperate effort to hold onto white male dominance in the face of the intimidating career woman. Jake believes that Melanie's success in New York has come at the expense of her authenticity and rural values (at one point addressing her as a "hoity-toity Yankee bitch"), reducing her to superficial, cosmopolitan materialism (as evidenced by the marriage proposal from her fiancée in the elegant, iconic New York City jewelry store Tiffany & Co.). Jake's attempts to reclaim Melanie's Southern identity for her illustrate Reed's argument that regional identification is defined by the community rather than the individual. Melanie is reminded of her Southern roots far more often by the men of her community than the women, echoing the dominant Southern white male's act of subsuming the threat of the woman's economic independence in the North by reeling her back into a regional value system whose culture is steeped in a history of white male dominance.

Though the tone of *Sweet Home Alabama* is light in the tradition of the romantic comedy, the reclamation of Melanie's Southern identity is treated quite seriously by her surrounding community, for the Southern white female as presented in this film represents one of the most important tenets structuring the South's commodified nostalgia industry: the Southern belle. According to McPherson, the belle operates as a cultural "asymptote" that reinforces "cultural and regional ideals of femininity and gentility," exercised most evidently in film history by the iconic figure of Scarlett in *Gone with the Wind* (1939) (4). With this celebration of the proper Southern woman, however, are the problematic social implications therein, namely the "traditional" function of the female as subordinated to a maternal role and the honoring of the female figure whom, according to Gilmore, is simultaneously rendered a central tenet for the South's various institutions of racial hatred, illustrating a complex process of cultural schizophrenia. However, even in the modern South, a figure as antiquated as the belle still holds the myth of the region together even as it makes transparent the problematic gender politics of her social function:

> The South, responding to its own feminized position vis-à-vis the North ... turned to a hyperfeminized figure of the Southern woman as discursive symbol for the region, with the land itself being figured as feminine as well. The myth of the Southern lady (which is no less powerful for its status as a faction) is central to Southern culture [McPherson 19].

This celebration of the belle sees its apex in the symbol of her white wedding dress, and her marriage to a white male, in which she remains pure, virginal, and uncorrupted through the employment of religious values as dictated by the moral consistency of the South. The status of the belle helps contextualize and reinforce the politically conservative South's history of both overt and covert antifeminism.

The film's ending features Melanie getting married to Jake in the ultimate symbol of the belle — a white wedding dress — in an Alabama dive bar, suggesting a full return to her roots and reclamation of her expected gender role. But the end credits of *Sweet Home Alabama* tell a more interesting and complex story. Still photographs accompanying the film's end credit sequence portray life for Melanie and Jake in New York City, going so far as to show Jake starting a Southern-style business in the metropolis. One still features the couple, baby in tow, in what seems like a rural location into one realizes they are strolling through Central Park with buildings peeking over trees in the background, an illuminating illustration of the conflict between the urban and the rural manifested literally. These stills suggest a miraculous reconciliation of the differences between Northern and Southern cultures that heretofore constructed the narrative's seemingly insurmountable sources of discord. Melanie has returned to the metropolis while simultaneously fulfilling her expected role as Southern belle by marrying her hometown sweetheart and fulfilling the maternal duty of procreation. This sequence suggests that an amalgamation of disparate regional cultures can exist without tension, a self-contradicting compromise considering that the narrative up to this point has illustrated the extensive conflict between regions as impossible to resolve. It becomes difficult to believe, for instance, that Jake would ever leave Alabama, yet this sequence portrays him doing exactly that. Thus, in order to satisfy both the urban and the rural audience, the film exhibits two separate endings for a given spectator to accept or reject: one ending in moving images that has the story conclude in the rural South, and another featuring a fairytale ending in an urban environment composed by still images. This allusion to a continuing confusion of place after the film's end exemplifies the process of cultural schizophrenia in the South's interaction within a larger American culture, and it reflects Reed's argument that such processes of regional identification can only be fully realized outside that region.

In tandem, *Sweet Home Alabama* addresses indirectly the relationship between whites and African Americans in a post–civil rights South. The three Southern African American characters in the film are seen having menial, subservient jobs (a maid, a postal worker, and a security guard), and have little if any dialogue. Most importantly, these three characters here are seen separately, rather than in a community, thus implying that while civil rights has afforded them equal rights within the law, the lack of an overt goal in combating any of the subtler, more recent incarnations of racial adversity and social struggle have separated a community once unified by culture and clear objectives for progressive social change. Civil rights laws are posited here to have successfully undone what the civil rights struggle did so effectively in disbanding a powerful minority group whose success was determined by their strength in number and unified cause. These points, of course, are never addressed explicitly in the film, but the portrayal of African American characters with fairly little attention placed on their role within the narrativized landscape of a contemporary South alludes to a post–civil rights misperception popularized by white domination in Southern political communities and one repeatedly echoed: that racism is, in effect, over. Such wishful thinking has been perpetuated in many of Hollywood's South-based narratives, especially those recent micronarratives depicting the overcoming of local and personal civil rights struggles which imply that, through victory over adversity exemplified by the narrative of the given community within the filmic diegesis, we currently live in a world where such race-based struggles no longer exist.

Furthermore, *Sweet Home Alabama* perceives racism as such a thing of the past that it sees no problem portraying the only African American female in the film as a maid of an estate that was formerly a plantation, having her character work as a servant to white males who reside in a house that symbolically contains the entire history of American slavery. That Melanie is always framed as distanced from these African American characters, barred by doors or windows, formalizes a contemporary reverberation of the sexual politics of gender and race articulated within the ideology of white supremacy, as argued by Gilmore. White women and black men are allowed to correspond in *Sweet Home Alabama*'s modern South as long as that correspondence takes place within a strict socioeconomic hierarchy (Melanie embodying the white plantation heiress and the Alabama town's African American characters occupying the servant class), thus preventing either group from realizing the powerful myth that cultivated a fear of miscegenation which ultimately enabled the thoroughly institutionalized socio-cultural subordination of both groups.[2]

Junebug's narrative exercises a central conceit similar to that of *Sweet Home Alabama* in that it comically explores regional differences when a migrant (from, in this case, Chicago) returns (with his non-Southern wife) to his Southern home (in this case, North Carolina), but the film contains a comparatively more critical function regarding the depiction of gender roles defined by Southern culture. *Junebug* lightly addresses the personal toll that gender-based subordination takes upon a pregnant woman within a Southern family while simultaneously exhibiting that family's discomfort with a female "Northern other." In the first respect, *Junebug* illustrates the hierarchy of subordinating functions that take place within expected gender roles. Married-and-pregnant Ashley (Amy Adams) becomes the signifier of the dominant heteronormative transcript through moments which feature Ashley acting as caretaker of her husband Johnny (Ben McKenzie), who reacts to all her efforts to create a comfortable, content family dynamic with passive-aggressive silence and continuing avoidance, shirking away or leaving the room every time she displays affection.[3] The troubled relationship between Ashley and Johnny signifies that the family dynamic expected within the employment of traditional gender roles and life-narrative expectations (job-marriage-procreation) do not necessarily create the alleged happiness attached to them (a happiness perceived to be a given with the ending of *Sweet Home Alabama*). At the same time, the family's fear and distrust of the "Northern" female character, Madeleine (Embeth Davidtz) is a result of her education level and the economic independence and agency that it affords, heightened by the fact that she does not have children, thus bestowing upon her character an implied rejection of what is traditionally expected from the Southern woman. The family's reaction to Madeleine (an English-accented character who hails not only from Chicago, but also Africa and Japan) exemplifies how "Northern" is often conflated to mean simply "not Southern" without regard to specifics of the other's exact geographical background, as many aspects of Southernness are defined merely as what is perceived to be elsewhere. In other words, Madeleine is simply not one of them.

When Johnny hits on Madeleine while she helps him study for the GED, his actions are based in the perception created by the myth of rural superiority. The North is perceived as being less bound by moral conviction than the South, so sexual promiscuity is inferred as an inherent aspect of the Northerner's personality. Johnny's reduction of Madeleine to a sexual object is also an attempt to overcome the threat of a woman clearly superior in intelligence. Thus, Johnny's attempt to reclaim supremacy by reasserting the narrative of white male dominance is reflected within the myths of Southern culture. Her rejection of him is a telling moment in which the perceptions and expectations of one's character as defined by their regional identification does not align with their individual, independent actions and modes of thought. This disconnect highlights a shocking schism between individual action and the perceptions injected by the influence of the regional culture's dominant narrative transcript. That this sequence is juxtaposed with Ashley simultaneously masturbating to a picture of herself and Johnny in a nonsexual photograph taken in the "better days" of high school, unaware of the attempt at infidelity occurring in the other room, reveals the extent of patriarchal subordination as demanded by regional mythos. This scene, and Ashley's futile attempts to make Johnny happy throughout the film, illustrate the futility within the belle's expected desire to please their husband through efforts toward an unattainable ideal state of domestic contentment, sacrificing her individual hopes of happiness in the process.

Furthermore, the extent of Ashley's subordination is most revealing in her interaction with her mother-in-law, Peg, because it is this matriarch, rather than the men of the family, who initiates Ashley's most forceful vocal subordination. Peg constantly condescends to Ashley, treating her like a child and a nuisance (played for comedy), showing impatience toward Ashley's unending enthusiasm and never treating her pregnancy with the seriousness that it necessitates (at one point dragging Ashley to the car by the arm as she is about to go into labor as if her pregnancy is a mere inconvenience to Peg). Thus, patriarchal hegemony and subordination is represented here as so thoroughly enmeshed in Southern culture that it is also articulated and structured within a hierarchal stratum of women rather than solely from men to women.

The differing ways in which both films address the Civil War's role in contemporary Southern society illustrate how each film perceives Southern heritage and reveals the differing levels of criticism within their respective means of address. The community of *Sweet Home Alabama* reenacts several famous battles from the Civil War, which is presented by the film as an absurd but harmless practice of paying respect to Southern heritage. Yet, according to Reed, it is the oft-articulated respect for heritage, tradition, and roots that inform the politics of southern regional identification (12–19). While race is never explicitly addressed in the film, the implications in honoring the Confederacy cannot help but allude to the racism and slavery of the Old South that led to the accepted race and gender politics, in its many incarnations, throughout Southern history. It is the schizophrenic aspect of this ritualistic respect for tradition that potentially perpetuates the region's regressive social politics despite the political trajectory of the rest of the nation.

Civil War reenactments are a potent site of cultural schizophrenia in the modern South, offering an occasion where history is selectively interpreted to enable a powerful culture of nostalgia and heritage while ignoring the problematic implications therein. McPherson argues that such attractions are essential to making the South into the influential cultural commodity it is today: "Museums, battlefields, and plantation homes stage sites at which the real and the mythic collide, and representations mediate how we know the places we inhabit" (11). Rebecca Bridges Watts attests in *Contemporary Southern Identity* that, while those who contemporarily appropriate the Confederate flag defend its cultural value in terms of the central tenets of regional identity outlined by Reed — honoring forefathers, lineage, ancestry, and Southern history — rather than an explicit exhibition of racism, the Confederate flag, in fact, was never reappropriated in the post–Civil War South until integration laws began to threaten its white male hegemony. Watts argues that, with the threat of integration laws, the white South saw itself again as a defeated minority and thus found the Confederate flag fodder for reappropriation, for they could no longer utilize broad "American" symbols to express regional pride (91). That modern Civil War reenactments became an iconic part of Southern popular culture simultaneously with the civil rights struggles of the early 1960s suggests a timely need for Southern whites involved to reassert regional (rather than national) identity and heritage (Hadden 4). While Civil War reenactments are presented within *Sweet Home Alabama*'s light comedic tone as a silly but innocent and given part of Southern culture, these traditions allude to a far more complex history of rejecting national values in favor of regional ones and further solidifies the impression of a North/South divide, a history referenced most explicitly when the preparation for these reenactments take place in the backyard of the town's former plantation home.

In *Junebug*, the Civil War is addressed through crude artistic renderings that uniquely interpret some of its famous battles by the film's eccentric painter character, David Wark (Frank Hoyt Taylor), whose work Madeleine attempts to purchase while visiting North Carolina. It is worth noting here that the name David Wark is also the D. W. in D. W. Griffith, alluding to another artist who used the unique utilities particular to an artistic medium in order to reinterpret Southern history, but the paintings made by Wark do not perpetuate Griffith's ideology of Southern white male hegemony. Wark instead depicts an absurd, crude, and strangely comic Civil War, illustrating generals and soldiers stabbing each other with gigantic swollen penises and superimposing white faces onto the black bodies of slave rebels including, at one point, the face of George W. Bush. Unlike *Sweet Home Alabama*'s simplistic, straightforward, but ideologically troubling recreation of the South's effort in accordance with strict attention to accepted history (i.e., these reenactments do not imagine a Confederate victory), and unlike Griffith's attempt at telling his idealized version of history, Wark's drawings can hardly be interpreted as a sincere ode to his heritage and regional identity. Wark's drawings potentially contain multifarious layers and meanings for the given spectator. While *Sweet Home Alabama*'s Civil War reenactments naively present themselves as uncontestable, uncontroversial, empirical recreations of truth, Wark's art forces a postmodern, interpretive, relativist approach to Southern history. Projecting the Civil War as a vulgar cartoon, Wark's crude paintings challenge the myth of Southern heritage and aim to deconstruct (or at least confuse) the conditions within which such a problematic history is honored and, like the film itself, in the process reveal the absurdities of accepted racial and gender social classification in the American South.[4]

The respective contemporary interpretations of the Civil War depicted in these films are integral to their structuring and perpetuation of Southern values, for the perception of uniform regional values are enabled by the institution of narrative myths within prominent cultural artifacts like that of the Civil War reenactment or painting and reinstituted into culture via continuing artifacts like popular Hollywood and independent American cinema. As the Civil War is an essential historical event influential to the creation of Southern value structures and perceptions of Southern regional identity, the gender and racial socio-politics defining the history of the New South are forever tied to this event. The Civil War is certainly the most extreme historical manifestation of the ideological schism between the North and the South, but the perception of a more symbolic division separating the United States into two separate nations has perpetuated and manifested itself in various contemporary forms. *Sweet Home Alabama* and *Junebug* not only address Southern history and the ongoing perception of the regional divide through their respective narrative diegeses, but through their distribution practices as well, illuminating that the marketing and exhibition practices of Hollywood and American independent films are predicated upon the impression of separately structured value systems between different areas of the United States even as the delineation of these areas and their conflation with perceived value systems become increasingly indefinite.

Notes

1. As Reed's text was published in 1983 and his studies are particular to evidence gathered in only one Southern state, it is hardly useful as a catalog of contemporary dialogs that inspire an ever-changing definition of Southernness. But *Southerners* is relevant for the purposes of this essay in that it illustrates specific processes of regional identification occurring in an established post–civil rights South, processes which continue to resonate as they laid the ground for the term's more recent delineations.

2. The only African American character Melanie is permitted to have something resembling a close relationship with is Frederick (Nathan Lee Graham), one of her New York fashion assistants. Such a friendship is permitted without controversy as this Northern character's overt homosexuality removes any resonant Southern fears of potential sexual threat in the closeness between a white female and a black male. When Frederick visits Alabama to help retrieve Melanie, the hint of a romantic link between him and closeted Southerner Bobby Ray (Ethan Embry) is played for comedy. Despite the South's rejection of homosexuality and progressive rights, the potential coupling of Frederick and Bobby Ray is presented here as acceptable and less threatening than any potential interracial heterosexual coupling because a relationship in which a female is uninvolved is detached from Southern mythology's associations of rape and loss-of-innocence so integral to the region's historical fear of miscegenation.

3. According to James C. Scott in his *Domination and the Arts of Resistance*, language is an important tool that dominating factions of society use to subordinate social minorities: "hierarchies of gender, race, caste, and class are encoded in the domination of talk" (30). We see this take place in the vocal routines of subordination by Jake ("hoity-toity Yankee bitch") and other Southern males of the Alabama community in their attempts to convince Melanie that she has lost her authentic cultural roots as a result of her newfound independence through migration and embrace of materialism. It is of particular and notable significance that the husband of *Junebug* instead turns to silence to implement just as powerful an act of subordination upon his wife, signaling that a lack of language can be just as powerful a tool as language itself to impose rigid social expectations upon Southern women.

4. As Madeleine is perceived by the Southern community featured in *Junebug* as a Northerner (despite the lack of specificity in her geographic roots), her fetishization of Wark's artwork and her desire to show it in Chicago as an esoteric work of regional art is an example of impressions of Southern regional identity being actively formed by somebody outside that region. Also, Madeleine's temporary migration and ongoing appreciation for Wark's art as product of regional culture effectively characterizes the Southerner as an "other" even as he resides in his own territory.

Works Cited

Comolli, Jean-Luc, and Jean Narboni. "Cinema/Ideology/Criticism." *Film Theory & Criticism.* Ed. Leo Braudy and Marshall Cohen. 4th ed. Oxford: Oxford University Press, 2004. 812–819.

Gerster, Patrick, and Nicholas Chords. "The Northern Origins of Southern Mythology." *Myth and Southern History—Volume 2: The New South.* Ed. Patrick Gerster and Nicholas Chords. 2nd ed. Urbana: University Illinois Press, 1989. 43–59.

Gilmore, Glenda. "Gender and *Origins of the New South.*" Origins of the New South: *Fifty Years Later.* Ed. John B. Boles and Bethany L. Johnson. Baton Rouge: Louisiana State University Press, 2003. 218–237.

Hadden, Robert Lee. *Reliving the Civil War: A Reenactor's Handbook.* Mechanicsburg: Stackpole Books, 1999.
Junebug, Dir. Phil Morrison. Perf. Embeth Davidtz, Alessandro Nivola, Amy Adams, and Ben McKenzie. Sony Pictures Classics, 2005.
McPherson, Tara. *Reconstructing Dixie: Race, Gender, and Nostalgia in the Imagined South.* Durham: Duke University Press, 2003.
Reed, John Shelton. *Southerners: The Social Psychology of Sectionalism.* Chapel Hill: University North Carolina Press, 1983.
Scott, James C. *Domination and the Arts of Resistance: Hidden Transcripts.* New Haven: Yale University Press, 1990.
Sweet Home Alabama, Dir. Andy Tennant. Perf. Reese Witherspoon, Josh Lucas, Patrick Dempsey, and Candice Bergen. Touchstone Pictures, 2002.
Watts, Rebecca Bridges. *Contemporary Southern Identity: Community through Controversy.* Jackson: University Press Mississippi, 2008.

VII.

The Screen Kallikak: White Trash for White Guilt in Post-Vietnam American Film

C. SCOTT COMBS

Near the end of Quentin Tarantino's *Pulp Fiction* (1994), Marsellus (Ving Rhames) chases Butch (Bruce Willis) into a junk store with a Confederate flag on the wall and a little altar of southern license plates. The man behind the counter, Maynard, takes the gangsters hostage at rifle point and calls up his friend Zed. Something like the town sheriff, in blue uniform with star badge, arrives on the scene. Together Maynard and Zed rape Marsellus while Butch is gagged and bound to a chair in the adjacent room where the "Gimp" looks on, squirming with pleasure. Donned in leather bodysuit and black headgear concealing his face, the Gimp functions as the spectator's focus during the violation; his body screens the visuals of homosexual rape behind the door. Maynard and Zed have brought him out of a metal crypt inside a box vault. He is, in other words, figured as their undead child. Butch escapes and dashes upstairs, but hesitates. Panning the wall for a suitable weapon, he picks up hammer, baseball bat, and chainsaw.[1] His gaze rests on what appears to be a samurai sword, the closest approximation to a saber, the Confederate's weapon of historical choice. Butch descends, slices and slays Maynard, and frees Marsellus who promises his perpetrating "hillbilly boy" that he will bring "a couple of hard pipe-hittin' niggers to go to work" on him "with a pair of pliers and a blowtorch." Marsellus grants Butch permission to leave L. A. (and flee to, go figure, Tennessee!), and the two men depart from one another on equal footing.

The Gimp's unspoken horror (Maynard and Zed don't situate him within a narrative, and the gagged Butch and Marsellus cannot verbally react to his appearance) blots out both the sex act and, more importantly, the cultural politics of the violation. It would be a mistake to depoliticize Tarantino's desire to one-up the audience's generic expectations. Though scantly organized to produce a laugh and the reassuring appearance of absurdity, this vignette is carefully vetted to display a far worse crime than any committed by the gangsters at just the moment of gangster reconciliation. The men who commit that awful crime seem readymade for the job: a pro–Confederate duo of rapists whose screen image Tarantino does not own, a duo that was drafted thirty years earlier by James Dickey for his *Deliverance* script. For Tarantino, who has come increasingly to prefer the western's hand-to-hand combat over gun violence, and the related samurai film's pre-technological showdown over distant destruction (think of Darryl Hannah's close-up popped-out eyeball in *Kill Bill 2*), the recycling of Southern rednecks precipitates a neat alliance between two gangsters — one black, one white — who have committed their share of dishonorable killings. The only characters who outperform the dueling gangsters in committing horrible acts are men decidedly without honor — one redneck confederate and his partner the sheriff. To paraphrase Richard Slotkin's well-known distinction between populists (townspeople, gunfighters) and progressives (industrialists, capitalists) in the western, *Pulp Fiction* suggests that gangsters form a populist fraternity through their mutual disgust elicited by white trash sadists who remain progressive in their self-gratifying bodily actions (Slotkin 379–404).

My interest in this essay is not Tarantino in particular, but rather a larger trend found in his cinematic predecessors that established the cultural patterns a film like *Pulp Fiction* embraces. The movie's connection to the western reminds us of the portrayal of white trash stereotypes in post–Vietnam Hollywood movies that visualize whiteness for a presumed multicultural audience — multicultural, if not in composition, then in orientation. Indeed, these stereotypes have political underpinnings and effects. When white filmmakers confront racial and ethnic diversity, they are more than willing to conjure up battered clichés of poor or regionally prideful whites. The stereotype seems needed to solidify other white characters' assimilation when such assimilation cannot be based on power, privilege, or normalcy. No fewer than four times, Tarantino's own character Jimmy screams the word "nigger" to Samuel Jackson's character Jules. The effeminate bourgeois Jimmy exhibits unusual power dynamics in this arrangement, and his use of the ethnic slur makes him the most unlikely of mafia characters. However jarring this breech of social etiquette may be, it slips under the radar of the film's detection of white horror. It seems very much Tarantino's fantasy to achieve not just black acceptance but black status, and the Jimmy/Butch dyad furnishes a barely concealed wish fulfillment.

How many rednecks does it take to justify the word "nigger"? This quantitative exchange may better be understood as qualitative: how bad must backwards whites behave so that mainstream whites can appeal to cultural acceptance by expunging the former? This essay tries to understand what is so alluring about the political currency of white trash for so-called liberal, or multicultural, cinema by reading a number of visual narratives. Novel as its effects may seem, *Pulp Fiction*'s cultural displacement can be traced to earlier moments in visual culture — first, to Hollywood multiculturalism during and after the Vietnam War, and before that, to anthropology's budding investment in the visual equation of poverty with white rural America. These two episodes in trash demonology inform contemporary configurations of white guilt displacement. That displacement continually centers around three thematic concerns: multiculturalism (the plea for racial legibility of those historically denied access to equality), war guilt (the projection of military violence onto the redneck), and sexual deviance (anthropology's and popular cinema's equation of sodomy and incest with poverty). These three modes of displacement — multiculturalism, war guilt, and sexual degeneracy — afford mainstream cinema a visual and narrative repository that continues to prove relevant in contemporary cultural politics.

Recently, critical work in whiteness studies has looked to the historical and cultural formations of white trash in order to cultivate a more nuanced theoretical identity for whiteness. Broken apart, the term white trash combines a racist epithet or "ethnoracial signifier" with a classist slur or "signifier of abject class status" (Wray 3). In their *White Trash* anthology, Annalee Newitz and Matt Wray claim that white trash can function positively in a multicultural context by making whites racially visible. "Unlike many white people," the authors claim, "white trash have the potential to perform the work of racial self-recognition and self-consciousness" otherwise missing "in dominant forms of whiteness" (Wray and Newitz 5). With their language of victimization and recognition, they envision a kind of self-inflicted melodrama whereby some whites recognize their own lack and suffer virtuously for the race. The suffering remains indirect at best, however, for those who lose moral status are the poor. I am not optimistic about white trash melodrama's capacity to restore virtue to whites, for any racial legibility enacted through poor people functions by denying the material conditions of class and looking away from poverty. This project of reparation within multiculturalism assumes a white middle-class audience as subject of consumption and ignores the particular ways moving image culture has formed and propagated the visual and aural stereotypes of the white underclass. As Jim Goad rather imaginatively puts it, "When JumboTron movie screens smack your head on every corner with images of buck-toothed, straw-chompin', pellagra-stricken, swine-schtuppin' yokels, does it have the air of people poking fun at *themselves* or at *others*? The answer should be obvious to anyone but an urban supremacist — the mainstream consistently depicts the redneck not as itself, but as a cultural weirdo. The redneck is the *watched*, not the *watcher*" (76). Goad's tone may be a bit hysterical, but it clinches the general point that cinematic address ensures an "us" looking at a "them." Confounding this problem is the near invisibility of self-representations of the white rural poor that might counter mainstream images with authored alternatives from within. A closer look at both the formation and circulation of white trash by mainstream cinema is in order so that we can understand why the conventionalized figure of the redneck proves so useful for white multicultural politics.

Since the Vietnam War, the western has been a hot spot for demystifying older founding American myths embodied with the western, including of course the story of violent opposition between pioneers and Native Americans (Cawelti 2–5). The period after 1967 reveals an adjustment in the generic terrain of American cinema that we can see clearly in the western, particularly in the antiwestern's vivid expressions of war's futility. Time and again, we find in the revisionist westerns bellicose critiques of intervention waged by some of the most progressive American filmmakers, including Sam Peckinpah, Arthur Penn, and George Roy Hill. While the genre was gesturing toward a multicultural embrace of ethnic and racial minorities to remap the psychic terrain of "us" and "them" on which the classical western was founded, it also mobilized a highly coded version of the uneducated, uncivilized, and unclean poor white (Goad's "cultural weirdo") to maintain a critical distance from white privilege. If a band of whites could be seen to behave badly — if they were, for example, complicit with slaughter, if they were ethically and bodily unselfconscious — the other whites could emerge in a better light.

The stereotype of the white rural poor proved irresistible for cinematic assaults on military involvement in Vietnam. Slotkin has argued that major restructuring in the western's embodiment of the gunslinger myth emerges after the My Lai massacre in 1968, a moment when Americans at home were forced to recognize the fact of violence committed by American soldiers, in this case, the massacre of Vietnamese civilians, including women and children. Some accounts included accusations of rape (a point to which I will return). Slotkin claims the massacre proved a pivotal point in the domestic reception of war imagery, turning the unseen foreign enemy into the very visible victim of disorganized American violence, and thereby switching the binary terms of cowboy and Indian that had been employed to make sense of the war against the Communists, one crucial political context of the western's nadir. In the absence of black and indigenous people as scapegoats, a new category would emerge. In the revisionist western, the war protest turned the tide on the white rural poor.

Let me set the scene with a brief flashback from a film that, while not a western, conflates Vietnam with life in the backwoods, in this case, Appalachia. In Haskell Wexler's *Medium Cool* (1969), a poor white mother Eileen and her son Harold struggle in a subsidized housing district in Chicago. Eileen's missing husband has died in Vietnam, but Harold does not yet know. At one point, a social worker comes to visit the apartment while Harold is home alone:

> SOCIAL WORKER: Where's your father?
> A long pause.
> HAROLD: Vietnam.

But then, loud gunfire triggers a flashback to a man and the kid walking through rusted shells of automobiles, shooting at Jim Beam bottles. The flashback to their West Virginia home forms the only moment in the film where Vietnam is represented. The flashback from Harold's response "at Vietnam" offers a kind of correlate object — these are not the jungles of Southeast Asia, but the hills of rural America, the second uninviting terrain mapping onto the first. West Virginia is where men like Harold's father are from, absentee dads who have left children and wives to fend for themselves. Set against the backdrop of the 1968 Democratic National Convention in Chicago, *Medium Cool* argues that mother and son have been jeopardized by a culture of media that ignores their class predicament in favor of passively exploiting subcultures at home and abroad for sensational footage. But Harold and Eileen find themselves in that predicament because they were abandoned by the gun-friendly, misogynistic, white trash father. Turning Vietnam into boondocks further distances the film, its characters, and its medium from responsibility for the war.[2]

The idea that American soldiers were poor mountain men gained special status during Vietnam, but it made its way to the screen earlier in *Sergeant York* (1941), a film that exaggerated Alvin York as an "unsophisticated yet instinctual child of nature" (Williamson 213). The equation of vet with hillbilly tends to thicken around Southern signifiers. An exploitation film from 1972 makes the connection quite palpable for us. The film is titled *Poor White Trash, Part II* (the original title was *Scum of the Earth* but changed for redistribution). In it, a city girl Norma has lost her first husband in Vietnam. She takes her new husband to a Southern lake to vacation. An unseen assailant — some woods dweller — kills her husband during a picnic and she flees to the woods in shock, only to be taken captive by the Pickett clan. We have Papa Pickett, who has sex with his daughter and rapes Norma; we have his pregnant under-age wife; and of course we have Bo, his mentally retarded son, the only boy left who did not leave home, presumably to go to war. One by one the

Picketts are picked off by the same unknown assailant. He shows great skill, using an array of weapons — axe to the chest, barbed wire around the neck, cemetery gate spike, and finally Papa Pickett's own gun. Only in the end do we find out that the killer is Jim, Norma's first husband. He has returned from Vietnam where he was held hostage in a POW camp which, as Jim tells us, "is its own dyin'."

Obviously a film with "white trash" in its title is quite aware of the exploitative possibilities of the stereotype, not to mention the money-making gimmick. But what is interesting is that the first-person camera during each murder intimates the point-of-view of the veteran killer. As the Pickett clan treats Helen with increasing sadism, we are positioned to want their destruction. Revenge is offered with glee. But we get revenge from the point-of-view of the returning vet, indicating at least in those moments that we are aligned with a disturbed soldier in our wish to stop poor whites from their acts of terrorism without ethics. While the film gives a nod to a hierarchy of evil, with maladjusted Vietnam vet coming in a few inches above white trash, it is a distinction most likely forgotten by the viewer, who has spent the majority of the film witnessing heinous backwoods culture. There is great slippage, in other words, between the figure of the stalwart vet bringing the war back home (note that he kills only in the woods) and the scum of the earth.

Poor whites may make only a subtle appearance in the revisionist western, but their appearance is always memorable. In Peckinpah's *The Wild Bunch* (1969), that privileged text in Slotkin's analysis of My Lai's impact on the western, a clan of professional killers uses townspeople as defense (clearly echoing the massacre) during a sudden ambush while they are robbing a bank. In the camp of ambushers, we find two particularly fanatical killers — T. C. and Crazy Lee — eager to plunder the fallen bodies for worthy trinkets. These two members of Thornton's clan argue over their spoils ("It's mine. You just dig out that bullet and see if it ain't mine.") in frivolous disrespect for the innocent bystanders. They are giddy with violence. They also equate townspeople with pigs as they pounce onto fallen bodies, a connection made by the even more pronouncedly half-wit in the Bunch, Crazy Lee, who practically explodes with excitement over the massacre and exclaims, "It's better than a hog killin'." Pike and his gang represent mechanically organized violence and theft that disintegrates in the presence of an unreadable ethnic other figured as the Mexican Mapache and his gang. Mapache demonstrates cruelty on the body of his ethnic cousin — the Mexican Angel riding along with the Bunch. If there are good and bad Mexicans, there are also good and bad whites. However, it is only the white camp — the Bunch — that recognizes the horrific displays of violent rhapsody within its group, the point being that whites are aware of their own regional horrors. Accordingly, Crazy Lee is killed within the first ten minutes. *Medium Cool*'s acknowledgment that the media manipulates images of inner-city black neighborhoods works similarly. The film's appeal to the rights of minorities in the face of white cameramen falls short of illuminating poor whites with its "explanation" of Harold's frustration with father figures — namely, that it is the result of hearing confusing misogynistic messages from his redneck dad. As long as white imperfection remains isolated in stereotyped trash, it fails to deliver the blow to whiteness as a race in the way Newitz imagines, and it certainly fails to create an identity worth celebrating in the ways Constance Penley has esteemed in her essay, "Crackers and Whackers: The White Trashing of Porn." Rather, white imperfection merely provides a device to exonerate the "normal" white characters from the crimes they commit.

Popular films have continued to exploit the connection visually more than logically, the most obvious example being *Southern Comfort* in which the entire war is blamed on gun-crazed Southerners living well below the bar of socialized etiquette. The connection has endured ever since: it can be found on Internet chat rooms addressing the current Iraq War. Though not explicitly concerned with overseas war but rather domestic violence, Michael Moore's *Bowling for Columbine* spends much of its time in interviews with a farm-dwelling gun-owner, though that time is rarely logged as part of the film's cultural politics. If it is in lowbrow genres like horror where we find the most transparent equation of redneck with vet, it is because higher forms tend to sublimate their acts of political demonology.

Whether soldiers sent off to Vietnam were predominantly minorities and poor whites, whether the army was indeed what John Gregory Dunne has called "a rainbow coalition of black, brown, and redneck," I leave to other scholars. However, if the actions surrounding the 1968 Democratic Convention serve as a kind of primer for domestic anxiety, then it would seem to indicate that while blacks and whites were thrown into the jungle together, back home there was no such reconciliation. Blaming Vietnam on blacks proved untenable because the public denigration of that group was becoming less viable at the same time. Black soldiers were generally regarded as "victims" of the war effort by the liberal antiwar movement. Several antiwar westerns seem to reason that where blacks could not be blamed for social ills, whites could, and not just any whites, but poor whites, or to choose a few signifiers that appear on chat rooms, "hillbillies," "rednecks," and "baby killers." It would not be the first time that filmmakers emphasized white degeneracy in order to alleviate racial concerns. As Michael Rogin has pointed out, David Selznick's cleaning up Margaret Mitchell's *Gone with the Wind* for the screen included turning Scarlett's black assailant and attempted rapist into "dirty, lower-class, white trash." Striving to eliminate the racialist claims of *The Birth of a Nation*, Selznick mounted this corrective onto another, less obvious, concern: "I feel so keenly about what is happening to the Jews of the world that I cannot help but sympathize with the Negroes and their fears" (Rogin 164). Turning black rapist into white degenerate has been something of a logical next step for at least a century; according to Rogin, *Gone with the Wind*'s white trash afforded Selznick a salve for white immigrant claims to mainstream assimilation.[3]

White trash characters, and the shield they provide for other whites engaged in questionable endeavors, were hardly invented for the screen. Photographing poor whites emerged within early twentieth-century fieldwork studies in eugenics, and especially within that movement's tendency to produce visible evidence of the "phenotype" of hereditary degeneracy. Studies funded by the Eugenics Records Office (ERO) in Long Island — modeled initially on the work of Charles Darwin's cousin Francis Galton — augmented the cultivation of a mainstream white American identity. The most dangerous study subjects were those who could reproduce and pass on the gene for feeblemindedness that manifested in low intelligence and moral standards. The danger was "cacogenics," or unacceptable sexual reproduction, including consanguinity (relations between cousins) and incest. Matt Wray writes: "Eugenicists were extremely effective in portraying white trash as racially degenerate and biologically inferior and therefore incapable of making any positive contribution to a democratic society" (Wray 19). To keep integration from happening, sterilization and institutionalization were implemented in varying degrees. Visualizing the conditions of white poverty to inculcate the impression of incest belongs to a venerable academic tradition and finds its emblem in eugenicist Herbert Goddard's study of the "Kallikak" family. Goddard — known for popularizing Alfred Benet's standard intelligence test in the United States — contributed to the Eugenics Records Office's field studies on genetic predisposition toward social deviance that linked criminality and ethical lapses with low intelligence. In 1912 he published *The Kallikak Family: A Study of Genetic Feeblemindedness*, which argued for the inheritance of feeblemindedness, characterized by such unwanted traits as laziness, reticence, and incapacity for learning. Goddard moved from the two lowest scoring groups on the Binet-Simon test (idiots and imbeciles) to focus on the group just below that of normal whites — those that could perform menial labor and were indistinguishable from normals. He named them "morons" from the Greek word for foolish. As Stephen Jay Gould points out, Goddard imagined intelligence to be a "single, measurable entity" (189). In the study Goddard traces the moronic gene back to the American Revolutionary War, where he finds a soldier — "Martin Kallikak" — who had an affair with a barmaid before returning home and fathering children with his wife. The child to whom the barmaid gave birth was mentally retarded, and that child in turn yielded generations of the feeble-minded. Meanwhile, Martin Kallikak and his wife churned out generations of senators, doctors, and the like. Loving the Greeks, Goddard chose for his etymological basis two conflicting Greek roots: "kalos" for beauty, "kakos" for bad. Hence, one good lineage and one bad, dangerously intertwined. This sexually promiscuous female blamed for perpetuating the feebleminded gene recalled the gendered analysis found in the work of one of Goddard's significant forerunners. In 1877, Richard Dugdale published his study of the "Jukes," a family of degenerate criminals discovered in an upstate New York penitentiary. Unclear on environmental links between poverty and pauperism, Dugdale was nonetheless clear that cacogenics was a threat posed by the Juke women, claiming their "impudicity" exceeded that of normal women twenty-nine times over (Wray 66). Goddard illustrated the point of contact around the female figure. The good and the bad converge upon that once-errant Revolutionary soldier, an otherwise respectable veteran from a good war who properly married and produced middle-class offspring.

Though nowhere in his prose does Goddard mention severe physical retardation beyond the dead-end gaze of a few Kallikak children and one father, photographs published to supplement the book filled in the gaps. The children featured on front porches of shacks or framed alone in doorways were visibly deformed, some with distorted grimaces, some with bulging eyes. Subsequent critics including Gould have claimed the photographs were fraudulent, that they had been tampered with to exaggerate degenerate features. Gould sought the expertise of Smithsonian photographer James H. Wallace, who assured him the images had been retouched around facial features to give "the appearance of dark, staring features, sometimes evilness, and sometimes mental retardation" (Gould 201). Predictably, counter-arguments have been waged in turn, claiming that touching up photographs was a common practice at the time for book publication. Whether faked or not (they were certainly staged, and it seems fairly clear they were touched up), these images of the menacing Kallikaks (Gould: "Their mouths are sinister in appearance; their eyes are darkened slits") have had great staying power in the popular imagination, forming a kind of available rebus for future visual exploitation. The inbred and toothless offspring of Dock Tobin in Anthony Mann's 1958 western *Man of the West*, and even more dramatically, the banjo-playing dueler at the beginning of John Boorman's *Deliverance* (1972) who refuses to shake the city man's hand, are but two prominent examples of the "cacogenic" tradition in popular cinema. And as we see in *Pulp Fiction*, that tradition leans heavily on the Southern bias, even when there seems little narrative justification for that regional accent. The Eugenics Records Office's studies of northern areas "incorporated and expanded upon the shared perceptions of Southern poor whites as immoral, lazy, dirty, criminal, filthy, and perverse and offered an explanation that could be generalized to the entire group" (Wray 95). Eugenics can be compared to multiculturalism in at least one way, namely the collapse of differences (ethnic or regional) under a larger signifier, the one based on class, the other on race.

What cinema offers that eugenic field studies could not is the image of poor whites moving or *being in* their bodies. Moving images commit these bodies to narrative form. Goddard hired women to visit Ellis Island to pick out promising candidates for feeblemindedness and administer to these immigrants Binet's test — women because they were more "intuitive" than men. Reading the appearance of poor white trash in isolation (i.e. picking them out of a line) becomes in the cinema a lens for narrative clarity. If the "Bunch" is bad for crossing the line of civility in that movie's opening sequence, then T. C. and Crazy Lee read as modern day Kallikaks. Whatever crime the civilized white man commits, he is one-upped by his Kallikak cousin. This hierarchy of class evils persists throughout the new western. Ditto *McCabe and Mrs. Miller*, in which the white capitalist buying out McCabe has help from a poor, vacuous, gun-hungry young man called "Kid" who blows away a gentle cowboy just to see dying in action. Ditto *The Outlaw Josey Wales* and later Clint Eastwood fare, a point to which I will return.

Outside the western proper, the atrocity committed by Kallikaks becomes more clearly an awful act that justifies retaliation by middle-class whites — the crime needed for absolution. Not only is trash not quite white, to echo Matt Wray, but it is also more or less Southern. Often when poor whites move in their bodies, they are genitally offensive. In her book on the slasher film, Carol Clover has argued that the rape-revenge films popular in the 1970s that were told along a city/country axis deal squarely with the problem of American class warfare. The unending dispute between the "haves" and "have-nots" is staged in a familiar plotline: white middle-class tourists visit the South and meet degenerate locals; the travelers speak to natives in slurs and epithets; natives attack both physically and sexually; outsiders fight back. In these films, poor whites are represented as lawless, uncouth beings in order to justify an act of vengeance, providing the "haves" the opportunity to acknowledge and then assuage their guilty privilege over not being "have nots." Usually the guilt in question is bad conscience over the destruction of rural America, of reaping the benefits of the poor man's invisible labor, of infiltrating and abusing the land. But that paean to class guilt — *Deliverance* — must also be understood as a revisionist Vietnam western, one that makes clear the genre's inherent sexual concerns, and one that haunts countless subsequent screen renderings of sexually exuberant trash: *Natural Born Killers, Pulp Fiction, Freeway,* and *Harold and Kumar Go to White Castle* (to name a few). *Deliverance* follows a middle-class foursome of men who visit the Cahulawassee River — the "last wild, untamed, unpolluted, unfucked-up river in the South" — before it is destroyed by a dam to provide electrical power. Lewis (Burt Reynolds, with biceps on display) and company deal not-subtle blows to the region's citizens. Bobby, played by Ned Beatty, jokes "we've got a live one here" when he first sees a cabin inhabitant. Lewis in particular invokes sexual metaphors when talking up their adventure. Once the dam is put in place, he reasons, "we're gonna rape this whole goddamned landscape." Metaphor becomes practice when Ed (Jon Voight) and Bobby rest ashore and Bobby is sodomized by one mountain man while another holds them at rifle point. Ed looks on, tied up to a tree by his own belt. Tarantino's Gimp as screen for homosexual rape is originally the gunman in this scene, one of Ed's dreaded "hillbillies" who, when he smiles in a close-up during the rape, shows us his missing upper-row and bracketed bottom row of teeth. (These teeth become quite important later on, as I discuss below.) Lewis arrives silently, shooting dead the rapist with his recurve bow. Fearing they may be pursued by the gunman, the four men hide the body and flee, but they cannot see that well canoeing down the river. Their big adventure turns them into target practice for mountain men.

With middle-class whites fighting hillbillies in a Southern wilderness, the film turns backwoods America into a combat situation of limited visibility. Deaths do not occur neatly: when the rapist is shot he falls turgidly onto an oblique branch where he begins to resemble the contours of the woods. Later when Drew's body is found twisted like a knot and erect in the middle of that formerly "unfucked-up" river, they search his body in vain for bullet holes to prove that he was indeed shot, to justify their attack on the man on top of the mountain.

Just as the woods will make combat illegible, so too will they be full of Kallikaks. The canoers' first encounter with a Kallikak native features an albino but virtuoso banjo-picker played by Billy Redden (who is neither a product of incest nor a banjo-player — shades of Goddard). Later, Ed peers through a cabin window and sees an older woman with varicose veins and physically debilitated child. The sodomizing hillbillies may be the worst inhabitants, the most dangerous, but they are part of the general human landscape. When the protagonists have to fight them, they drop a notch in class. The countryman, the film suggests, has always been good at violence — it is a part of his way of life; the land requires it. The foursome must find that early settler grit they first romanticize but soon discover requires a hunter's detachment. The city man has to learn violence, in other words, whereas the countryman already knows it.

This act of regeneration through violence falls a bit short of resetting

VII. The Screen Kallikak (Combs) 117

social boundaries, however. After climbing a cliff through the night to kill the hillbilly they believe to be chasing them, Ed wakes to the sight of a lone mountain man in the distance with rifle drawn. Ed pulls out Lewis's recurve bow and this time is able to release the arrow for a successful shot through the neck. (He proved less capable earlier in the film with a deer.) Bending

Killed in a case of mistaken identity? This mountain man (Herbert "Cowboy" Coward) dies when Ed shoots an arrow through his throat in John Boorman's *Deliverance* (1972, Warner Bros.).

down, he opens the dead man's mouth to confirm his identity. To his horror, he finds a set of upper-row dentures. The assailant he believed he was pursuing turns out to be just another mountain man. Blending into one another, the natives thwart Ed's efforts at separating himself from them through vision. Here *Deliverance* steps outside the exploitative tradition of the white trash stereotype. Ed lies down by the dead man, their two heads drawn close together. Unable to identify the hillbilly as his enemy, he must recognize him as his victim. His intimate moment with the corpse allows him to step over the boundary the film otherwise polices. It is not a complete transgression, clearly, since the victim is already dead. However, the dead man's teeth underscore not only Clover's point that "the country is a world beyond dentistry" (125), but that it is a world beyond identification.

For a moment the two men, and the two shades of white, share equal footing, the enduring difference being that one shot the other. *Deliverance* suggests that what propagates the white trash stereotype is a mixture of fear of and desire for proximity with the white "other," a need to establish a form of intimacy with rural strangers. Mainstream culture's investment in white trash eroticism runs both ways: however disturbing the proposed sexual conduct may be, it is also somewhat exciting. Remember that incest was visually projected onto Goddard's Kallikaks. It is little wonder that the connection between poverty and sexual degeneracy is so unbreakable. Kindred sexuality — Goddard's cacogenic horror — is just another unwanted form of embodiment that middle-class whites project onto poor whites, but it is a special case at least insofar as desire remains legible in the *act* of projecting. The landscape of American film history is dotted with examples of a forbidden non-white sexuality that also arouses. Not knowing where the line can be drawn between white and not-white, unable to protect the boundaries of whiteness through sex, is exactly what worries sovereign whites in Griffith's *The Birth of a Nation*, Ford's *The Searchers*, and Boorman's *Deliverance*, three genre-structuring films that insist on defining whiteness as a clean slate despite their anxieties about the nature of white sexuality. *Deliverance* expands on the others as it suggests that it knows the white protectorates have already "fucked" the natives and echoes, perhaps, Martin Kallikak's fling with the barmaid. In eugenic studies, that point of genetic divergence of two lines can be rethought as a point of convergence — dreadful, perhaps, but nonetheless one that stages the erasure of the very barrier it proposes. The unacceptable habits and history of the "haves" can be pushed onto the "have nots" and disfigured beyond recognition, but not without the residual effect of living through the fantasy of the other to the brink of overinvestment.

President Reagan would later revise the War on Poverty when he said, stealing meter from a popular song, "We fought a war on poverty, and poverty won." The U.S. also fought a war on North Vietnam. The logical conflation of these two losses proved just too irresistible, as we can see in both revisionist and exploitation cinema during and after Vietnam. Before the war, those whose social conditions offended the eye could be framed as an alien threat to outsiders. During and after the war, the allegory moves in another direction: popular culture (both high and low) aligns the war-shocked killers at My Lai with their gun-carrying rejects back at home. Whatever bad deeds committed by the country, whites could displace their discomfort and guilt — over not fighting the war, over privilege, over not being quite exemplary in whatever way — onto their white trash ethnic neighbors, always already giddy with violence. Poverty as precondition for sexual degeneracy is this tradition's great master myth, and it reminds us how easily the formation of "white trash" maps on top of the incest taboo. The fantasy of policing the latter boundary helps keep the former boundary in check.

The act of defining white integrity by expurgating awful rednecks continues in American films from high to low, and it shows no signs of decline. Though *Pulp Fiction* is exemplary, I would like to end with a brief assortment of recent films that follow the cultural patterns of multicultural projection discussed here. Western motifs continue to be as relevant in neighboring genres as in westerns proper, and the regional flare of the South as location in earlier films has become a technique of postmodern citation. Clint Eastwood recycles the western myth of the lone gunfighter with his female boxer Maggie Fitzgerald in *Million Dollar Baby* (2004), a film that defends euthanasia as a last-ditch effort to save America from welfare-greedy white trash families like Maggie's. Protecting whiteness in the era of racial equality may not seem to be this film's main agenda, but viewed beside the Dirty Harry series, it is hard not to read Maggie's would-be-fatal bout with a black boxer as a gesture toward Eastwood's own racialized discourse that he rescinds when the money-grabbing rednecks step into the second half of the film. In the last decade or so, American films have been more brazen with their eroticized investment of white trash. In *Harold and Kumar Go to White Castle* (2004), second-generation Asian-American and Indian-American protagonists gain recognition by enduring a series of horrors committed by whites. They face a poseur dude camp, a racist police officer, and, not least of all, they face Freakshow, an oozing, zombie-like, hymn-singing repairman who picks them up to fix Harold's tire. The boys are stunned to hear Freakshow invite them to go inside, have something to drink, watch TV, and "fuck" his wife. When they do, sex-kitten Liane greets them with an impatient request, but as the two young men settle for blowjobs for fear of their "balls rubbing together," Freakshow lurches in and, after some confusion, invites Harold and Kumar to have a foursome. "Who gets the first reach-around?" he asks, and the boys flee. Liane's sexual bravado mediates Freakshow's bodily disgust in more than one way, reinforcing the "impudicity" of the Juke women and the infectious disease of his skin/class.

But it is *Pulp Fiction*'s neighbor, Matthew Bright's self-proclaimed "artsploitation" film *Freeway* (produced by Oliver Stone after *Natural Born Killers* and released in 1996), that thoroughly exposes the systematic punishments that liberal guilt dishes out on sexualized poor whites. The film concerns white trash heroine Vanessa Lutz (Reese Witherspoon) as she hitchhikes unknowingly with a child killer named Bob (Kiefer Sutherland) to Southern California to see her grandmother who lives, not surprisingly, in a trailer park. Vanessa herself lives in a motel: in an early scene her methadone-addicted mother is picked up for soliciting and her stepdad Larry is making moves on Vanessa in his bed. Bright himself based this police intrusion scene on the television show *Cops*, a show Newitz has singled out as particularly retrograde to the identity politics white trash could potentially mobilize (Newitz 137–8). The mise-en-scene of trailer trash moves up a level in discourse as Bob holds Vanessa hostage in his truck on Highway 5 and forces her to narrate her sexual abuse with his words. After proclaiming her a "victim" ("I do got trauma huh?" she asks naively), Bob pounces on her. His initial liberal acceptance of Vanessa's sexual past is revealed later as a frame for his own projection: if Vanessa can be dehumanized through the revelation of incest, then she cannot look back at him as he beats, kills, and rapes her (and in that order, too, for he also practices necrophilia). Furthermore, as a stock pedophile he helps her so that he can switch his view of her from human to object. His insistence that she is a victim, in other words, translates her into a liberal hate-object and affords her melodramatic legibility in his mind, only to clear his conscience as he himself victimizes her. Bob's equation of white trash with incestuous desire breaks down to reveal a liberal safeguard so that he can exonerate himself of his own unacceptable desire. Though it revels in the exuberance of Reese Witherspoon's white trash performance, and though it traffics in hypertrophy, *Freeway* also offers an object lesson in multiculturalism's screening whiteness, of distilling it through the projected figure of people like Vanessa.

Notes

1. This last — the chainsaw — reminds us of the slasher film's nod to gender equivalency. Carol Clover's *Men, Women, and Chain Saws* (1993) argues that the last one standing in the slasher film is frequently a female character who equips herself with a phallic weapon (axe, chainsaw, knife) that supplies her with masculine authority over the killer, offering the (presumed) male viewer a violated female body with which to identify at the moment of retribution. Although the perpetrators in Tarantino's scene are Southernized and the

sword finally chosen reads as a correlate weapon for Confederate history, this "class" association of the weapon does nonetheless lend Butch a level of masculine authority over the crime at hand, which is, after all, a male-male anal rape.

2. I read this film more cynically than does J. W. Williamson, who sees the film's equation of white and black poverty to be at least a potentially conscientious treatment of class inequalities across racial lines. Williamson does, however, pause at these flashbacks. In his *Hillbillyland* he writes: "Wexler tried valiantly to raise his audiences' consciences about unequal power in America, but his definitions of powerlessness, especially in the hillbillies' case, seem decidedly more cultural than economic (especially in a couple of brilliantly photographed memory sequences in which the boy learns the rules of manhood from his now-missing-and-presumed-dead father)" (Williamson 252).

3. In fact, the corrective employment of sexually degenerate whites occurs closer to the root source. Oscar Micheaux's *Within our Gates* (1919), an African American production that responds to Griffith's film, places the mulatto protagonist's Sylvia Landry's flashback (to her separation from her Southern black family) within the mind of Alma, her conniving sister-in-law. Sylvia's father was wrongly accused for killing slave owner Gridlestone, a crime actually committed by an unnamed poor white with a rifle. Sylvia's father and family are lynched for the crime. Later, she is held up in a shack by another slave owner who tries to rape her. He stops only when he recognizes an identifying mark on Sylvia's neck proving that she is, in fact, his own daughter. Incestuous rape is interrupted in the nick of time. In order for this scene to serve as a corrective vision of sexual crimes committed in the antebellum South, another unnamed white must be moved to the margins.

Works Cited

Cawelti, John. "Chinatown and Generic Transformation." *Film Genre Reader II*. Ed. Barry Keith Grant. Austin: University of Texas Press, 1995. 243–261.
Clover, Carol. *Men, Women, and Chainsaws: Gender in the Modern Horror Film*. Princeton: Princeton University Press, 1993.
Deliverance. Dir. John Boorman. Per. Jon Voight, Burt Reynolds, Ned Beatty, and Ronny Cox. Warner Brothers, 1972. Film.
Dunne, John Gregory. "The War That Won't Go Away." *The New York Review of Books* 25 Sept. 1986.
Freeway. Dir. Matthew Bright. Per. Reese Witherspoon, Kiefer Sutherland. Roxie Releasing, 1996. Film.
Goad, Jim. *The Redneck Manifesto: How Hillbillies, Hicks, and White Trash Became America's Scapegoats*. New York: Simon & Schuster, 1998.
Gould, Stephen Jay. *The Mismeasure of Man*. New York: Norton, 1996.
Harold and Kumar Go to White Castle. Dir. Danny Leiner. Per. John Cho, Kal Penn. New Line Cinema, 2004. Film.
Medium Cool. Dir. Haskell Wexler. Per. Robert Forster, Verna Bloom, Peter Bonerz. Miramax, 1969. Film.
Newitz, Annalee. "White Savagery and Humiliation, or A New Racial Consciousness in the Media." *White Trash: Race and Class in America*. Ed. Matt Wray and Annalee Newitz. New York: Routledge, 1997. 131–154.
Penley, Constance. "Crackers and Whackers: The White Trashing of Porn." *White Trash: Race and Class in America*. Ed. Matt Wray and Annalee Newitz. New York: Routledge, 1997. 89–112.
Poor White Trash II. Dir. S. F. Brownrigg. Per. Gene Ross, Ann Stafford, Norma Moore, Camilla Carr. Magnum, 1974. Film.

Pulp Fiction. Dir. Quentin Tarantino. Per. Samuel L. Jackson, John Travolta, and Bruce Willis. Miramax, 1994. Film.

Rogin, Michael. *Blackface, White Noise: Jewish Immigrants in the Hollywood Melting Pot.* Berkeley: University of California Press, 1996.

Slotkin, Richard. *Gunfighter Nation: The Myth of the Frontier in Twentieth-Century America.* New York: Harper Perennial, 1992.

The Wild Bunch. Dir. Sam Peckinpah. Per. William Holden, Ernest Borgnine, Robert Ryan. Warner Brothers, 1969. Film.

Williamson, J. W. *Hillbillyland: What the Movies Did to the Mountains and What the Mountains Did to the Movies.* Chapel Hill: University of North Carolina Press, 1995.

Wray, Matt. *Not Quite White: White Trash and the Boundaries of Whiteness.* Durham: Duke University Press, 2006.

Wray, Matt, and Annalee Newitz, ed. *White Trash: Race and Class in America.* New York: Routledge, 1997.

VIII.

The Haunting of a Black Southern Past: Considering Conjure in *To Sleep with Anger*

PHILLIP LAMARR CUNNINGHAM

The opening scene of Charles Burnett's gothic film *To Sleep with Anger* (1990) is pregnant with significance: the film's protagonist Gideon (Paul Butler), who is in the midst of a deep slumber, dreams of being consumed by flames as he sits idly, clad in a brilliantly white suit and shoes. The flames foreshadow the looming presence of evil, which will eventually manifest itself in the form of Harry (Danny Glover), Gideon's old friend from Memphis. When he awakens, he finds that he is barefoot and has fallen asleep while reading the Bible in the backyard garden of his modest South Central Los Angeles home. The slow dissolve between the dream sequence and real-time hints at the conflict that runs its course throughout *To Sleep with Anger*: Gideon and his family are embroiled in a struggle between tradition and modernity, conjure and religion.

Conjure serves as the basis of this conflict: Gideon and Harry have lost their tobies, totemic charms which ward off evil spirits. As Harry laments, "You don't want to be at a crossroads without one.... In my travels I misplaced it. I have been looking over my shoulder ever since." For Harry, life without his toby has been precarious; for Gideon and his family, the loss of the charm brings about misfortune in the form of the wayward Harry, who represents a Southern past that breaks the tenuous hold the family has on peaceful coexistence.

Due to the prevalence of blues music and the connections to Memphis in the film, scholarly work on *To Sleep with Anger* casts it in the mold of a blues allegory, one in which the South is a point of contention. Jacquie Jones notes, "Burnett's blues return to the rural South as the point of origin not only of the conflicts represented but also of the tensions that exist with regard to family and social mobility" (23). The African American gothic has long looked to the South as a site of terror. As Teresa Goddu notes, "The gothic, like race, seems to become most visible in a Southern locale.... The South is a benighted landscape, heavy with history and haunted by the ghosts of slavery" (76). Slavery, however, is an afterthought in *To Sleep with Anger*: while slavery is the vessel that brought conjure to the South, the "peculiar institution" has little bearing on the film. The haunting in *To Sleep with Anger* is done not by a slavery-ridden South, but a postbellum black South steeped in traditions, particularly a continued adherence to conjure.

Situating *To Sleep with Anger* in the Gothic

To Sleep with Anger is centered upon a somewhat disjointed yet close family presided over by Gideon and his wife Suzie (Mary Alice). Gideon, a retired railroad worker, and Suzie, a midwife, are Southern transplants who now reside in South Central Los Angeles, where they raised their sons, Junior (Carl Lumbly), an industrious family man in the mold of his father, and Babe Brother (Richard Brooks), who is self-indulgent and money hungry. The family, which, for the most part, retains its Southern values, has become splintered over how Babe Brother and his wife Linda (Sheryl Lee Ralph), a modern-day power couple, continue to neglect their son Sunny (DeVaughn Nixon). Harry's arrival follows shortly after the family confronts Babe Brother for not helping to repair the roof and for not getting Suzie a birthday gift.

Enter Harry, who asserts that he is on his way to Oakland from Detroit. Weary from the lengthy trip, he decides to stop in Los Angeles to rest, so he looks up Gideon, his old friend from "back home" in Memphis. Gideon and Suzie welcome Harry into their home and offer to let him stay as long as he would like. Harry, who, like Gideon, has lost his toby, immediately makes his presence felt by beguiling Babe Brother with tales of his sordid past, which includes drinking corn liquor, frequenting juke joints, and apparently murdering a few people back in Memphis. As Harry's stay prolongs, he begins antagonizing everyone with whom he comes into contact, particularly Hattie (Ethel Ayler), an old girlfriend and blues singer who also has relocated to Los Angeles and is now a practicing Christian. Harry tempts her with memories of her own seedy past, which she vehemently rejects. During his confrontation with Hattie, Harry proposes a large fish fry to gather old friends, including Okra (Davis Roberts), Suzie's former boyfriend. At the gathering, Gideon finally admonishes Babe Brother about his lackluster parenting skills, which further damages their already fractured relationship.

Shortly after the fish fry, Gideon grows quite ill from a rather mysterious illness. With the family patriarch removed, Harry continues negatively influencing Babe Brother. As the rest of the family attends to Gideon, Harry appeals to Babe Brother's greed by teaching him how to cheat in high stakes cards. Babe Brother's demeanor darkens as he spends more time with Harry, eventually leading him to slap Linda over a minor accident. Having grown weary of Harry's disruptive presence, Suzie finally asks Harry to leave. However, before he leaves, he tempts Babe Brother with promises of good times and money if Babe Brother returns to Memphis with him. Babe Brother goes to his parents' home to inform his family that he is leaving with Harry, leading to a violent confrontation with Junior. As Junior chokes him, Babe Brother brandishes a knife, which Suzie stops him from using by gripping the blade. The brothers cease fighting in order to rush Suzie to the hospital. The incident reunites the family and returns the focus back to Gideon's health. After returning from the hospital, the entire family attends to Gideon; meanwhile, downstairs, Harry, who has returned to gather his possessions, slips on Sunny's marbles and eventually dies from an apparent heart attack. As the family awaits the coroner, Gideon rises out of bed for the first time in three weeks, seemingly unaware that he had even been sick.

Harry's arrival, of course, is the catalyst for the tensions in the household, for his disruptive presence begins the series of unfortunate events that follow. Hattie, the former juke joint singer, laments, "Harry, you know you remind me so much of what went wrong in my life." For Hattie and Gideon's family, Harry is the living embodiment of the South, a site of conflict for the protagonists of *To Sleep with Anger*. Harry's interaction with Hattie highlights his ability to haunt with the past:

> GIDEON: Haven't the years been good to Hattie?
>
> HARRY: It hasn't been the years; it's been the men in her life.
>
> HATTIE: Harry, that's not nice. I'm in church now.
>
> HARRY : Why run out and close the barn door when the horse is gone? I remember when you weren't saved. That was way back yonder when the Natchez Trace was just a dirt road.
>
> HATTIE : Some people grow up and change their ways.
>
> HARRY : I know your mother ain't still operating that house of hers.
>
> HATTIE: My mother passed on years ago.

In one fell swoop, Harry has drudged up Hattie's former promiscuity, her mother's career as a whorehouse madam, and her mother's death. His reference to the Natchez Trace firmly situates a sordid past within the South, for the Natchez Trace, a 400-plus mile route between Natchez, Mississippi, and Nashville, Tennessee, is a path fraught with peril. As J. Kingston Pierce notes, the Natchez Trace is also known as "the Devil's Backbone," due to the illicit activities — excessive drinking, gambling and prostitution — that took place there (31–32). Therefore, linking Hattie to the Natchez Trace is not coincidental: in doing so, Harry not only indicts Hattie for her own checkered past but traces its roots and Southernizes it in the process. He also manages to call attention to the frailty of her newfound conviction here, for as Hattie suggests, Harry does indeed bring out the worst in her: when Suzie asks Hattie about what she should do about Harry's negative influence on her family, Hattie states coldly, "If it was up to me, I would poison him." While Harry has proven incapable of drawing Hattie back into a life of debauchery, he has managed, at the very least, to reveal a chink in her religious armor.

In Harry's presence, eggs and jars suddenly drop and break, a trumpet virtuoso cannot play in tune, an unborn child violently flails in his or her mother's womb, a mysterious illness strikes an old friend, and a tightly knit family breaks apart at the seams. These occurrences suggest that the origin of Harry's corruptive power is in the supernatural. In many regards, Harry is the ultimate conjurer, a trickster with the power to darken the soul. As Ellen L. O'Brien notes, Burnett, the film's writer and director, based Harry on "Hairy Man," a Southern folkloric character known for stealing the souls of those who are most vulnerable (114–115). Hairy Man's origins can be traced further: as Sojin Kim and R. Mark Livengood note, the Hairy Man tale most likely emanates from a folklore motif associating the devil with a hairy man that Stith Thompson has indexed in his well known *Motif Index of Folklore* (73).

As Jones suggests, "*To Sleep with Anger* opens with a spiritual blues that fades from city to country, and back to a composite of both, thus preparing the viewer for the psychic ambiguity at the film's core" (22). Given that the film is a blues allegory, Harry as the devil seems fitting. One of the first indicators of Harry's connection to the devil is his mentioning of the crossroads. The crossroads are a standard in blues lore, most notably as the place where legendary bluesmen Robert Johnson and Tommy Johnson sold their souls in order to play a mean blues. Ayana Smith writes of the crossroads, "In the blues, the crossroads are therefore the locus of an American [Esu-Elegbara, the Signifying Monkey and trickster of West African mythology]. The interpretational uncertainty represented by the crossroads creates a spatial and temporal realm of ambiguity. This is the realm of the trickster figure. In the blues tradition, this trickster figure is often represented as the devil" (184). Harry mentions the crossroads as a rationale for having a toby; he tells Babe Brother, "When we were children, there used to be an old man that came around and would snatch your soul if you didn't have something on you that didn't make a X." That Harry is now the harvester of souls speaks volumes:

it not only indicates the power of the toby, but also it indicates that, as Harry suggests of Hattie, the penchant for wrongdoing is in his lineage. Furthermore, it perhaps explains why Harry has arrived in Los Angeles, where Gideon's family stands at a crossroads themselves as a result of division amongst them over Babe Brother's irresponsible behavior.

A toby took the form of an X or cross largely because of conjure's connection to Christianity. Often, conjure is presented as incongruous to traditional religion; however, for many Southern blacks, often, black magic and Christianity went hand-in-hand. Yvonne Chireau highlights the relationship between conjure and Christianity: "Conjurers often appropriated rituals and sacred symbols from Christianity. Many charms were endowed with magical potency 'in the name of the Lord.' Religious accoutrements adopted from Christian traditions were enlisted by black specialists for purposes of protection and prediction" (234). However, one must also consider the converse: talismans such as the toby can also be wielded for evil purposes. Having lost his toby, Harry has chosen to replace it with a rabbit's foot. O'Brien notes the significance of the rabbit's foot in *To Sleep with Anger* as an ambiguous object that both protects its holder and might be used "to practice evil magic" (120). Chireau writes, "For many blacks, illness was viewed as the work of the devil, and Conjure was associated with the universal contest between the forces of good and evil" (236). Considering this, one can deduce that Harry has utilized his rabbit's foot for evil purposes, namely the corruption of Gideon's body and the corruption of Babe Brother's soul. Without his toby, Gideon and his family have no means in which to maintain the balance between good and evil; thus, they succumb to it.

Conjure and the Dichotomy of Tradition and Modernity in *To Sleep with Anger*

Harry's ability to haunt with a Southern past is perhaps most evident in the scene in which he walks along the railroad tracks with Harry. As the two former railroad workers stroll down the tracks on a hot afternoon, Harry remarks, "I can sit here and look at train tracks all day. We laid enough of them, didn't we? So many memories are stretched along tracks like these." As a weary, sweat-ridden Gideon gazes into the distance, the ghostly specters of men singing a work song while laying tracks appear. Harry, however, remains unaffected; that the heat does not weaken him is yet another indication of Harry's devilish nature.

This scene is pivotal for a number of reasons: first, it serves as the moment of affliction. The next morning, Gideon, a usually strong and virile person, is unable to get out of bed. On the surface, it appears as if Gideon has been worn out by the previous evening's fish fry and his long walk in the summer sun. However, conjure is implicated here, as well, for in conjuring forth the ghosts of their careers as tracklayers, Harry haunts Gideon with the distance between Gideon and his Southern roots. Harry thus evokes the film's central conflict: the dichotomy between tradition and modernity.

Though the actual distance between Los Angeles and Memphis is just short of 2,000 miles, in terms of spirituality, the distance is nearly immeasurable. As Jones notes, a great deal was lost in the black migration from the South to more industrial locales: "The great Black migrations, which took African American people from Southern plantations into large cities like Los Angeles, New York, and Chicago, came at great spiritual and communal cost, distancing African Americans from family and roots" (23). In *To Sleep with Anger*, this "spiritual and communal cost" is greatest for Gideon and Babe Brother, both of whom struggle to balance tradition and modernity. Gideon is as out of sorts with modernity as Babe Brother is with tradition. Of this conflict, O'Brien writes, "Burnett warns us that wherever one's self definition comes from in terms of cultural values, the individual must learn to live with the new ways as well as cherish the old ways, otherwise that person is vulnerable to evil forces" (117). Indeed, as the two most affected by Harry's presence, Babe Brother and Gideon clearly lack this balance and, as a result, are the most vulnerable.

Gideon's struggle with modernity is evident in his being linked to John Henry, the legendary railroad worker of African American folktales: "Gideon represents John Henry, a supporter of traditional ways, and the steam drill represents the modern way of industrialization. Gideon, like John Henry, refuses to accept modern ways and fights them. This makes him vulnerable to Harry's evil manipulations" (O'Brien 115). Though there are many variations of the John Henry myth — ranging from his death as a result of an orgasm to his not dying at all — the most popular form sees John Henry achieve a pyrrhic victory over the steam drill in a race to complete the digging of West Virginia's Big Bend Tunnel. Though John Henry manages to defeat the steam drill, evidencing the power of the worker over technology, he ultimately dies as a result, thus becoming a victim of modernity.

The film's invocation of the John Henry folktale helps punctuate this conflict. Staging Gideon as John Henry and Harry as Hairy Man highlights the struggle between tradition and modernity. Of this conflict, Karen Chandler writes, "*To Sleep with Anger* fulfills the instructive and epistemological role of folklore, inviting viewers to consider racial and gender roles and responsibilities, as well as generational tensions and influences, in black communities" (300). This cultural crisis is writ large in Gideon, who, through his labors, has managed to transplant his family from poverty and the old-fashioned ways of Memphis into the working class and modernity of Los Angeles. However, in the move westward, Gideon remains immersed in the South: he maintains a chicken coop in his backyard, he relates folktales to his grandchildren, and he believes that the toby his grandmother crafted for him will protect him from harm.

One of the more striking conflicts between the past and the present pits conjure versus religion in a battle to heal Gideon. Gideon's illness grows more severe, noticeably after Harry serves him a bowl of chicken soup which, as O'Brien notes, resonates with traditional African healing practices (120–121). However, given O'Brien's earlier finding that magic meant to cure can also inflict, one can assume that Harry has malicious intent. After Gideon's doctor's office visit does not alleviate his symptoms, Suzie begins treating him with home remedies, a form of conjure in itself. Shortly thereafter, Gideon and Suzie's preacher (Wonderful Smith) appears with members of the congregation to pray for Gideon at his bedside. Suzie reveals the treatments she has given Gideon:

> SUZIE: I put some Plummer Christian Leaves under his feet to draw the fever out.
> PREACHER: What else have you been giving him?
> SUZIE: I crossed his stomach with cold oil and gave him some cow tea.
> PREACHER: Suzie, I would think you would depend on prayer rather than these old fashion remedies. Let us read from the Bible.

As O'Brien suggests, "In the film, the Baptist church plays a role in symbolizing the differences between traditional ways and modern ways, and specifically, the division among the characters" (118). The preacher and his parishioners regard Suzie with contempt for her and Gideon's continued adherence to the old ways. Suzie's decision to treat Gideon with conjure and the preacher's negative reaction shows how antiquated conjure appears in the face of modern organized religion.

Religion is one of the points of conflicts in the family, particularly for Babe Brother and Linda. Part of Gideon's anger towards Babe Brother and Linda is that they do not take Sunny to church:

> GIDEON: Tell me, how come me and Suzie have to be mother and father to your child? You never take the boy to the park, circus or anything. If we did not take him to church, he wouldn't have any sense of religion.
> LINDA: I think forcing him to go to church when he really doesn't understand is not saving his soul. When he gets old enough to make up his own mind about religion, that will be better. It will be his intellectual decision.

As distanced from modernity as Gideon and Suzie are, Babe Brother and Linda are equally distant from any sense of tradition, particularly any ties to the South. As Gideon chides him for his lackluster parenting skills, Babe Brother laments, "I don't need that kind of love. And I don't want to be reminded all the time that Big Mama's grandmother was born in slavery. If you really care about me, just tell me how I can make money." Babe Brother's interests are in the present and the practical, not the past and the spiritual, and serve as further evidence of the family's problematic break from the South.

Harry, with his proclamation that "I am more modern in my ways," appeals to Babe Brother's greed and desire for power. While the rest of the family attends church, Babe Brother's family remains home to hear the gospel according to Harry, who preaches, "I don't believe in sin, though there is good and evil. And evil is a thing you work at." He beguiles Babe Brother with tales of his turbulent past, emphasizing his ability to determine his own fate simply by playing a good game of cards and wielding a knife when necessary. Harry gives Babe Brother a more material and modern form of protection from harm: an old knife that Harry implies has been complicit in a few of his misadventures in Memphis. That this scene is juxtaposed with a scene of the rest of the family attending a baptism is telling, as Chandler indicates: "This arrangement of scenes offers an ironic commentary on Harry's status as interloper and upsetter of the status quo, for his transgressive, disruptive influence is juxtaposed with the Christ of Matthew 10:34–35, who threatens to turn family members against one another" (306).

The knife is not the only gift Harry offers, for he also gives Babe Brother the gift of knowledge. As the rest of the family attends to the severely ill Gideon, Harry provides Babe Brother with a lesson that Babe Brother can appreciate:

> HARRY: Never play with someone else's cards. You always get a new deck. Look at this card. See anything?
>
> BABE BROTHER: It is just a regular card.
>
> HARRY: Son, I can take everything you got with that deck.

When Harry (Danny Glover) arrives in Los Angeles, he brings a dark Southern past and conjure that threaten a family in Charles Burnett's *To Sleep with Anger* (1990, Samuel Goldwyn Company)

It is marked. Now I'm going to show you how to make some money in case you get stuck somewhere.

Harry's words are prophetic, for in offering Babe Brother the deck, Harry does indeed threaten to take all of what Babe Brother has, most notably his family.

In effect, Babe Brother, by learning the tricks of the trade from Harry, is offering his soul to the devil. Without coincidence, every card game played between Babe Brother and Harry sees Babe Brother wagering more of his soul: his disposition darkens with each hand dealt. During the initial card game, Babe Brother scolds Linda for merely touching one of his cards. In the next card game, after chastising Linda for not seeing that Sunny's shoes are tied, he slaps her when she tries to prevent him from cutting a piece of roast before it is ready. Immediately afterwards, he forces Linda, who has rejected domesticity throughout the course of the film, into a domestic space by making her serve dinner to him, Harry, and Harry's friends. Chandler notes, "[T]he film suggests the inevitable continuity of certain masculine poses in black life, given the persistence of such social formations as segregation and black alienation from the mainstream. Yet *To Sleep with Anger* also clearly upholds Gideon as the man best able to facilitate familial well-being and stresses the nihilism and misogyny of Harry's model" (302). Harry's misogynistic beliefs are made clear toward the film's conclusion. Amongst all of the other offerings to Babe Brother, Harry also offers a rather dated form of patriarchy as evidenced in his final conversation with Babe Brother:

> BABE BROTHER: Had Moms and Pops given me my share of what was mine, I could have been rich by now. Linda and I had it all worked out.
>
> HARRY: I know your mind is on your wife but you should never treat a woman as an equal. You want to get your wife back, get another woman, one of those big hip women that will ride you till you sweat.

He follows this chestnut with another purposeful exchange with M.C. (John Hawker), the host of the card game:

> HARRY: M.C., you ever heard of a real man having one woman?
>
> M.C.: No, Lord!
>
> HARRY: When one woman puts you out, you have another to take you in. You don't drive around without a spare tire, do you? The more mules you have hitched, the easier it is to plough.

In demeaning women, equating them to mere whores at best and disposable goods at worst, Harry makes his final offer to Babe Brother: "It's important to know the difference between the incoming fire and the outgoing fire. As Amos and Andy might say, 'We is the outgoing fire.' Come with us, son. We'll show you some steaming hot juke joints, steaming hot women." Though following Harry would result in his eschewing all of his father's teachings and forsaking his family, Babe Brother finally agrees to join Harry and his friends in their journey back to Memphis.

Conclusion: Striking a Balance

Babe Brother's decision to leave with Harry, coupled with his overall irresponsible behavior throughout *To Sleep with Anger*, leads towards a confrontation with his older brother Junior, the better-adjusted of the two. As the brothers fight each other, Babe Brother draws the knife given to him and inches it closer to his brother's throat. To stop the fight, Suzie grabs the blade of the knife. In doing so, she not only shows her willingness to risk her life for her family, she also breaks the hold Harry has on Babe Brother. Her bloodshed reinvigorates the familial ties, for, in the end, the film leads its viewers to conclude that family is key in the natural progression between past and present.

Indeed, every member of Gideon's family plays an essential role in bringing about reunification. The mothers of the film play a particularly important role in maintaining the family structure, especially considering that it is Suzie and Linda who bring Babe Brother back into the fold. Furthermore, the mothers in the film are least susceptible to and most skeptical about Harry's influence. Even the children in the film have a role. In fact, Harry's heart attack and eventual death is caused by his slipping on marbles inadvertently spilled on the kitchen floor by Babe Brother's son, Sunny. As such, Jones notes, "Burnett finds a conclusion that resides within the continuum of African American experience and not in resistance to it. Rather than opting for an individual solution, as *Boyz n the Hood*'s 'go to school' conclusion does, or blaming current crises like crack cocaine, Burnett makes the family necessary for recovery" (24).

While the film does emphasize an acceptance of modernity, *To Sleep with Anger* does not suggest a complete break with the South or tradition. On the contrary, the film emphasizes the need for balance, even in terms of conjure. Conjure by itself proves inadequate in protecting one from the devil just as organized religion proves incapable of healing one befallen from conjure. Instead, the need for a reciprocal relationship is suggested, which is very much in line with the African worldview. Conjure and religion do not have to be adversarial. Chireau writes, "At the heart of black spirituality is an inner quest for fulfillment, an abiding search for security. In African American culture, the worlds of Conjure and Christianity converged, creating empowering responses to misfortune and other persistent needs in human experience"

(240). A degree of retention of a Southern past is necessary for navigating the present.

The restoration of a balanced family notwithstanding, *To Sleep with Anger* still remains a gothic film: as the film's conclusion suggests, not all is well for the reunited family. As Harry's dead body remains on his floor for hours on end and the coroner's office never arrives to retrieve it, the family is left to deal with a new haunting, that of being black in South Central Los Angeles. The film leaves the family's ability to deal with this new threat uncertain; however, it also hints at a solution. As the neighborhood becomes aware that Harry's dead body is still in the family's home, several neighbors throw an afternoon picnic for Gideon's family to get everyone out of the house. This suggests that the community, family on a larger scale, is essential in contesting this new haunting.

Works Cited

Chandler, Karen. "Folk Culture and Masculine Identity in Charles Burnett's *To Sleep with Anger*." *African American Review* 33.2 (Summer 1999): 299–311.

Chireau, Yvonne. "Conjure and Christianity in the Nineteenth Century: Religious Elements in African American Magic." *Religion and American Culture* 7.2 (Summer 1997): 225–246.

Goddu, Teresa A. *Gothic America: Narrative, History and Nation*. New York: Columbia University Press, 1997.

Jones, Jacquie. "The Black South in Contemporary Film." *African American Review* 27.1 (Spring 1993): 19–24.

Kim, Sojin, and Livengood, R. Mark. "Review: Talking with Charles Burnett." *The Journal of American Folklore* 111.439 (Winter 1998): 69–73.

O'Brien, Ellen L. "Charles Burnett's *To Sleep with Anger*: An Anthropological Perspective." *Journal of Popular Culture* 35.4 (Spring 2002): 113–126.

Pierce, J. Kingston. "Along the Devil's Backbone." *Historic Traveler* 5.4 (April 1999): 30–38.

Smith, Ayana. "Blues, Criticism, and the Signifying Trickster." *Popular Music* 24.2 (May 2005): 179–191.

To Sleep with Anger. Dir. Charles Burnett. Perf. Mary Alice, Paul Butler, Danny Glover. 1990. Sony, 1997. VHS.

IX.

Practice in a Cemetery: Ross McElwee's North Carolina Documentaries

STEPHEN BROOMER

In *Smokey and the Bandit*, the Southern stud-hipster is pitted against the corrupt and stupid law. The Southern hipster character, made iconic through Burt Reynolds, is as important to Southern representation as its opposite, the corrupt and xenophobic yokel-idiot. The dominant conflict in the Southern road movie is between these two types, who engage in a contest of wits. In this genre, deception and maneuvering advances plot. Another example of this is television's *The Dukes of Hazzard*, with the Southerner represented in the dueling roles of the sly Duke boys and moronic Rosco Coltrane and Boss Hogg. In their chases, the law is inevitably lacking in brains and motor power, their endgame loss as dependent on their self-assuredness as it is on their lackluster machinery. The Southern road movie is a fantasy built of positive (masculine, noble) and negative (bigoted, stupid) stereotypes of the Southerner. Jim Goad writes of the representation of Southerners as having "a limited ability to achieve and a massive capacity to destroy" (86), which is evident in the small victories of these protagonists and the massive rampage left in their wake. Destructive glee is as omnipresent in the Southern road film as the empty or uncertain futures of its characters, oppressor and oppressed.

When Ross McElwee began to make documentary films in North Carolina in the 1980s, he did so as an expatriate Southerner. He had spent years as a student at MIT in Boston, Massachusetts, a monument of northern liberalism, and had grown distant from the traditional, conservative values of his upbringing. In the opening scenes of his *Backyard* (1984), he relates his return to the viewer, in which he tells his father that he might work in black voter registration, or with the peace movement, or he may become a Buddhist monk. These are career options that his father, a doctor, regards disdainfully. McElwee returns to a South that does not share in those zany characteristics of the South in film and television: its citizens bitterly feel the effects of the Civil War and the civil rights movement. McElwee's South is traumatized by this past. The Southerner is deposed as a stranger in his own land, witnessing the wealth of an immoral labor system dry up. This is not Burt Reynolds's South, a land that celebrates stud-hipster, masculine fantasy. This is a land of racial and economic unrest where the many who pray for the Reynolds fantasy to be reality are in profound self-denial. Ross McElwee arrives in his homeland not quite as a tourist but never as a resident. He visits with his family and people from his past. His identity is that of the Southerner exiled by his independence from tradition.

While McElwee has made a number of autobiographical films about reconciling his origins and raising his family, all of which involve his home state of North Carolina to some degree, this essay focuses on the three films in his oeuvre that deal substantially with Southern representation, culture and trauma (*Backyard*; *Sherman's March*, 1986; *Bright Leaves*, 2003). Each film addresses one of three legacies of the South: segregation, the failure of the confederacy, and tobacco cultivation respectively. When Godfrey Cheshire writes about the films of Ross McElwee, he contends that the Southern films of his and McElwee's youth were interminably offered from an outsider's perspective; one imagines he is speaking of *A Face in the Crowd* (1959) and *To Kill a Mockingbird* (1962), though the same holds true for *Smokey and the Bandit* and Southern "exploitation" cinema that emerged in the 1970s. It was not an indigenous Southern cinema that was issued to theaters — accents were faked, locations staged, the rhythm of the drama lacking an indefinable authenticity that Cheshire senses in McElwee's calm, observational style. If this style lends the work an elusive authenticity as indigenous Southern cinema, McElwee's films become an auto-ethnographic cycle, adopting a distinctly Southern conception of time and revelation to critique past and present Southernness.

Backyard (1984)

Ross McElwee had made three films by the time *Backyard* was released. His first, *Charleen or How Long Has This Been Going On?* (1978), is a portrait documentary about a former teacher of his, Charleen Swansea, as she prepares her poetry class for a public performance. He followed that with *Space Coast* (1979), three portraits of Cape Canaveral residents, and then collaborated with Alexandra Anthony and Michel Negroponte to make *Resident Exile* (1981), described by Cynthia Lucia as being "about an Iranian student living in Texas after enduring brutal torture under the Shah" (32). Unlike McElwee's later films, *Backyard* does not deal with past representations of Southerners on film, but it does introduce some major themes of his work, as well as his observation-driven structure.

McElwee hammers out a dirge on an out-of-tune piano as his narration explains his visit as an attempt to film his family. This piano returns as a motif, the physical disrepair of the piano becoming a symbol of the metaphysical disrepair of the home in the wake of McElwee's mother's death. His brother is preparing to begin medical school to become a doctor like their father, and McElwee attempts to film his father working, in surgery and in visits to patients. However, whenever McElwee attempts to film his father performing surgery, his camera malfunctions. As this becomes a lost cause, he films the activities of his family and their black staff who helped raise him. The staff performs household chores and maintenance. The family is shown primarily in preparation for the brother's departure. The family teases McElwee: his brother calls him a yankee and his father is critical of his uneconomic use of film stock. McElwee successfully films his father's visits to patients, but while filming a telephone consultation, the camera again malfunctions. On hanging up, his father says, "I'll be happy when that big eye's gone," a turn of phrase that implicates the camera as an extension of McElwee's vision, which is dysfunctional. This gives the impression that his unsuccessful attempts to film his father speak to the misunderstandings of their relationship, epitomized in the father's frequent apprehension of McElwee's self-documentation, an apprehension that is reprised in later works. The functional camera would succeed in preserving the father, while through the dysfunctional camera, the father deteriorates into the abstract patterns of a broken machine. The intended image would not only document the present, but also exist for posterity as a future memorial. These scenes are conceived with McElwee's consciousness of his mother's death and the certainty that his father, too, will die.

As a doctor, McElwee's father encounters mortality regularly, and though it does not hang a pall over their activities — which involve ordinary, joyous recreation — it is a fact of his profession and McElwee's brother's future profession. In a late scene, McElwee decides to speak with his brother about their mother's death which occurred suddenly during an optimistic period of a battle with cancer. He believes that the brother's pre-med training might give him some insight into what the exact cause of death had been, as this is a subject that he does not wish to broach with his father. The brother admits to not knowing the precise cause of death, save to attribute it to cancer.

McElwee's hesitation to bring this up with his father recognizes how devastating an event it was for the family and how delicate a subject it is to be breached. At the same time, that hesitation speaks to the widening gap between the two signified through his camera malfunctions and in his inability to create a whole representation of his father. The portrait photographer Richard Avedon wrote of a series he produced of his own father that he attempted to show his father as he was and not as he would like to be seen, in order to get to a truth of his father's being that was absent from his father's self-image (2). By not seeing these images, Avedon's father avoided confronting mortality and reveals the insincerity of how we wish to be seen. In McElwee's case, he wrestles with representing his father not because his father has an inflated self-image but because their connection has, through their separate political and professional identities, grown so weathered and tenuous that he doubts the accuracy of his representations of his father. Similarly, McElwee doubts his ability to represent his homeland of the South, specifically North Carolina, after his time away from it. This is not so much a matter of objectivity as it is of subjective accuracy; McElwee's absence has estranged him from both his family and a whole past identity, one marked by a traditional ideology and unfulfilled expectations.

McElwee films his grandmother singing a song about a black mother who warns her child to "stay in [his] own backyard":

> Honey, don't you mind what them white childs do,
> And honey don't you cry so hard,
> Go out and play as much as you please,
> But stay in your own backyard.

The black staff tends to the grounds. Melvin is the housekeeper Lucille's husband, and Clyde Cathy is a beekeeper, who, as McElwee tells us, "relies on visions from God to help him locate swarms of bees." Cathy who, in his professional life, has inhabited the backyards of wealthy whites, is shown weeping at the wedding of a client's daughter. On their way home from the wedding, the father of the bride, who is a neighbor of the McElwees, jokingly asks McElwee where he lives, and then says, "you live in my backyard, that's what I tell your daddy." Despite the end of official segregation the blacks and whites of Charlotte appear to occupy separate worlds, both governed by self-denial. When McElwee asks Lucille if she would like to sit with him as he eats, she refuses, saying that she prefers the kitchen; she is, by McElwee's admission, a second mother to him, but she maintains a distance that suggests a fear of the past social order of segregation. Clyde Cathy's service has turned him into a kind of holy man, preaching of a mystical connection with insect life even as his connection to the human world appears tenuous. While they occupy the same space, *Backyard*'s blacks and whites continue to live by the rules of a past social order.

McElwee observes these proceedings by embracing the coincidental. His films are spontaneous in form, with camera malfunctions, the end of reels, and occasionally incorrect color temperatures interrupting throughout, and similar interruptions litter and enliven the film's content. One may be inclined from this to dismiss the compositional elements of McElwee's filmmaking, which have always taken a backseat to his literary sources in criticism. The aesthetic is that of the home movie — zoom and manual focus are employed; the "big eye" becomes McElwee's sole physical perspective. Cheshire's idea of a distinctly Southern observational style need not be restricted to the calm of revelation in narration, dialogue and narrative perspective — all elements that were absent from those northern "Southern" films of his youth. McElwee's films are littered with glancing blows, inconstant and non-rhythmic revelations and thematic recurrences. It is the thematic recurrence that gives *Backyard*'s title power — not the pro-segregation song, but the backyard as a site for black labor and family recreation. These visual cues allow the viewer to revel in the same apparent coincidences as McElwee, coincidences that indicate an ideology embedded in the culture. Diane Stevenson has written on coincidence in McElwee's films and describes the coincidence as metaphysic, to be discarded in the ontology of causality, to which fate and universal accordance are laughable concepts (63). But the coincidental is at the core of McElwee's narrative and aesthetic, which explores subjects (the Civil War, segregation, tobacco farming) that have emblematic causal explanations. The visual cue, the casual phrase, the interruption and overlap of one subject on another, these elements join together from a coincidental basis but contribute to a greater thematic structure. Perhaps this coincidence-laden structure is the only authentic approach to exploring a South where slavery economy has become enmeshed in a national mythology of the Civil War, the morally ambiguous realities of war eclipsed by a fable of northern good dispelling Southern evil. Complex reasons are reduced to a single moral conundrum with the dominance of abolitionism; the Civil War came about through a number of factors that, perhaps through coincidence, perhaps causality, amassed to turn North and South against one another in 1861, but it is the emancipation of black slaves that made the North's victory moral. It may be that Southernness can only be authentically communicated in such forms that resist causality and embrace fate, because the history of the South is so marked by the emblematic moral victory of the North. This is coincidence as determinism, a Southern style evidenced in the phenomenally doomed characters of Carson McCullers and William Faulkner. On the surface, their narratives occur in coincidence. The final image of *Backyard* speaks to McElwee's assembly of coincidences that have loaded the film's simple title: Melvin tends to the grounds on a riding mower in the family's backyard, filmed through an ornamental window of the darkened house.

Sherman's March (1986)

As *Sherman's March* begins, a narrator (Richard Leacock) tells us of the campaign that General William Sherman led in the closing days of the Civil War, a path through the Carolinas and Georgia that left cities in ruin, humiliating and shattering the pride of the South. Ross McElwee appears in a large, empty New York loft, explaining that he had intended to make a film traveling Sherman's route but has become disillusioned due to a recent romantic entanglement. He tells us that he has decided to visit his family in the South to try to get perspective on his situation. As the film progresses, he tries to shake his unrequited love by engaging in a series of brief relationships with Southern women as he follows the path of Sherman's campaign and attempts to keep his work in sight. He establishes parallels, sometimes tenuous, between his and Sherman's lives. McElwee's encounters include an interview with a man who wants to be Burt Reynolds's stand-in and an attempt at interviewing Reynolds himself on a movie set, which results in the crew threatening to have McElwee arrested.

The coincidental becomes more pronounced in *Sherman's March*, as McElwee follows a path that is perpetually derailed by prospects of love or by financial necessity. The resulting film is intensely conscious of Southern representation on film as explicitly introduced in McElwee's pursuit of Burt Reynolds, a figure whose importance in the narrative enters coincidentally through one of McElwee's lovers (Pat Rendleman) who wishes to act with Reynolds. Later, McElwee is stranded by his failing car in Atlanta where Reynolds is filming a movie. McElwee's broken car strands his fractured masculinity near the great archetype of Southern manhood and "car-hood." McElwee seeks an audience with Reynolds, and though fate appears to draw them together repeatedly, the actor's security staff conspires to keep them apart. McElwee films his fans instead, a legion of aging Southern women intent on catching a glimpse of Reynolds. One proudly dis-

Pat Rendleman is an actress who aspires to act with Burt Reynolds in Ross McElwee's *Sherman's March* (1986, First Run Features; credit Michel Delsol).

plays her sleeping baby, saying that Burt Reynolds kissed it. Through the inaccessible Reynolds and the fantasy that he inspires, the film develops a commentary on the falseness of Southern representations with McElwee himself standing in as reality and opposite.

Sherman's March was released in 1986, inspiring some critics to regard McElwee as the Southern Woody Allen. *The Boston Globe* declared, "a Tarheel Woody Allen leads 'Sherman's March'" (Carr B1). There is a desire in that comparison to make McElwee somehow less Southern, an exception among "tarheels" (a slang term for North Carolinians). By his own admission the style of his narration follows in a tradition of Southern writers, notably Walker Percy. In April 2009, he told the *Kitty Snacks* literary journal:

> [M]y narrative style has probably evolved from the sense of being introspective and somewhat ill at ease and out of the loop — perhaps an overall Southern condition. Many Southerners have sailed this ship — Thomas Wolfe, Eudora Welty, but Walker Percy appears to lead the flotilla [18].

The women that McElwee encounters on his journey have personas that seem to have emerged from Southern literature. Rendleman, who is pursuing a career as an actress, describes a rich fantasy life wherein she is a movie-star astronaut, a self-described "female prophet" who evokes the alternately joyous and melancholy self-deceptions of Blanche DuBois. She and others among McElwee's Southern belles would be suitable company for the unreliable narrator of Welty's "Why I Live at the P.O.," whose caustic relationship with her divorcee sister Stella-Rondo forces her to move into her workplace. There is a fragile vanity about a number of these women, several of whom are aspiring celebrities, that seems linked in an unstated way to the humiliation of the Civil War. Southern womanhood is dichotomous, ruled by expectations of formality on the one hand (a notion that few of these women conform to) and completely free-spirited on the other. This womanhood does not have a set type and is ultimately unpredictable as McElwee discovers in the case of Karen, the woman who had inspired his journey by suddenly leaving him and returning to her former lover. The irrational and defensive justifications of a humiliated South emerge in other conversations with women. McElwee films one of his lovers in conversation with her girlfriend who declares that slavery should never have been abolished, but rather, turned into a right. She suggests a constitutional amendment: "If you want to be a slave, be a slave." This woman's South is paralyzed by the new social order that condemns past social order in much the same manner as *Backyard* shows Southern social order as a palimpsest, new practices cohabitating with old practices. Those who wax nostalgic for the confederacy era did not live in it, but they nevertheless see it as preferable to the present and deny the horrors of that past. In this case, the horrific imposition of slavery is misrepresented as a choice. Such self-denial manifests at its most extreme in a group of isolationists that McElwee visits.

McElwee intimates to the viewer that he has dreams of nuclear war, that such dreams have haunted him, infrequently, since he was a child (the film's subtitle is *A Meditation on the Possibility of Romantic Love in the South During an Era of Nuclear Weapons Proliferation*). Nuclear proliferation made the apocalypse a growing possibility in the Cold War era, but it is economic and moral disparities that seem to have inspired haphazard militias to move into the wilderness and build bunkers in defiance of the federal government. Such is the case of a group of men whom McElwee is introduced to by one of his lovers. Members of this isolationist commune answer McElwee's questions about the women in the commune, but they are more interested in discussing their survival in the face of what they believe is a hostile and immoral America: specifically, a post–Civil War America which has, in their view, been eroded by northern liberal economic and social practices. They tell McElwee that they have everything they need "to survive in style." They are an armed collective who view the federal government as an antagonistic force and one of their principle goals is their own emancipation from taxation. They are not by appearances wealthy, but they are creating their commune in a harsh economic climate from the fear of losing their property and their rights, even as the specter that they fear is by logic non-existent, a government of conspirators imagined and defied by a nation of paranoiacs. Such social conservative fringe militias may not be restricted to the South, but less than a decade after *Sherman's March* was released, the conflict between Branch Davidians and the ATF in Waco, Texas (1993) associated such isolationist practices with the South in popular consciousness. One sees in McElwee's subjects the same fear that his other subjects demonstrate: that the change in Southern economy and social values effected after the Civil War is an injustice.

There is never a dispensation of the personal perspective from the film, even in its opening moments when Leacock introduces the viewer to William Sherman over an image of a map. Even this sequence ends with McElwee intruding on Leacock, directing him. This short interruption exposes the opening as part of a process. The act of filmmaking and the personal journey are intertwined as processes that never reach a tidy completion. Film and journey are both interrupted, and in the end neither process has ended. The journey does not end in the North — the concluding passages have McElwee meeting a date, not a bride — and the film that he had apparently planned and began to make will never exist, the introductory narration enclosed here as a trace fragment of an abandoned documentary. The objectivity of that documentary, with its attention to historicity, is false to the present-day South. No objective documentary could truthfully investigate the effect of the South's defeat, or even the reduced scale effect of William Sherman's march. While those contradictory elements of Sherman's persona, the conflict between his love of the South and his loyalty to the North, remain unresolved and, one senses, irresolvable, the war is unfinished.

Bright Leaves (2003)

In the decades between *Sherman's March* and *Bright Leaves*, McElwee made a pair of intimate films about childbirth (*Time Indefinite*, 1993) and childrearing (*Six O'Clock News*, 1996). In 2003, McElwee released *Bright Leaves*, in which he returns to North Carolina after a second-cousin shows him Michael Curtiz's *Bright Leaf* (1950), a film about the dawn of tobacco tycoons in the South. The lead character, tobacco baron Brant Royle (Gary Cooper), appears to be based on McElwee's own great-grandfather, John Harvey McElwee, the supposed developer of a tobacco formula whose career ended in ruin when his formula was stolen and marketed under the Bull-Durham brand. McElwee mounts an investigation into the film and its sources. At first, they indicate that his great-grandfather was, as the film depicts him, a victim of the cutthroat practices of James B. Duke in building his own tobacco empire.

McElwee deals with the legacy of tobacco in the South, his apparent exclusion from the glory of the Duke cigarette empire a bitter aside to his sense of guilt over the contribution of his ancestor to tobacco addiction. McElwee views footage of his now-deceased father and admits to the viewer that his father seems less real to him over time, that the landscape of Charlotte has brought McElwee the familiarity that he expected from the home movies. And there in that beautiful landscape is tobacco. It is not simply that the carcinogenic legacy of tobacco has analogously corrupted the land. The poisonous crop itself ruins the soil for future agriculture. Intrusions persist. The observation-driven form continues: Charleen Swansea, McElwee's frequent subject, exclaims in the middle of a recollection, "There's a black cat in the grass!" causing McElwee to spin 360 degrees. McElwee, whose narration throughout his filmmaking has been comic, asks a cousin, sole living grandchild of his ancestor-subject, if John Harvey McElwee had a sense of humor. He pursues such routes to link his character to that of his ancestor, much as he attempted to link his motivations, victories and failures to those of William Sherman. John Harvey McElwee's role as a tragic historical figure interests Ross McElwee as much as their blood relation. *Bright Leaf*'s representation of McElwee's ancestor is either far more complex or coincidental than it first appears, and by the documentary's conclusion, the wife of the novelist who wrote *Bright*

Leaf insists that the story does not have a basis in any kind of research, let alone the life of McElwee's ancestor. McElwee even produces a convincing alternative: that Brant Royle is based on James B. Duke, and the film's antagonistic tobacco manufacturer is based on his own great-grandfather.

McElwee characterizes his trips South as a blood "transfusion of Southernness." He finds that blood, in the sense of ancestry, holds only more questions and few answers, as *Bright Leaf*'s sources come into dispute and no objective reality of his ancestor's ruin can be known. *Bright Leaf* is an example of that very style of filmmaking that Cheshire holds up as the false Southern film of his youth, a film in which Northerners portray Southerners, made with a non-indigenous perspective and rhythm, which stakes a claim to the telling of a distinctly Southern story. *Bright Leaves* reclaims it, and its characters, through McElwee's indigenous observational style.

McElwee spends time with smokers suffering from cancer and reflects on his own family's more recent history with smoking, in the death of his grandfather from cancer and his own father's resulting resistance to smoking. The mortality theme that he explores in his relationships with family in prior films is here extended to the social landscape of the Carolinas where death seems to be stitched into the landscape. He spends time on tobacco plantations, interviewing farmers about their work and their own families. The film deals with the idea of family business — McElwee and wife Marilyn Levine are both filmmakers — and in one scene McElwee brings his teenaged son Adrian with him to a hospital, in the capacity of a sound recordist, to interview a terminal cancer victim. The tobacco farmers that he encounters lead family businesses. One insists that, despite her mother's death from cancer, her crop has nothing to do with anyone dying. Like the Burt Reynolds fans that McElwee encountered in *Sherman's March*, who were so devoted to Reynolds's stud-hipster fantasy, these farmers appear to be coping with their complicity in tobacco addiction through self-denial.

Toward the end of the film, McElwee visits his great-grandfather's grave with his cousins and finds the tombstone crooked, perhaps knocked by a lawnmower. McElwee subsequently finds himself at a tobacco-funded North Carolina beauty pageant, where vehicles driving down a town street include lawnmowers: "some sort of lawnmower precision drilling team ... I wonder if these guys happen to practice in a cemetery." Practice in a cemetery seems an appropriate term for McElwee's own filmmaking practice, where chronology is annihilated and the ghosts of history — be they the personified ghosts of John Harvey McElwee and William Sherman, the architectural ghosts of once-ravaged Civil War-era landscape, or the analogous ghost of declining regional ideology — mingle with the present. McElwee documents the everyday activities of his family and his encounters with friends, lovers and other subjects, and though these encounters are rarely morbid or ominous, McElwee's vision is marked by past and future death.

Self, Scale and Personal Filmmaking

In Ross McElwee's films, the self is a site of investigation to uncover greater truths of history. There is an inescapable falseness to the epic film. The historical-religious epic was shaped as a genre through the work of Cecil B. DeMille, later to become a vehicle for movie stars to transform the visages of the great figures of history (Elizabeth Taylor as Cleopatra). Nowhere is cinema's investment in the unreal more on display than in its bent fantasy representation of historical sources. That genre's origins are in, among other works, two contentious films about the South and the Civil War: D. W. Griffith's *Birth of a Nation* (1915) and David O. Selznick's *Gone with the Wind* (1939). McElwee's work employs his family, friends, lovers and the chance encounters that he has in the process of making his films in order to interpret the relationship between the commonplace and the epic, the everyday and the historical, and through that interpretation of this greater scale, come to an understanding of love and death.

Personal filmmaking has its modern origins in the New York underground film *David Holzman's Diary* (1967), a film that takes on the form of the diary of Holzman, a fictitious invention of writer/performer L. M. Kit Carson and director Jim McBride. Within that same climate of independent filmmaking Jonas Mekas and Stan Brakhage, among others, were fashioning intensely personal work. McBride's film was formally conventional and received relatively mainstream attention and esteem. A similar example emerging from the same period is Milton Moses Ginsberg's *Coming Apart* (1969), in which a fictitious psychiatrist (Rip Torn) surreptitiously records his sessions and dalliances with women. A more direct influence on McElwee is his mentor Ed Pincus, best known for his *Diaries: 1971–1976* (1981), who preceded his own personal filmmaking with documentaries on the civil rights movement of the 1960s (*Black Natchez* and *Panola*). These filmmakers cannot be unified into one coherent aesthetic or narrative trajectory; however, they collectively represent an emerging personal filmmaking that came after the increased accessibility of filmmaking equipment in the 1950s and 60s. Such works share the origins of the home movie. Their unconscious descendant is the YouTube webcam soapbox. McElwee's work is grounded in reflection, and at times he turns his camera into his confessor. While *Sherman's March* is a foundational work in the point-of-view documentary tradition, that tradition has much in common with investigative journalism and often little in common with autobiographical impulse. Among those who would follow him is Michael Moore, who adopted McElwee's structure but substituted cynicism for wit and polemic for rumination.

There is also the auto-ethnographic dimension to McElwee's work, which is distinct from personal filmmaking. Kidlat Tahimik, a Filipino auto-ethnographic filmmaker, directed *Perfumed Nightmare* (1977), a semi-autobiographical hybrid film that bears uncanny thematic similarities to *Sherman's March*. In it, Tahimik describes daily life in the Philippines employing the analogy of a bridge that he tells us his grandfather built, which has been torn down, replaced, and altered by colonial powers so that it has become a Frankenstein palimpsest of a bridge. Tahimik's subject is post-colonial Filipino culture and he instigates a culture clash by traveling to Paris, where he finds employment with a fictitious bubble-gum machine magnate. Tahimik's journey to the West is itself a perverse homecoming owing to the habitation of the Western values in Filipino culture, shown in the film's opening scenes of Easter parades, of signs and rituals absorbed from its Spanish and American colonists. *Sherman's March* inverts this journey, traveling from the victorious land through the defeated. The South that McElwee travels has retained the characteristics of a colony after the departure of its empire-master, its economy crushed by the success of the North, the eyes of its citizens filled with the ghosts of their former glory as evident in the crippling anxiety of the isolationists he encounters. Like McElwee, Tahimik positions his ostensibly autobiographic fiction in the shadow of epic historical drama. *Perfumed Nightmare* is about a personal struggle that stands in for a greater struggle, between the Philippines and its former occupants, between the present identity of a colonized region after it has been granted autonomy and its role in a global future.

One of McElwee's lovers reminds him that there is a great difference between William Sherman's failed real estate business and McElwee's own failed love affairs. He attempts an analogy between their journeys, his and Sherman's, because the parallels that he identifies link Sherman's love of the South with McElwee's romantic love. This is where self and scale distort in the personal-political spectrum of autobiographic filmmaking. McElwee cannot explicate the events of his life from the events that shaped his homeland. Analogies between the small scale of everyday experience and the epic scale of history are not tenuously arrived at nor invented without evidence of their truth. The experiential, in McElwee's terms the "corpse of the present" (Rhu 10), speaks from the epic scale of the past to that of the future.

The Compson family of William Faulkner's *The Sound and the Fury*, doomed by history, struggle with the dissolution of their family and its respectability. Ross McElwee's family portraits demonstrate a gentle severing of tradition most clearly on display in the comic apprehension and displeasure that his family expresses at his decisions. This is compromise of tradition in *Sherman's March*, which ends with McElwee embracing the prospect of love in the North. There is also a continuity of the everyday in McElwee's films where, whether he is intimidated by the prospects of nuclear annihilation (*Sherman's March*) or a culture that revels in tragedy (*Six O'Clock News*), his relationships with his family and friends continue, his self-documentation continues, and that Southern rhythm that Cheshire identifies in McElwee's patience and his embrace of coincidence continues to inhabit his work.

Matthias Muller writes of the diary film as a public expression of something that is usually considered private, "under lock and key" (167). The same might be said of any autobiographical filmmaking. At the time of my writing this, McElwee has been keeping his celluloid diary — a cycle, Cheshire calls it — for three decades. This cycle ties the ruins of industry and past social order that persist in the consciousness and self-representation of the South, to events as intimate as childbirth and the death of family. It absorbs a great many characteristics of Southern literature, and acts as an intensely personal investigation of universal truths, of the role played by familial and regional forces in shaping McElwee's life and all lives.

Works Cited

Avedon, Richard. "Statements." *Avedon*. Exhibition Catalog. Minneapolis: Minneapolis Institute of Art, 1970.
Backyard. Dir. Ross McElwee. 1984. First Run Features, 2006. DVD.
Bright Leaves. Dir. Ross McElwee. Homemade Movies, 2003. First Run Features, 2006. DVD.
Carr, Jay. "A Tarheel Woody Allen Leads 'Sherman's March.'" *The Boston Globe* 15 Nov. 1985: B1.
Cheshire, Godfrey. "Ross McElwee." *Exile Cinema: Filmmakers at Work Beyond Hollywood*. Ed. Michael Atkinson. Albany: SUNY Press, 2008. 111–115.
Goad, Jim. *The Redneck Manifesto*. New York: Simon & Schuster, 1997.
"An Interview with Ross McElwee." *Kitty Snacks Literary Journal* 1.2 (Spring 2009): 17–19.
Lucia, Cynthia. "When the Personal Becomes Political: An Interview with Ross *McElwee*." *Cineaste* 20.2 (1993): 32–37.
Muller, Mattias. "Films of Life and Death: Remarks on the Diary Film." *Landscape with Shipwreck: First Person Cinema and the Films of Philip Hoffman*. Ed. Karyn Sandlos. Toronto: Insomniac, 2001. 167–171.
Perfumed Nightmare. Dir. Kidlat Tahimik. 1977. Flower Films, 2006. DVD.
Rhu, Lawrence. "Home Movies and Personal Documentaries: An Interview with Ross McElwee." *Cineaste* 29.3 (2004): 6–12.
Sherman's March. Dir. Ross McElwee. 1986. First Run Features, 2006. DVD.
Stevenson, Diane. "Coincidence in Ross McElwee's Documentaries." *Three Documentary Filmmakers: Errol Morris, Ross McElwee, Jean Rouch*. Ed. William Rothman. Albany: SUNY Press, 2009. 63–71.

X.

The *Junebug* Dilemma

BRYAN GIEMZA

Junebug (2005) is a film of multiple dilemmas — of low-boil class resentments, of unbridgeable generation gaps, of the occasional sheer maddening stupidity of love. But the most difficult dilemma that the film posits is an identity crisis rooted in the same obstinate sort of paralysis that James Joyce diagnosed in his *Dubliners*. Whether this is a problem that attaches to a so-called post–Southern worldview, or is simply a more perennial concern endemic to human affairs, is hard to say. Regardless, this sort of malaise is concomitant with a period of rapid cultural transition. But the reason one may write about *Junebug* in terms of not just "a" dilemma but "*the*" dilemma is that this Joycean paralysis stands out as the most central problem confronting Southerners today. It has become manifest in all sorts of Southern artistic production; it hangs over Southern literature, and it is brilliantly understood in *Junebug*. And again, in keeping with Joyce, the refracted parental relationships that Joyce represents through the symbol of the *gnomon* appear once more in *Junebug*. Along with the *gnomon* and paralysis, the third key to unlocking the world of *Dubliners*, announced in the first story of the cycle, is simony, "the sin of dealing for personal gain in things spiritual" (Joyce and Jackson 10). It proves equally relevant to the paralysis of *Junebug*, as the film investigates the commodification of Southern culture and the often damaging substitutions of contemporary relationships. These substitutions are demonstrated in *Junebug* by characters who live vicariously through loved ones. Some characters love things and use people (rather than vice versa), some conflate sex with intimacy, and some trade on family and identity for success. The film also raises multiple questions of value and authenticity that bear on the spiritual lives of its characters. Curiously, the reactions of audiences and critics have also turned on issues of authenticity — is this *really* the South? Is it patronizing in its stance? Is it sincere? These questions are very similar to those raised by Joyce's probing exploration of his native soil in his time.

Indeed, like Joyce's *Dubliners*, *Junebug* is a film dedicated to what is unrealized in ordinary relationships and what happens when paralysis impedes aspirations. When newlyweds Madeleine and George Johnsten visit George's family in North Carolina to announce their elopement, one might expect it to be a joyous occasion. Instead, tensions thicken the air in a house that soon seems claustrophobic: George's generally disapproving mother is not eager to embrace Madeleine; George's brother Johnny seethes with unspoken resentments; and, until the end, characters are incapable of either receiving or extending gestures of genuine love. Many significant events are held in abeyance: the child that Ashley Johnsten expects to "fix" her marriage, the tantalizing deal that Madeleine hopes to clinch with outsider artist David Wark. Characters refuse to speak about what is most important: Madeleine discovers how little she knows of her Southern husband; Johnny is incapable of expressing affection to his bride or communicating to his brother, and in the middle of it all, their elders move about like paradoxically familiar strangers. All are left to curdle in the heat of a North Carolina summer.

Scriptwriter Angus MacLachlan might have arrived at his sense of paralysis in ways not so different from James Joyce, for his screenplay speaks to a strong sense of duty inherited from the generations of Southerners whose family- and community-oriented worldview were transmitted across the twists and turns of a difficult history. This is, at times, a mixed blessing, and it is visibly out-of-step with modernity. The state of things is roughly comparable to Joyce's Dublin. There is, on the one hand, a sensibility of grievance in Irish and Southern subordination to British and American hegemony, respectively, along with the sense of enclosure bred by community expectation, with its implicitly and sometimes oppressively pious restraints. And on the other hand, there is the chance to live life more deeply through those connections. There are the enticements of a new world unfolding and the comforts of an old, with a conservative culture that resists the former and is too often nostalgic about the latter. These concerns are hardly new — scholars of Southern culture have argued about them for generations now, with many a backward glance. Yet it seems that the dilemma is becoming more acute in ways that *Junebug* so inventively captures. Ask a Southerner to freely associate with the word "Junebug," and you are likely to get a phrase beginning "crazy as," or perhaps childhood memories of tying the beetles to strings. The film pursues both notions — the tethering and the unstrung. It is the latter, the tethering, the going around in circles, and in Faulknerian terms, "the old fierce *pull of blood,*" that drives Junebug *to offer yet another take on what is stultifying and redeeming about Southern life.*

The film is directed by Winston-Salem, North Carolina, native Phil Morrison, who, explains *New York* magazine, "moved to New York at 17 to attend NYU and got sucked into the indie-rock scene, shooting videos for Yo La

Tengo and Sonic Youth" (Hill). Having moved to Manhattan, Morrison was well poised to have an expatriate perspective on his native region. In a *New York Times* interview he explained, "It's almost like being ashamed of being ashamed.... When you're in New York, you want to make it absolutely clear where you come from, and you're ready to explain that it's a lot more complicated. And then, when you go home, you really do have the feeling that to some degree, by having left, it is some betrayal" (Halbfinger). The piece describes Morrison as "the sort of introspective Southerner who feels a constant tug of war between the values of his childhood home and those of his current one and an impatience for stereotyping in either direction."[1] As a reviewer for the English *Observer* astutely noted, "This is a truthful film about difficult relationships that brings to mind a famous statement by North Carolina's most celebrated novelist, Thomas Wolfe: 'You can't go home again'" (French). For James Joyce this truism became the truth of his life's work, yet it might also be said that many Southerners today can't go home again, either — to the nostalgic agrarian past that never was, or to the interchangeable no-places of contemporary American life.

Southerners, black and white, are more than mildly self-conscious about where they now stand. There are still the old expectations of community, but there is a sense that we should be a little more urbane, a little more fashion-conscious, a little more go-aheadative. The film follows a pair of newlyweds, a mixed marriage, in fact — Yankee and southern — descending into this uneasy peace. And Southerners soon see how tenuous their compromises between traditions of Southern community and new urbanity are. How fully do we give ourselves over to the old time religion, the life of the spirit, the shared joy and grief of community? Even in the industrial South, do we not long for the all-in-it-together spirit that pervades so unlikely a place as Replacements, Ltd., where troubled Johnny Johnsten works? This is a deft touch, because the film toys with the notion of the acceptability of "replacements" in human love, in the exchanges between the Johnsten brothers and their wives. The broken knickknack at the film's start is replaced with a handcrafted one at its end in a startling comment about the nature of old love and new. The piece has been meticulously crafted by Eugene Johnsten, the quiet observer who wants to mend fences. Does the bird augur a new day for the Johnstens? It raises many other questions besides. Does our culture abet us in settling for substitute love? What will replace the old order? Is simplicity more to be desired than the endless seductions of "going Gatsby" and forging a new American identity? The South has always held out a unique set of answers to these questions; even the most rootless Southerners might feel their urgency.

Another point of anxiety comes from the commodification of Southern culture. Phil Morrison explains the opening "hollering" sequence this way:

> The people in the opening shots are hollering. This was once a practical form of communication in the North Carolina hills. I think it's an appropriate start for this movie in two ways. First, "Junebug" is about people communicating across great divides. Second, I'm interested in the moral challenges posed by the relationship between makers and connoisseurs. Hollering is still practiced because it has been recognized as an art form and incorporated into a "folk tradition." It has been aestheticized by its appreciators, who have become its patrons and, often, its practitioners. "Junebug" is meant to explore the difficulty created by relationships based on patronage, however well meaning ["Epoch" 4].

The notion is very skillfully realized in the way that the film's Madeleine quite shamelessly courts a visionary artist for export to New York. It turns out that he can be bought only by Christian testimony — and a fruit basket. In a *New York Times* interview, Morrison observed, "We Southerners are complicit in defining our region by what is peculiar about it." The interview cites the example of those who have "exalted barbecue or Elvis for effect," with Morrison opining, "It quickly becomes kitsch.... It's broadcasting what is idiosyncratic, as opposed to just being good" (Halbfinger).

In an expanded sense, what is at stake here is not simply phony materialism, in the bygone phrase, or the fetishizing of Southern culture, but simony as Joyce understood the term. As John Wyse Jackson and Bernard McGinley explain, Joyce's work explores simony in its many different guises, beginning with prostitution as a form of simony in *Stephen Hero* (the temple of the Holy Ghost desecrated for money). Selling out, in the spiritual sense, might take many avenues:

> exchanging love for money or status, betraying or buying friendship, exploiting of the poor, lonely or miserable, reneging on political principles, abuse of high office, nepotism, and many forms of pandering and hypocrisy are all covered by the term. For Joyce, it is no longer merely a personal sin; it is also a crime against society and against life. This expanded simony is the root cause of much that will follow in [*Dubliners*], and the reader, like the boy [in "Sisters"], will "look upon its deadly work" [Joyce and Jackson 11].

It is interesting that the deadly work of the film's failed birth occurs just after Madeleine has indulged in simony. Following this broader definition of simony, Madeleine seems to have lost her way in exploiting a friendship for the gain of her studio, and in pursuing her work at a time when she might have been sharing in her family's joy (and sorrows). George has his own sins to answer for, as his closing repudiation of his home place is transparently a selling-out. Even an accent can become a kind of fetish. In one interview Morrison explained of George, "He's moved away, and his Southernness is currency. It's something he can pull out to make himself special when he wants" (Halbfinger). In another interview, he acknowledged that "when he conceived George, the Southerner who has the ability to be a New Yorker and then come south and turn on the Dixie charm, [he] had a certain former president in mind. Like Bill Clinton ... George 'has this ability to compartmentalize'" (Thomson). Simony's justifications come from "compartmentalizing," and these ways of walling off others lead to paralysis not just of the individual but of society.

True to form, nothing is too easy in this film: faith is tested, and ethical obligations are weighed not against the self but against family and community. Ashley Johnsten comes closest to having faith like a child, yet her unshakable faith falters with her miscarriage. The film closes with George Johnsten declaring that he is glad to be leaving the South again, but with clear "I-don't-hate-it-I-don't" undertones.[2] The same visionary artist who depicts gory scenes of (in his words) "nigger-slaves" being dispatched will in the same breath add, "bless their hearts." Later, when painting a scene of slaves gleefully torturing their tormentors, he explains of their white faces, "I put my own in there — or somebody I like." Apparently, George Johnsten is one of them; as Wark will gleefully announce to Madeleine later, the face of her "hubby" graces a black body. George is naturally a part of the community, but what will Madeleine do with that knowledge? Wark earlier says that he likes Madeleine's legs — pointedly not her face — but it is George that he likes well enough to place in the painting. Madeleine likes the artist's work, but can she really like him, with his anti–Semitic leanings? How much of her friendship is her own projection, or an effort to exercise some sincerity from one she hopes will bring her profit? She claims to have always felt a connection to the South, but is she ready to embrace the complexities rendered visible in Wark's apocalyptic art, in which her husband is now complicit?

In my view, the inscrutability of Southerners, and indeed, their two-facedness, so often remarked by outsiders, receives the most intelligent treatment that has yet been visited on the screen in *Junebug*. This, according to Morrison, was his express intent; as a *New York Times* profile explains,

> [he] was not content to merely dash or discard Southern stereotypes. He calls that a "fool's errand" and ridicules the clichés that await those who try: "Salt of the earth. Simple people have greater wisdom. Blah, blah, blah."
>
> Instead, his film, which was written by an old friend from Winston-Salem, Angus MacLachlan, quietly skewers not only Southern caricatures, but also the Northerners who condescend to them, and the Southerners who allow and even encourage them to do so [Halbfinger].

In the audio commentary of the DVD, lead actress Embeth Davidtz (Madeleine) describes the film as offering "Such a loving portrayal of the simplicity of these people, and the complexity of them, too." At one point in the film, Eugene Johnsten explains of his wife, "That's just her way. She's not that way inside. She hides herself. Like most." In this Southern tableau, every character is more hidden than apparent.

Parts of the characters are pointedly missing in a way that evokes the *gnomon* of Joyce's *Dubliners*. Jackson and McGinley give the definition from geometry — "a regular four-sided figure with a smaller piece of the same shape missing from one corner" — and emphasize that the term connotes incompleteness. Even the pastor of the Johnstens' Methodist church acknowledges that he is missing something, admitting that it has been a long time since he was drunk on joy. Characters from *Dubliners* frequently do damage by attempting to replicate themselves in others, a recognizable dilemma among the incomplete searchers of *Junebug*. "As the simoniacs have lost their 'wholeness' through their simony," explain McGinley and Jackson, "so too the paralytics are incomplete by virtue of their paralysis" (Joyce and Jackson 10). In the essential narratives of both the film and Joyce's story cycle, family denotes the fact of brokenness and incompletion. Every marriage in the film serves to remind how marriage fails to bring individual completion. Without the viewer perhaps realizing it, the film insistently points to absences: the missing bird, the missing wedding, the missing brother (George), the missing husband (Johnny), the missing father, and the ultimate gnomon, the miscarriage (i.e., the missing child).

Certainly a quality of the gnomon is that the invisible part is rarely noticed. Joyce famously declared, in attempting to write a chapter of the "moral history" of his country, that he offered a portrait written "for the most part in a style of scrupulous meanness" (Joyce xlii). Likewise, *Junebug*'s portraiture consistently points to the missing parts. William Wordsworth loved to speak of the "invisible world" but rarely glimpsed by mortals. He explained in "Latitudinarianism" that for the artist/visionary,

> Come secrets, whispered nightly to his ear;
> And the pure spirit of celestial light
> Shines through his soul — "that he may see and tell
> Of things invisible to mortal sight."

David Wark's mysterious muse visits him in dreams; he calls this being "the Glow-ray," a phrase reminiscent of Wordsworth's "celestial light." Wark explains that his purpose in life is "to make the invisible visible," so it is only fitting that he should be the one to make Madeleine see the gnomon, and thus to fully realize what she has been missing.

For his part, Morrison believes that audiences might appreciate moments of incompletion in a film, places and moments where character and motivation are not fully explained. He elucidated the paradoxes of family thus:

> It's possible for people just to live their life and be the way they are, and pursue legitimately what they wish to pursue. But the nature of their relationship and their proximity to each other — also known as family — make that kind of resentment just a given. John feels small, feels inconsequential in the face of George, period [Thomson].

In human experience, brokenness is the norm, with love and resentment mutually inseparable. Of course, Johnny might well resent George for simply moving away and leading a more glamorous life. Life exacts its damages, and the damages of others must often remain mysterious to us, the film seems to suggest in the unexplained dimensions of its characters. Some critics, like the *Boston Globe*'s Ty Burr, saw this as a fault: "[*Junebug*] is a textbook case of filmmakers who can't make up their minds about their characters; it's a failure of nerve disguised as dramatic ambiguity." Not surprisingly, the film generates a certain amount of anxiety in its viewers, perhaps especially so for those from the South. Southerners are eager to see if they will be misrepresented with the usual Hollywood distortions, or pandered to, or condescended to, and so forth. I've gauged these reactions in many viewers of the film. Most are won over, particularly after realizing that the film does not patronize, and that the film is uplifting in a way that avoids Hollywood feel-good formulas.

Instead, the film draws closer to the paradoxes of triumph in defeat, and life in death, offering, like Joyce who canvassed the same territory so masterfully in *Dubliners*' capstone "The Dead," not mere criticism but a way to see the splendor of it all. If the true character of despair, per Kierkegaard, is that it is unaware of itself as despair, MacLachlan's masterful script anticipates that the true character of exuberance, the opposite of paralysis, is often mistaken for something else. The preacher of *Junebug* asks, "Y'all, when was the last time you were so filled up with the holy spirit that people mocked you, and said, That person must be drunk? That person must be filled with new wine." He alludes to Acts 2, and the fact that some dismissed Pentecostal fire as nothing more than drunken behavior. Pentecostal fire seems to hang over *Junebug* at multiple levels; there are flickers of it in the apocalyptic outsider art of Wark, in the hymn singing scene, even in the self-destructive behaviors of characters who want to scourge an old self in search of a new.

Again, to point to common ground in changing agrarian cultures: in James Joyce's *Dubliners*, alcoholism presents a persistent problem, and too often serves to palliate the misery of paralysis — or else is a confederate to a violent escape from paralysis. Confronted with the Real Presence of Christ in the tabernacle of a Catholic church while drying out on a church retreat, Mr. Kernan will sit well back from the "distant speck of red light," having earlier dismissed the miracle at Knock as "magic lantern business" (171). Like the characters of *Junebug*, he seems nearly impervious to Pentecostal enlightenment. Among *Dubliner*'s gallery of disgraceful alcoholics, though, Freddy Malins is an important exception. As a soothsayer and a true gentleman he elicits more of fear than respect. Of all those who attend the party in "The Dead," he alone seems attuned to the significance of the Feast of the Epiphany; his healing and courageous words, lovingly delivered, bear the power of reju-

An outsider at the church supper: Embeth Davidtz as Madeleine in *Junebug* (2005, Sony Pictures Classics; credit Robert Kirk).

venation and point to the value of all souls. But he is counted a fool and his exuberance is dismissed as that of the drunkard. MacLachlan's *The Dead Eye Boy* treats the unfolding relationship between a single mother and an ex-con who meet at a Narcotics Anonymous session. The following stage directions accompany their initial appearance: *"They enter, falling through the front door, laughing so much they can hardly walk and talk. They may appear drunk, who can tell"* (7).

Audiences might well wonder if Ashley Johnsten is drunk when she makes her first ecstatic appearance in *Junebug*; her spontaneity, good humor, and exuberance make her the Freddy Malins of the film. Indeed, some commentators wondered if her character might stereotype the flighty Southern woman, but in commenting on the film, Embeth Davidtz is quick to defend it against charges that it makes fun of its subjects. In a telling remark, she notes that people not from the South are more likely to misapprehend the film in that way. She adds in her audio commentary, "He doesn't poke fun. He's just showing it." Academics might be inclined to say that this authenticity should not matter, since culture *is* performance. But perhaps this notion is child's play to the age-wise emotional intelligence of Southerners. In an era that favors irony over sincerity, it is easy to dismiss cynically what is most vital.

Yet there *is* a great irony at play here: in some respects, this most authentic of Southern films is remarkably ersatz. The outsider art which so wonderfully complements the film's aesthetic was created not by a recluse *savant* but by a professionally trained artist who tailored it to the script. The mild-mannered George Johnsten is played by Alessandro Nivola, an Italian-American Bostonian; his bride, by Davidtz, a globetrotter whose roots go to South Africa. In the DVD commentary she supplies along with Amy Adams, Davidtz admits that she had never laid eyes on a junebug before the three weeks she spent filming in North Carolina. Indeed, she marvels at the naturalness of real Southern actors as she reviews one scene, to wit: "All authentic — listen to the accents — all from the area. In fact, I get embarrassed seeing myself act next to them, because I feel like these guys were so natural and so good. You know?"

Of course, Davidtz's outsider status might well have helped her play her part, but even the captivating Amy Adams (Ashley)— whose hypnotic portrayal of an off-kilter and uber-intense Southern woman won her an Oscar nomination and a heap of best supporting actress awards — has no direct connections to the region, though she professes to "love" North Carolina. A military brat, she comes from a Mormon family by way of Colorado. Neither did she consult the customary dialect coach for her flawlessly executed part. To her credit, she came to the part with her own insights. She explains in one interview, "I was concerned at times about going too far, being too much of a stereotype ... But Phil [Morrison] wanted that, and then he wanted to shatter it and create an effect that I wasn't necessarily aware of while we were shooting" (Taylor). As to her passion for portraying Southern women, Adams explained, "They have a sense of tradition, and yet they're still modern women underneath it, so it creates a built-in layer and you hardly have to work at it. They're fierce, but you would never know it."

As one who grew up among Mormons, Adams might have some insights in that department. And in playing a Southerner Adams had an ace up her sleeve by acting alongside Celia Weston (Peg Johnsten), a native Southerner who went to college in Winston-Salem. Certainly much of the film's verisimilitude comes from the Southerners who were involved in its creation, including Ben McKenzie (Johnny) and Scott Wilson (Eugene). The film declares itself very much Angus MacLachlan's brain-child, as MacLachlan made certain to get his native Winston-Salem, not to mention nearby Pinnacle, into the film. A church flyer on the refrigerator in one scene advertises Twin Cities Baptist, a local church, faithfully in the twin cities of Winston and Salem. His is the rare case of the writer deeply involved in the direction of the film. Yet in its sophistication, MacLachlan and the filmmakers faced a dilemma of their own. They ran the risk of creating the sort of highbrow, arthouse film that would betray the sensibilities of the very people they wanted so earnestly to portray. MacLachlan explained in an interview, "The delicate line of non-denigrating humor and true feeling and depth that I was aiming for in the script and Phil illuminated in the film may be specifically Southern, may be North Carolinian, I don't really know. But for this story it was very important to be true to the people I live with" ("Epoch" 6).

MacLachlan walks this line with a playwright's dexterity, drawing on his experience with such critically-hailed works as *The Dead Eye Boy*. He can get away with it precisely because he knows the character of the people and place so well. Though *The Dead Eye Boy*'s "Place" is given simply as "North Carolina," and "Time" as "The present," MacLachlan's eye for detail is of a piece with Morrison's vision of the interiors of *Junebug*:

> *A family room in a rental house in the Piedmont of North Carolina. Painted-over plywood paneling, shag carpets of an indeterminate color. A living room area; couch and coffee table bought at This End Up—a kitchen door, two bedroom doors, and the front door. It is busy, messy, beaten up. But clean* [7].

Junebug is brilliant in its details. MacLachlan would say of his piedmont North Carolina, "We [Phil Morrison and I] know those kitchens, those church suppers" ("Epoch" 6). Indeed, they know the specific regional nuances that rarely find their way to film. Morrison explained, "The dialect Frank [Hoyt Taylor] uses for David Wark is very particular to a part of northwest North Carolina between where I grew up and where Frank lives at the Virginia border. Wark's accent is particularly inspired by N.C. storyteller Ray Hicks" ("Epoch" 10).

Reviewer Ann Hornaday noted, "Morrison, who is from North Carolina, filmed *Junebug* on location there, and the movie is suffused with the sense of place, language and culture that might be called the cinematic equivalent of a wine's *terroir*." These small details of place complement the small cinematic details that imbue the film with humor and deeper meaning. For example, as Johnny stews, channel-surfing in the basement of the Johnsten home, he comes across a program on meerkats, his wife's favorite animal. As he goes into a fury, casting around for a cassette so that he might tape it for her, one might easily forget about the very brief commercial clip that precedes the meerkat special. It is a commercial showing bread being baked—literally, a bun being popped in the oven, offering viewers who are paying attention a kind of visual pun. Similarly, one might not notice that the naturalist droning on about meerkats is speaking specifically about "non-reproducing females who contribute to the welfare of the community," a motif that is crucial to understanding the problem of sterility in the film, and Madeleine's torrid but infertile marriage. The pastor's baby cries when introduced to her, and she does not recognize herself when he addresses her as "Mrs. Johnsten."

Of course, Ashley and Johnny's marriage is torrid in a different and yet unfulfilled way, as Ashley demonstrates with a photograph. One of *Junebug*'s dilemmas is its degree of unwonted but real intimacy. Its many silent interiors, that take us into the much lived-in spaces of a middle class home are transporting, sometimes uncomfortably close. *Junebug* is indeed a film of pregnant silences. We grow subconsciously aware of the empty cribs and cradles of its interiors. The characters study one another, wordlessly, in close shots; they make love, at times, soundlessly; they travel in silence in their cars; they sometimes eat without speaking; words of love are met with heartbreaking, heartfelt silence. Neatly trimmed lawns repose in suburban silence; in this quietude, the churning of the katydids at night takes on the same urgency as a Greek chorus. If Walker Percy could have brought his vision of paralysis and Southern quietude to the screen — and he did see it with cinematic relish, as *The Moviegoer* suggests — this would be it.

I do not mean "silence" in quite the sense that we have critically applied it to unheard voices, though this is undoubtedly laudable work. Silence in Southern literature is always contentious and two-faced, tied at once to submission and to privilege. In white Southern culture silence can be virtuous; so virtuous, in fact, that what is rotten is described as "loud" (as in, "That potato salad has gotten a little loud"). Black writers often write in a different register. But I am thinking here in simpler, more archetypal terms, of silence as death, as the movement toward entropy, since "we are such stuff as dreams are made on, and our little life is rounded with a sleep." Such is the suffocating silence of Edgar Allan Poe's entombed South, a South so inward-looking that it threatens to collapse in upon itself. For all our human puniness, its refutation is joyful noise and exuberance; in its way, *Junebug* brims with these things. Not by accident, it begins by sounding an immortal yawp with a Southern accent, in a sequence of clips from the great Spivey's Corner Hollering Contest.

The silences of *Junebug* are the silences of the snow falling in Joyce's "The Dead"; we literally hear the same classical airs accompanying them. Yet life will not be denied, even when, as in *Dubliners*, snow is general over Ireland, or when the Johnstens lay themselves down in the paralyzed quiet of the Carolina hills. This is the great affirming hint at the end of *Dubliners*, when Gabriel, lying down "cautiously" beside his wife like one freshly shriven for burial, thinks, "Better pass boldly into that other world, in the full glory of some passion, than fade and wither dismally with age" (224). It is the shout of ear-piercing joy that Ashley Johnsten sends dancing down the telephone wire when, after her miscarriage, her husband, trembling, says, "Let's try again." When Ashley greets her brother-in-law, in a beautifully improvised line, she says, "You're here you're here you're here — *right where we live.*" She, at least, is certain that she is living.

A paralytic culture is an abortive culture: abortive in its inability to love fully, and much inclined to fear. Fear obtrudes in every one of *Junebug*'s marriages, and love is shown to be defectible in equal degree. The passion of Madeleine and George, married in a whirlwind just weeks after meeting, is transparently a groping in the dark, notwithstanding David's pastor's prayers for their "spirit-filled union." Ashley speaks the truth, although she does so out of fear, when she says, early in the film, "Children are the most important thing—they're so important." One wonders whether Madeleine and George feel the same way.

But perfect love casteth out fear, or so the notion goes. The way out from paralysis—and it is paralysis more than the he-ing and she-ing that keeps the family awake of nights in *Junebug*—could again be tied to Joyce's *Dubliners*. If the dilemma here is much the same, so is the solution, which goes to faith. It is Eucharistic in nature, the simultaneous acceptance of death-in-life and life-in-death. In the worldview of David Wark, there are no barriers between the living and the dead. Madeleine says of him, "He gets confused— his own personal history and that of the world." No wonder Wark can see into Madeleine's soul "as clear as well water." He peers into a world that most of us, like Gabriel in *Dubliners*, only rarely glimpse:

> His soul had approached that region where dwell the vast hosts of the dead. He was conscious of, but could not apprehend, their wayward and flickering existence. His own identity was fading out into a grey impalpable world: the solid world itself which these dead had one time reared and lived in was dissolving and dwindling [225].

Paralysis and death, again, but the artist makes us see it clear: "Maybe the ultimate verity that *Junebug* clings to is that darkness and light are inseparable," Morrison declared of his film ("Epoch" 4). MacLachlan makes a deliberate choice in "Softly and Tenderly" as the central hymn of the story. Beneath the silences of the film, there is a still quieter call to "Come home, come home; / Ye who are weary come home," even as "Shadows are gathering, deathbeds are coming, / Coming for you and for me." The scene where Madeleine realizes a new side to her husband as he sings is an affecting scene— so much so that many of the film crew wept, along with the auditors, as it was filmed. In her commentary on the scene, Amy Adams says, "Every time I watch it I start crying. I don't know—maybe I'm lacking something in my life." A gnomon? During the commentary Embeth Davidtz expresses uncertainty about MacLachlan's Christianity, asking, "Is he a churchgoing chap?" At that moment one realizes that Los Angeles may as well be on the other side of the moon. Certainly it is fascinating that these actors genuinely appreciated something of MacLachlan's spiritual South. According to Morrison, Amy Adams absorbed some of it on-site: "While we were in Winston-Salem, we went to Green St. Methodist Church. One Sunday the minister said 'God loves you just the way you are, but too much to let you stay that way.' There

Curiously child-like: Amy Adams as Ashley Johnsten in *Junebug* (2005, Sony Pictures Classics; credit Robert Kirk).

was no way we were going to let the shoot end without Ashley repeating that" ("Epoch" 9).

My reading of the film, then, suggests that *Junebug* is profoundly Christian in its worldview, and that it offers a balm for Southern angst. I do not wish to suggest that the film proselytizes — it does not, as David Wark's anti–Semitism and Madeleine's courting of him complicate any facile reading of the film as a conversion narrative — and neither am I trying to proselytize by pointing to its Christian core. Rather, I want to point out how the film replaces the anxieties of the moment with first things, offering a solution to the dilemma of enclosure in one's own heart. From pregnant silences it goes to the hope of pregnancy. In her irrepressible love, Ashley Johnsten shows exactly what it means to have faith like a child.

Yet the way out of the *Junebug* dilemma is not pat or, as stated earlier, easy. The movement toward change for most of the characters is inchoate and tenuous. The phone call is a start, but will Johnny grow up or reconcile with his brother? Can George ever be reconciled to his family? Eugene gives the bird he has carved to Peg, but can there be healing there? Madeleine helps make sandwiches, and reaches out to George in bed and in the car; will he understand what she wants?[3]

In sum, *Junebug* simply cannot be fully appreciated, or apprehended, without reflection on how its Christian contexts speak to love, incompletion, and paralysis. Its aesthetic achievement is grounded in its verisimilitude and thoughtfully diagnostic (not to say Joycean) themes. It is a profound meditation on paralysis, and the jockeying of fear and love that underpins our silences. It remains brilliant in its understanding of the culture, and beautifully insightful in its dilemmas.

Notes

1. Ty Burr felt that this was precisely the film's weakness: "What 'Junebug' reflects isn't ambivalence about the American South so much as young filmmaker's torn between loving and hating their roots (which, not coincidentally, plays very well to audiences who want to condescend to the small towns they've left behind while still feeling guilty about leaving them)." So at least one critic felt that Morrison did not avoid the trap of patronizing his subjects.

2. The much-quoted phrase is from Quentin Compson at the close of William Faulkner's *Absalom, Absalom!*

3. I am indebted to Joseph Flora for many good discussions that contributed insights on incompletion and paralysis in the film.

Works Cited

Burr, Ty. "A Confused Trip South in 'Junebug.'" *The Boston Globe*. The Boston Globe, 12 Aug. 2005. Web. 27 July 2010.
"Epoch Films Presents *Junebug*." Presskit, 2005. Web. 13 Nov. 2009. <http://www.sonyclassics.com/junebug/_content/downloads/junebug_presskit.pdf>.
French, Phillip. "Junebug." *The Observer*. The Observer, 16 Apr. 2006. Web. 27 July 2010.
Halbfinger, David M. "Bridging North-South Divide." *New York Times*. New York Times, 5 Aug. 2005. Web. 27 July 2010.
Hill, Logan. "Debut Director: Phil Morrison." *New York Magazine*. New York Magazine, 24 July 2005. Web. 27 July 2010.
Hornaday, Ann. "'Junebug': Welcome to the Rural World." *Washington Post*. Washington Post, 26 Aug. 2005. Web. 27 July 2010.
Joyce, James. *Dubliners*. New York: Penguin. 1993.
_____, John Wyse Jackson, and Bernard McGinley. *James Joyce's* Dubliners*: An Illustrated Edition with Annotations*. New York: St. Martin's, 1993.
Junebug. Dir. Phil Morrison. Perf. Amy Adams, Embeth Davidtz, Ben McKenzie, Alessandro Nivola, Frank Hoyt Taylor, Celia Weston, and Scott Wilson. Sony Pictures, 2005. DVD.
MacLachlan, Angus. *The Dead Eye Boy*. New York: Dramatists Play Service, 2002.
Taylor, Ella. "Judging Amy." *LA Weekly*. LA Weekly, 4 Aug. 2005. Web. 27 July 2010.
Thomson, Desson. "'Junebug,' Squashing Southern Stereotypes." *The Washington Post*. The Washington Post, 26 Aug. 2005. Web. 27 July 2010.

XI.

Imagined Realities: Appalachia, Arabia, and Orientalism in *Songcatcher* and *The Sheik*

THOMAS R. BRITT and USAME TUNAGUR

Muslims and Appalachians — at first glance this seems an unlikely pairing. We have traditionally perceived these peoples as a world apart from one another, with no apparent connections. However, these seemingly disparate groups share a history of negative representation. Both have been demonized through common stereotypes, which provide an intersection for critical analysis of the "Moon-Shining, Wife-Beating Hillbilly" and the "Seventy-Two Virgins-Seeking Terrorist." Fiction and non-fiction accounts about these groups create, situate, and exploit them as the cultural other. This takes place through identifiable conventions of character and setting as well as narratives that suggest education or extermination as the only means of handling these populations.

In this paper, we will explore *Songcatcher* (2001) as an Orientalist text akin to *The Sheik* (1921). These films embody the insidious approach that narrative films sometimes use to portray Appalachians and Muslims as the cultural other. *Songcatcher* exhibits an internal otherness that characterizes Appalachians as uncivilized, primitive savages. Its protagonist recognizes the mountain folks' songs as commodities to be mainstreamed for the educated class, but she rejects their passion when it threatens to consume her. Her academic perspective is the context through which the audience is supposed to determine which characters are tamable and upgradeable. Similarly, *Sheik* presents an external otherness and views Muslims through the myopic lens of Orientalism. Both films complicate their already problematic representations of region and race with asides about religious practices, violence and the "proper" place of women.

Our goal in analyzing *Songcatcher* as a continuation of *Sheik*'s legacy is to examine the process through which these narratives shape cultural realities and understandings. By choosing films at opposite ends of the film history spectrum, we hope to highlight the persistence of this pattern and its effect on sociopolitical discourse. The first decade of the twenty first century has seen an increase in the politicization of broader Middle Eastern and southern American identities, yet these populations rarely have a chance to control the content. Despite technological advances in media production, many films and television programs stick to convenient, stereotypical narratives about both groups. Only occasionally does an individual from these cultures have the opportunity to correct the record for mainstream audiences. As a result, conventions of representation and cultural misconceptions continue to thrive in narrative films when the represented cultures are not speaking for themselves.

Appalachians, although coming to North America as European colonists, were soon appointed as the uncivilized mountain people, pushed to the background, and even used as a justification for slavery, with the argument that the "white trash" mountainfolk were so lazy and incapable of labor, that the slaveholders were obliged to use black slaves as a workforce. Since then, the media image of the uncivilized mountainfolk emerged with two inseparable attachments: moonshine and the family feud. In his informative book, *Hillbilly: A Cultural History of an American Icon*, Anthony Harkins reprints a portion of an editorial from the *Baltimore Sun* of 1912, which was written in reaction to a deadly shootout in Hillsville, Virginia:

> There are but two remedies for such a situation as this, and they are education and extermination. With many of the individuals, the latter is the only remedy. Men and races alike, when they defy civilization must die. The mountaineers of Virginia and Kentucky and North Carolina, like the red Indians and the South African Boers, must learn this lesson [35].

Ironically, a secondary image of the Appalachian was being popularized at the same time. This image is of the one who stands up for true rugged individualistic American attitudes. The Appalachians were presented as a possible alternative for the iron-caged industrialized people who were tired and wornout by modernity, urbanization, and strict bureaucracy. In 1896, Pencraft, the lead character in Francis Lynde's travelogue *Moonshiner of Fact*, takes a trip through the mountains in eastern Tennessee. He finally acknowledges (albeit condescendingly), "These people are poor and ignorant and simple and primitive — anything you like along that line ... but they are as hospitable as the Arabs, as honest as they are simple, and as harmless as unspoiled country-folk anywhere" (qtd. in Harkins 40–41). This characterization suggests that Appalachians enable and embody a sort of retreat from civilization. It is against this backdrop of assumed hospitality and simplicity that the comparatively sophisticated lead characters of *Sheik* and *Songcatcher* seek adventure.

Whereas Pencraft learns that not every mountain family is made up of warring moonshiners, the lead character of director Maggie Greenwald's *Songcatcher* embarks on a travelogue of paint-by-numbers Appalachian backwardness. In the film, musicologist Dr. Lily Penleric (Janet McTeer) flees her university in the wake of professional and romantic frustration and escapes to the Appalachian Mountains for the purpose of retreat. A second (soon to be dominant) goal of her trip emerges, which is to collect the songs of the people in this untouched (read: unwashed) environment. A surface reading of the inciting incident and the ensuing journey is that Dr. Penleric needs to forge her own path if she is going to distinguish herself in the academic world. A deeper reading of the entire set of narrative events suggests that in order to assert her identity as a strong modern woman, Dr. Penleric needs to exercise control over an entire group of people. That control involves appropriating their precious, if not sacred, songs, offering reams of unsolicited aid and advice, and taming one of its more feral men — this is how she will drag them into the realm of civilization.

Perhaps the original model for this sort of negative representation is Orientalism. To understand how such exaggerated and savage portraits could be painted of a culture within America's own borders, one could look to the image of certain outsiders that previously captured the imagination of western minds. In the seventeenth century, as the Orientalist project took shape, the overtly negative perception of Islam had already been strongly instilled in the minds of Europeans. Orientalists developed various media around this "imagined East," including paintings, novels, essays, travelogues, and finally films. The image content of this invented Orient was, as the late Edward Said describes it, "a place of romance, exotic beings, haunting memories and landscapes, remarkable experiences" (1).

The Orientalist discourse "establishes a set of polarities in which the Orient is characterized as irrational, exotic, erotic, despotic and heathen, thereby securing the West in contrast as rational, familiar, moral, just and Christian" (Lewis 16), and it is also through this binary spatial construct that Europe, and later the United States, identified and expressed themselves. This sheltered expression enabled the Orientalist artists the freedom to cross boundaries, express repressed sexual desires, reestablish nostalgic masculinities and femininities, and unearth the bottom of the iceberg of the Freudian id, all in the disguise of the Orient. As Montgomery Watt observes,

> The war of light and darkness sounds well but in this post–Freudian world men realize that the darkness ascribed to one's enemies is a projection of the darkness in oneself that is not fully admitted. So in this way the distorted image of Islam is to be regarded as a projection of the shadow side of European Man [83].

This same fantasy projection is what fuels familiar narratives today, especially in film. The concept of an imagined reality does involve some small degree of actuality (perhaps a direct observation, a sensory experience, or a relationship). Yet these small seeds frequently become representative of whole populations when they are turned into concrete images. John Boorman's 1972 adaptation of James Dickey's *Deliverance* is a thrilling wilderness survival film. Yet the legacy of the film within popular memory and imagination is a fear of a specific environment and people. Thus, the common imagined risks associated with enjoying the land of hillbillies include rape and death. Further, the trivialization of the text's horrors, specifically the decontextualized rape scene as a source of pop culture dark humor ("squeal like a pig") ensures that successive audiences remember only the most sensational and damaging images of the South in the movie. Later films such as *Wrong Turn* (2003), *The Descent* (2006), and *Timber Falls* (2007) continue the inbred hillbilly horror trend. The abundance of these films ensures that for many audience members, the imagined environment, born from a fragment of reality, becomes the "real" in toto.

With regard to our comparative example of Muslims and Islam, the highlighting of reality's fringes creates a very similar cycle of "subjective actuality." Orientalist perceptions can be found at the root of assumptions made by contemporary figures such as Pope Benedict XVI—"Show me just what Mohammed brought that was new, and there you will find things only evil and inhuman, such as his command to spread by the sword the faith that he preached" (qtd. in "Aula Magna")—and more recently Swiss lawmaker Ulrich Schluer, who advocated November 2009 legislation banning the construction of minarets, which he describes as "a political symbol against integration; a symbol more of segregation" (Lauter 1). These contemporary expressions of the Orientalist discourse influence spectators' impressions of the whole, despite the fact that in both cases, the content of the statements refer to exceptions rather than rule. Within film history, there is one work (adapted from an Orientalist bestselling novel) that set the tone for years to come in its elevation of western fantasies and fears concerning Arabs. This film is *The Sheik*, which could also be called Orientalism 101. Directed by George Melford, the 1921 blockbuster production carried Rudolph Valentino to super-stardom and also initiated what Jack Shaheen calls Sheik, one of five character types along with Villain, Maiden, Egyptian, and Palestinian that are featured in popular films about the Middle East (19).

The Sheik is a story about Lady Diana (Agnes Ayres), an independent and upper-class French woman, who is abducted in France by Sheik Ahmed Ben Hassan (Rudolph Valentino), an Arab tribal leader. She is then taken to what seems to be the deserts of Arabia. Initially, Diana is imprisoned in Sheik

Agnes Ayres (Lady Diana) and Rudolph Valentino (Sheik Ahmed) star as an independent woman and a handsome kidnapper in *The Sheik* (1921, United Artists Corporation).

Ahmed's tent and prays for her freedom. First, he attempts to rape her. However, he is unsuccessful with an implication of impotence. Diana's prayers come true in another way, and Sheik Ahmed falls in love with her. However, his darker-skinned opponent Sheik Omair (Walter Long) abducts Diana to rape her — and he is definitely not impotent. With his army, Sheik Ahmed attacks Omair's tribe, and saves Diana seconds before she is raped, but Sheik Ahmed is attacked by the darkest-skinned African slave and rendered comatose. He recovers slowly, opens his eyes on his bed and finally declares his love to Diana. She replies positively to this and announces her love. The audience is challenged with a white woman declaring her love to a non-white man, but then they are immediately relieved, as Sheik Ahmed's best friend tells Diana that actually Sheik Ahmed is not an Arab. He is the son of a British man and a Spanish woman. After such an active visual and narrative climax, the disclosure of Sheik Ahmed's European ethnicity ultimately represents the final struggle being resolved. Equipped with this information, both Diana and the audience are able to move beyond that remaining barrier and bask in the fulfillment of desire.

As with shoot-from-the-hip representations of Muslims, the treatment of Appalachians in the media has moved only negligible degrees away from the traditional stereotypical characterization. In this case, the Orientalist attitudes are imported and applied to portions of the United States and its people: "The other of internal orientalism belongs to the state where the othering is produced" (Jansson 267). When the Sago Mine accident captured the attention of America in 2005, the cable networks' freshest faces were sent to West Virginia to report from the front lines. And while their reporting was for the most part reverent with respect to the event itself, their descriptions of the native people were virtual echoes of Pencraft's statement, extolling the simple virtues of a simple, hospitable people. Additionally, arbitrary representations of Southerners in lightweight Hollywood fare are signs of lazy writing and reveal ingrained prejudices. In *Someone Like You* (2001), when the script requires a character to give commentary on cows, the finished film makes the obvious choice and gives him dirty overalls and a Southern accent. Even in an innocuous romantic comedy, Appalachians and Southerners receive no mercy.

The merciless *Songcatcher* (which has much in common with classically Orientalist desert romance novels) is a period piece whose narrative events depend on the dual oppression of women in the city and hillbillies in the mountains. The film perpetuates and invigorates a female character type defined by a liberal worldview and desire to liberate others, and it is also an example of internal Orientalism. It announces itself as a film that intends on exploring the pioneering spirit, but as the film unfolds that spirit quickly morphs into one of appropriation akin to colonialism. The film reinforces the notion that negative portrayals are almost certainly around the bend when the film itself "looks at privilege from the position of privilege and thereby excludes the disenfranchised" (Rocchio 117). To complicate matters, the film (and by extension, its maker) seems to mistake its protagonist as belonging to the sphere of the disenfranchised.

Perhaps the most problematic element of this film and other films that share a similar narrative type is a central contradiction: it is predicated on evolution yet rarely operates in a way that moves its supposed causes forward. And in many cases, the formulaic narrative thrust requires regression, often through the monolithic portrayal of disenfranchised characters that depend on the saving grace of the main character. The elements of the formula are almost always thus:

1. The protagonist enters a foreign environment and discerns certain needs of the native community.
2. The ability to intercede, speak and/or act on behalf of the *other* is regarded as a goal and function of the protagonist.

3. The protagonist's upward mobility occurs at the expense of the group(s) to whom she is offering aid.

4. The audience is not asked to consider the collateral damage left behind once the main character has achieved her goal and/or learned her lesson.

To varying degrees, films like *Norma Rae* (1979) and *Party Girl* (1995) use this formula with crusading female characters in very different environments. In both of these cases, the characters' passions threaten to disrupt the good they hope to do for others. Audience reaction to the films, then, depends on the degree to which viewers accept these stereotypes in the service of their protagonists' goals being met. When the formula works, the audience members become unconscious accomplices to negative representation through alignment with their heroine.

Interestingly, the central figures in these stories are women who hope to move beyond a traditional notion of females as passive and to activate practical changes in exotic environments. We suspect there is a degree of calculated justification at play here. For instance, one might say the worth of the films is found in their progressive gender representation, thus excusing the otherwise negative portrayals of race and culture. Yet even this gender evolution is self-defeated when the protagonists are inevitably overwhelmed by emotion and impulse. Suffice it to say that such films, and particularly the two films in question, suggest that the women cannot "have it both ways." Again, despite the seeming good intentions of the filmmakers, the cumulative meaning or message of the tale denudes the occasional or incidental step forward, and the films reveal themselves to be anything but progressive. Despite the pioneering efforts of these women, they ultimately fulfill only that which their proximity to a new masculine dominator allows. Hence, *The Sheik*'s Diana, who early on asserts her independence and seeks an unfettered experience in the desert, eventually becomes the prototypical swooning desert romance ingénue. Likewise, *Songcatcher*'s Penleric abandons her academic mission after severely disrupting the serene mountain environment, yet she enjoys a happy ending because she leaves with a rugged beau and a moneymaking voice prodigy in tow.

This liberated/liberating character type — which has parallels in the New Woman, suffragette, and flapper types popular in films from, and about, the late nineteenth and early twentieth centuries — is central to both the stories and ideological underpinnings of *Sheik* and *Songcatcher*. Additionally, these films share a number of traits in their representation of violence, sex, and religion. Within their fantasy projection narratives, both films use these as fundamental elements in shaping perceptions of Muslims and Appalachians.

The first two scenes of *Sheik* are Orientalism-in-a-nutshell and introduce

the audience to the implications that follow. The first scene opens with a shot of a minaret from where a muaddhin (caller) is announcing the call to prayer. Then, we are in a desert where a group of generic Muslims are performing the Islamic daily prayer. Not only is it performed incorrectly but also in a way that is disrespectful and insulting to an ordinary Muslim. The following scene is a slave-marriage in the desert where women are presented to Sheik Ahmed. He buys whichever — not whomever — he likes and for which he lusts. These women are sold and bought in the desert, to put it plainly. The combination of these two scenes forms a single-minded conclusion: they are Muslims, they pray, and they treat women like livestock or property. Steven Canton concludes that the editing of these two scenes together suggests, "that religion is to blame for this reduction of women to commodities" (114).

The following scene conveniently introduces Diana as a New Woman, who is clearly not interested in marriage due to its restrictive nature. The film's introduction highlights the extent to which she stands outside of the traditional woman's role at the time, as other, older female characters express shock at Diana's independence. However, what will turn out to be Diana's desert romance begins with her unconsciously fulfilling a fantasy type in the name of "independence." She chooses to disguise herself as a belly dancer in order to enter the realm of the other, and the film uncritically gazes at her covert mission as a mark of her enterprising nature. Ironically, the dominant impression of the scene is that of submission — Diana can gain entry only by fitting in to a harem and casting off her individual identity.

After Diana exchanges gazes with Sheik Ahmed for the first time and disguises herself, she goes into Sheik Ahmed's party in the hotel. Sheik Ahmed is gambling the women he bought in the previous scene. Here, again, the film reemphasizes the correlation between Islam and the commodification of women. Sheik Ahmed's guests are happy to gamble for a white woman. But she instructs the West on how to deal with the Orient: she takes her gun out and saves herself from rape. Ill-treatment of women is accompanied by violence and bloodshed. It is interesting to note that in the scenes featuring the tribe of Sheik Ahmed, they are armed with rifles. In a classic case of saber-rattling, they always carry their rifles and point them upwards, in an extra effort to make them visible for the camera. The second half of the story involves gunfights with the rival Sheik Omair and Sheik Ahmed's final assault on Omair's settlement. Cumulatively, the film shows Muslims' lives consisting of ill treatment of women, warfare, and prayers — or something that looks like it.

Opposite: Janet McTeer stars as Lily Penleric, a dedicated musicologist who falls in love with Tom Bledsoe, a rugged mountain man (Aidan Quinn) in *Songcatcher* (2001, Trimark Pictures).

The ready availability of guns, violence, and misogyny are impossible to miss in *Songcatcher*. Conflict is resolved by drawing one's rifle. When Tom Bledsoe (Aidan Quinn) first appears, he comes into the house wearing a readily identifiable hillbilly outfit, and of course, carrying his gun. Anthony Harkins summarizes the media-constructed hillbilly imagery in seven features: "A surly disposition, bare-feet, long scruffy beard, suspender-clad overalls, shapeless oversized felt hat, moonshine jug or flask, and long-barreled rifle" (39). Most of these tropes are evident in Bledsoe with a few upgrades to make him likeable to contemporary audiences. Honeycutt (Greg Russell Cook), a teenage boy hired by Dr. Penleric to assist with her belongings, breaks the fan she gives to Deladis (Emmy Rossum) as a gift. His violent reaction to the introduction of a high culture accoutrement establishes the movie's pattern of hillbilly psychology, based on pure emotion and violent reflex rather than reason or intellect. When an Appalachian is mad, he/she breaks something, beats someone, or shoots a gun.

As with *Sheik*, womanizing is also prevalent throughout *Songcatcher*. One of the main Appalachian characters, Alice Kincaid (Stephanie Roth Haberle), is a mother to many children. However, her husband, Reese (Michael Harding), is cheating on her with another woman and he is never around. When he fails to show up as Alice gives birth to their child, it is Miss Butler (Pat Carroll), the old lady of the town, and Dr. Penleric the liberal liberator, who deliver the baby. Although Dr. Penleric takes it upon herself to reunite the couple later, this dysfunctional mountain marriage is destined to fail. The womanizing and violence go so hand in hand that at the end of the movie Reese's mistress kills him in front of his family in a makeshift Appalachian church. Even the church does not provide sanctuary for this Appalachian family feud.

These movies portray religion as backward and simple and as a roadblock to civilization. While *The Sheik* presents Christianity as the cure for Islam, *Songcatcher* offers intellectualism and modernity as the cure for Appalachian fundamentalism. In *Sheik*, Christianity is presented almost as an antidote to this problem-ridden tribal society. As Canton argues, "the film means to leave no doubt as to the power of Christianity in saving this young woman and her lover and thus triumphing over its arch adversary, Islam" (115). After Sheik Ahmed's unsuccessful rape attempt, he orders Diana to get dressed for dinner, and she comes out with a large shining cross on her neck. After dinner, Sheik Ahmed tries once again to have her but is interrupted with the news that his horses have gotten loose during the sandstorm. When he leaves to attend to the problem, "Diana, visibly relieved, slumps by the side of the bed with her hands clasped in fervent prayer, her head raised heavenward, the cross around her neck gleaming like a beacon in the infernal darkness" (Canton 115). The cross is elevated above all other elements of the mise-en-scène, virtually becoming a tool of exorcism.

In *Songcatcher*, however, Christianity is no longer the cure but the problem. Not only is the mountain religion portrayed as accompanying low-culture barbarism, but also it is juxtaposed against rationalism, civilization and development. For instance, Reverend Merriweather (Taylor Hayes) knows the most ballads, but does not give even one song to Dr. Penleric because he has found the good old religion and now considers singing as the devil's work. When Honeycutt and his friend discover that the two female school teachers are in a lesbian relationship, they burn down the school in another fit of reactionary violence. The rage continues as Reverend Merriweather verbally attacks and rebukes the teachers during the Sunday service. Interestingly enough, Merriweather's daughter, who is also Reese Kincaid's mistress, kills Reese during the very same service. Absurd as it seems, this scene is the height of the movie's indictment of Appalachian Christianity as the meeting place for aberrant sexuality and violent nihilism. Yet there is a deeper function to these exorcisms and fiery baptisms. They prepare us for final revelations that both movies strategically use to separate the true indigenous hoi polloi from those who are capable of cultural salvation.

Only when the truth about Sheik Ahmed is revealed at the very end of *Sheik*, does the film's true intent become clear. He is the son of a British nobleman and a Spanish mother. This revelation completely recontextualizes the story, attaching a new set of characteristics and values to Sheik Ahmed's actions and attributes. At this point, the film's new argument is that the evil attributes of Sheik Ahmed, which are also shared by Omair, are original, primordial Muslim values. However, his virtues and his readiness for Western values are due to his ancestry. These values are further prefigured by his noticeably lighter complexion. Additionally, the film suggests that no matter how much Sheik Ahmed has devolved from his natural European sensibilities, he remains upgradeable. His otherness is erasable. The fact that he allows a slave girl to marry his associate Yousaef (George Waggner), that he never raped Diana, and that he fought for his love, are all attributable to his Western background. At the end, the real Arab/Muslim is not Ahmed but Omair: Omair abducted Diana, imprisoned her under a big black guardian, attempted to rape her, and was killed and corrected by a Westerner Sheik, Ahmed. Ella Shohat and Robert Stam summarize the revelation of Ahmed's background, "Valentino, as long as the spectator knows him only as an Arab, acts as the id. Revelation of his status as the son of Europeans, however, transforms him into a superego figure who risks his life to rescue the [European] woman from 'real' Arab rapists" (168).

While *Sheik* advocates the power of nature to redeem through one's racial identity, *Songcatcher* emphasizes nurture. After the fire, Dr. Penleric decides to return to civilization without completing her research. However, she takes Tom and Deladis with her. These two are the only Appalachians who are tamable, upgradeable, and civilizable: Tom has already been out of Appalachia as a youngster and Deladis is still young and impressionable. Penleric's initial plan to collect songs scientifically, introduce them to mass culture, and thereby promote Appalachian heritage changes course. Now equipped with Tom's guitar and Deladis's great voice and vast repertoire, Penleric recognizes the commercial potential of these songs. At the film's conclusion, the trio is ostensibly bound for fame and fortune thanks to the appropriation and commodification of the Appalachian people and their land. *Songcatcher* argues that as long as the mountaineer is exposed early enough, science and a modern urban lifestyle will cure his/her backwardness. More broadly, from Deladis to Britney Spears to Jessica Simpson's vapid variation on Daisy Duke, the myth of the exportable (exploitable) Southern girl continues to rank high amongst American fantasies. As an aside, Pierre Morel's 2008 film *Taken* could be considered the pinnacle of our efforts to trace this study's comparative fantasies, as it offers a young impressionable female, with aspirations of singing and independence, who pays for her yearnings by being kidnapped into sex slavery and sold into the harem of a ridiculously cartoonish sheik.

Taken is the latest, most barefaced proof that the reductive nature of the Orientalist context continues to be a problem within narrative film. Additional complications arise when films employ this context to tell the story of crusading women with good intentions, yet whose quest for self-awareness is unaccompanied by cultural awareness. Diana and Penleric are painted as liberated characters, eager to enter what they think are savage environments and liberate others in need of their civilized touch. When both women are "put in their place," even in uncharted territory, there is an implication that independence could (and should) backfire in order to maintain the "natural" balance of the sexes. This runs parallel to the problematic Orientalist dichotomy. Nothing improves, little is learned, and the audience gets a speciously happy ending in place of the progressive breakthrough they might have expected from these liberated, liberating characters.

In *Songcatcher*, Penleric's choice to explore and educate (rather than exterminate) evokes several filmic precedents, among them the work of Robert Flaherty. Early in his career, Flaherty, regarded as a key founder of the documentary tradition, "plunged with all his heart into the role of explorer and prospector" (Barnouw 45). His work as a prospector amidst exotic worlds and people reflected what Flaherty later interpreted as his participation in a kind of cultural destruction. His films therefore "[banish] the intruder from the world he portrayed" (45). Flaherty's own words reveal the perspective from which he hoped to shoot real-life subjects:

> I am not going to make films about what the white man has made of primitive peoples.... What I want to show is the former majesty and character of these people, while it is still possible — before the white man has destroyed not only their character, but the people as well [45].

In *Nanook of the North* (1922), for example, Flaherty succeeded in this mission. When he could have intervened with his rifle or other modern instruments to help his onscreen subjects secure food or temper harsh living conditions, he restrained for the sake of his documentary portrait.

To conclude, the role of intervention in films about "other" populations cannot be ignored, and there are no short cuts that allow a filmmaker to escape its implications. Satire reduces the real-life effect of negative representation, because the form requires exaggeration and is normally using the representation to make a reflexive point. When a one-eyed, inbred hillbilly shows up in the basement during Jon Hurwitz and Hayden Schlossberg's equal-opportunity offender *Harold & Kumar Escape from Guantanamo Bay* (2008), there are twists to the character and setting that seem to attack the convention (Southern stereotypes) rather than the region (the South). Likewise, in *American Dreamz* (2006), Paul Weitz pairs a young would-be terrorist and a blonde midwestern ingénue to poke holes in our fears and fantasies rather than to reinforce them.

Yet a film as po-faced as *Songcatcher*, which in several (backfiring) ways attempts to show off its own authenticity, comes with a greater responsibility of controlling voice. Once director Greenwald decides to speak for the mountain people, it should ultimately be her task to think critically about how she is representing her subject matter rather than using kernels of truth to paint sweeping, lasting misimpressions of Appalachian life. While some say Flaherty's approach was overly romantic — having his subjects reenact already outmoded practices for the sake of preservation — he nonetheless empowered them with the ability to convey their experiences *themselves*, free of too heavy an intervening authorial hand. His preservation of history (despite some fudged facts and timelines) still fulfills the goal of documenting an actuality and informing audiences about the lives of others.

Greenwald uses the story of Penleric to present a naïve, played-out view of pitiful others who will benefit from her sophisticated touch. The director's own intense touch distorts so much of the picture that scenes of apparently lesser intervention are quite refreshing. One scene in the film that succeeds in this regard is when Rose Gentry (Iris DeMent) sings "Pretty Saro" on her porch. The director relaxes her grip, the spectator temporarily loses the gaze of the liberated liberator, and an authentic performer is allowed to express herself in an uninterrupted take of a song that can be traced to early-1900s Appalachia. An appreciation of this actuality does not require the enhancements of imagination, and as a result the scene attains a level of perceptual realness often missing in the film. Although the tendency to exploit cultural others through formulaic Orientalist lenses remains rampant in feature filmmaking, *Songcatcher*'s "Pretty Saro" scene reveals how the simple act of ceding control to the film's subject can lead to transcendent results that go beyond the screen.

Works Cited

"Aula Magna." *The Holy See*. Vatican.va, 3 Oct. 2006. Web. 10 June 2010.
Barnouw, Erik. *Documentary: A History of the Non-Fiction Film*. New York: Oxford University Press, 1993.
Canton, Steven C. "*The Sheik*: Instabilities of Race and Gender in Transatlantic Popular Culture of the Early 1920s." *Noble Dreams Wicked Pleasures: Orientalism in America, 1870–1930*. Ed. Holly Edwards. Princeton: Princeton University Press, 2000. 99–119.
Deliverance. Dir. John Boorman. Perf. Jon Voight, Burt Reynolds, Ned Beatty, Ronny Cox. 1972. Warner Home Video, 2000. DVD.
Harkins, Anthony. *Hillbilly: A Cultural History of an American Icon*. New York: Oxford University Press, 2004.
Jansson, David R. "'A Geography of Racism': Internal Orientalism and the Construction of American National Identity in the Film *Mississippi Burning*." *National Identities* 7.3 (2005): 265–285.
Lauter, Devorah. "Swiss Voters OK Ban on Minarets." *Los Angeles Times*. Los Angeles Times, 30 Nov. 2009. Web. 14 Dec. 2009.
Lewis, Reina. *Gendering Orientalism*. London: Routledge, 1996.
Nanook of the North. Dir. Robert Flaherty. Perf. Allakariallak, Nyla. 1922. Criterion Collection, 1999. DVD.
Rocchio, Vincent F. *Reel Racism: Confronting Hollywood's Construction of Afro-American Culture*. Boulder: Westview, 2000.
Said, Edward. *Orientalism*. New York: Vintage, 1979.
Shaheen, Jack G. *Reel Bad Arabs: How Hollywood Vilifies a People*. New York: Olive Branch, 2001.
The Sheik. Dir. George Melford. Perf. Agnes Ayres, Ruth Miller, Rudolph Valentino, George Waggner. 1921. Image Entertainment, 2002. DVD.
Shohat, Ella, and Robert Stam. *Unthinking Eurocentrism: Multiculturalism and the Media*. London: Routledge, 1994.
Someone Like You. Dir. Tony Goldwyn. Perf. Hugh Jackman, Ashley Judd, Greg Kinnear, Marisa Tomei. 2001. 20th Century–Fox, 2003. DVD.
Songcatcher. Dir. Maggie Greenwald. Perf. Janet McTeer, Aidan Quinn, Emmy Rossum. 2000. Lions Gate, 2001. DVD.
Taken. Dir. Pierre Morel. Perf. Liam Neeson, Maggie Grace. 2008. 20th Century–Fox, 2009. DVD.
Watt, Montgomery W. *The Influence of Islam on Medieval Europe*. Edinburgh: Edinburgh University Press, 1972.

XII.

Adaptation and *Sunshine State*: Nature and Nostalgia in Contemporary Florida Films

MARLISA SANTOS

Though Florida is one of the southernmost states in the U. S., its identity is not often characterized as Southern. When one considers the diversity of its geographical regions, whether it is Disney-fied Orlando, the ethnic melting pot of Miami, or the quasi–Caribbean Keys, Florida may be thought of — and depicted on film — as many things, but these are usually not the typical markers of Southern life. However, the identity of Florida as a Southern state on film can be seen in certain contemporary films that portray the colorful ethnic and natural history of the state, depicted as both a state known for its eccentric uniqueness, and also as kin to its Southern state neighbors. The longing for the past that is often seen in Southern culture is visible in films such as Spike Jonze's *Adaptation* (2002) and John Sayles' *Sunshine State* (2002), in the sense that an Edenic (and wild) natural environment is mourned for as a symbol of a more unspoiled time — a time in which (in memory, at least) racial and class inequities and aggressive urbanization mysteriously coexist with pastoral elegance.

In Florida's rich and diverse history on film, one element is common: attention to the state's lush and dangerous natural landscape. The myths surrounding the state's history in American cultural consciousness provide the roots for such depictions — alternately paradisal and criminal, playground to children and the wealthy elite, leisure for the aged — but all against the backdrop of sun, sand, water, and exotic foliage. Whether comedies such as *Caddyshack* (1980) or *The Birdcage* (1996), dramas such as *Blood and Wine* (1996) or *Ulee's Gold* (1997), or neo-*noirs* such as *Palmetto* (1998) or *Out of Time* (2003), the environmental features of the state are portrayed on film with prominence, usually woven into the themes and motifs of the filmic narratives. When these portrayals go beyond the simple eye candy of tropical titillation, the depictions of Florida's ecology tend to turn either toward the sublime volatility of the state's weather—blazing, glorious sun and balmy breezes shifting instantaneously to hair-raising lightning and torrential downpours— or toward the idea of Florida's natural beauty as something endangered and disappearing. Susan J. Fernandez and Robert P. Ingalls argue that "[i]ncreasingly, Florida has become paradise lost, both in the popular imagination and in film" (7). Either because of over-development or crime and corruption, the myth of Florida's unspoiled paradise, where one could go for escape or rebirth, is seen as tarnished and tainted—often as the seamy underside to an outer veneer of beauty and purity. It is a yearning for this fantasy of an earlier pristine time that pervades modern films set in Florida. Whereas general Southern nostalgia hearkens back to gentility, class, and racial hierarchy, almost an aristocratic scheme of royalty, Floridian nostalgia centers on a lack of civilization, or at least a lack of planned civilization. From this perspective, human communities rightly grew organically out of the creative and pioneering desires of those who were brave enough to embrace the natural eccentricities of the state enough to deserve its bounty. Conversely, the dark side of the push for civilization involves the more modern practices of the rape and exploitation of the state's natural landscape, resources, and ethnic peoples.

Much of what commands attention in *Adaptation* are the narrative undulations of Spike Jonze and Charlie Kaufman, as they present an ambitious, innovative, and self-reflexive film that portrays the attempted adaptation of a book, while also representing the process of that adaptation. However, the transference of the rich Floridian landscape from Susan Orlean's book onto film is a necessary and compelling component of the film's ethos. The frame of the film depends on the idea of self-awareness and self-realization, and the role that the adaptative process has in these pursuits; this framework is necessary to understand in order for the importance of the Florida setting to be fully appreciated. Charlie's seemingly futile search for self-actualization, as he mournfully declares, "Today is the first day of the rest of my life—I'm a walking cliché," is bookended by the extremes of two other characters: his twin brother Donald (both played by Nicolas Cage), who represents all of the baseness and mediocrity that he is trying to transcend, and John Laroche (Chris Cooper), the itinerant and nonconformist orchid-hunter who is the focal point of Orlean's source material. Donald and Laroche represent the two components of the Darwinian framework that informs the film's narrative, with Laroche being the necessary mutation on the human norm, and Donald being the tried-and-true measure of success. As David L. Smith points out, "in evolutionary terms, Charlie is maladapted ... while Donald represents the genius of nature itself, the tautological triumph of what works" (432). Charlie's "maladaptation" is also subtly referenced when, in response to Charlie's assertion that "no one makes a movie about flowers," Donald says, "What about *Flowers for Algernon?*"—a film as Charlie points out, not about flowers but, as Charlie does not point out, about a functional mentally retarded man who is temporarily given great intelligence through a brain operation. And of course, the film version of the book is actually titled, *Charley*, a further connection to Charlie Kaufman's adaptative difficulty. By contrast, Donald's routine pick-up lines succeed with women and his formulaic script succeeds with Charlie's agent. Charlie is in real danger of becoming obsolete, of getting sucked under the evolutionary maelstrom of what "works."

Laroche is the other extreme of what "works" in the evolutionary scheme, as he is the unpredictable element that turns the organic process in a different and unexpected, but no less necessary, direction. He is the pathway into the mysterious Florida swamp where resides the rare and endangered ghost orchid that fascinates Orlean initially in the book and drives the narrative in the film, as it represents an elusive passion, a thing that can inspire powerful and sometimes irrational pursuit. Orlean delineates the complicated heritage of the orchid in both the book and the film, describing quests in China and Borneo that often result in disease and death, all to attain its otherworldly beauty. A montage of close-up shots of the ghost orchid against a black screen highlights Orlean's voice-over about her desire to see one, even though she does not really even like orchids that much, because she wants to see the thing that so many had risked so much for. According to Orlean (Meryl Streep), Laroche loved "the difficulty and fatality of getting them almost as much as he loved the orchids themselves." Laroche navigates the complex process of attaining the ghost orchid through his relationship with local Seminoles. Though theirs is a somewhat symbiotic relationship—they have employed Laroche to build their nursery and he in turn uses them, in their governmentally protected status, to remove the orchids and other endangered plant species from the Everglades—Laroche clearly seems to have the upper hand in the bargain, as he likely profits most by the enterprise. As he and three Seminole men venture into the Fakahatchee Strand in the Immokalee area near U.S. 27, Laroche is the dominant figure, as he tells them where to cut and when questioned by the state ranger, glibly cites court cases that would defend their actions. The Seminoles are depicted as sullen and slothful pawns in water-soaked shirts and pants, leaning against a car, smoking, and not interacting with the ranger until Laroche prompts them to repeat his assertions. Sergio Rizzo argues that "[i]n an apparent effort to enhance the fictional Laroche's cinematic virility ... Kaufman turns Orlean's portrait of the Seminoles into crude stereotypes," adding that "[l]ike other legendary white men from Natty

John Laroche (Chris Cooper) hunts the elusive ghost orchid with Seminole help in director Spike Jonze's *Adaptation* (2002, Columbia Pictures; credit Ben Kaller).

Bumpo [sic] to Carlos Castaneda, Laroche acquires the native Indian's primitive life force and makes it safe for consumption by other whites" (305). Indeed, Laroche seems most interested in appropriating the nature associated with the Seminoles for his own profit, and as he explains to Orlean his scheme to cultivate the ghost orchid and thereby ameliorate its endangered status (and the poaching that goes with this status), he proclaims, "Laroche and nature win!" He is endeavoring to make a rare feature of nature less rare and therefore, less valued, through artificial means. His unromantic attitude toward this enterprise parallels the disinterest shown when, in the swamp and a ghost orchid is sighted, the handsaw of Matthew Osceola (Jay Tavare) bumps carelessly against the flower before he cuts it down, unconcerned about its supposed sacredness. The film is ambivalent about the extent to which such value and sanctity is an artificial construct by the white, "civilized" world or a symbol of the overdevelopment of the state and the natural contortions that result.

The romantic exoticism of the ghost orchid is further tarnished with the introduction of the sensationalist "Donald" plotline that suggests Laroche's real motivation for collecting the plants is to harvest a hallucinogenic powder that the Seminoles use and, the implication is, could be sold to whites. This powder is certainly depicted as a liberator of them, as Orlean's character loses her urban inhibitions and affectations through the drug, abandoning herself to sex with Laroche and freely overstepping any number of cultural taboos, as she has no trouble suggesting that they kill Charlie when they discover him spying on them. Prior to this sequence of events, Laroche, like the orchid, is far more mystified, and represented as a force of native Florida nature himself, in his changeability and his wholehearted acceptance of natural adaptation. His single-minded obsessions with various objects turning instantaneously to complete rejection illustrate this characterization, as he demonstrates to Orlean by using the example of tropical fish. After amassing a multitude of fishtanks to house the hundreds of species of fish he had collected, to the point that he would "skin dive to find just the right ones," Laroche abruptly ends his quest, concluding, "Fuck fish. I renounce fish." To Orlean's incredulous query about his reasons, Laroche simply says, "Done with fish." Laroche's life has been filled with so many random — and tragic — turns of events, from the accident that led to the deaths of his mother and uncle and his divorce, to Hurricane Andrew destroying his beloved nursery, that it is no wonder that he has come to accept with resignation the somewhat divine underpinnings of the natural world. He says he loves plants "because they're so mutable ... adaptation's a profound process ... means you figure out how to thrive in the world." Orlean counters this argument by asserting that it is "easy for plants because they have no memory"; for humans, she says, "adaptation is shameful ... like running away." Smith asserts that the life advocated for here is "abandonment ... the human capacities associated with narrative only get in the way of the process of getting on. Memory and reflection not only falsify life; they impede it" (429). What is remembered in this world, whether good or bad, can mesmerize or paralyze, and therefore inhibits life from proceeding organically.

The specter of the past permeates the film and the natural Florida surroundings that frame it. The Seminole men seem shades of their ancestors. Depicted as being flunkies for a white con man, their only interaction with the nature of their heritage is the theft of lucrative plant life and the use of the drugs derived from the plants. When Matthew Osceola dreamily fingers Orlean's blonde hair and muses that he can "see [her] sadness ... it's beautiful," and that he can no longer speak to her because "it's the Indian way," the mystery of Native American culture is evoked, but cheapened, reduced to its most cliché (and drug-induced) effects. The two swamp scenes of Laroche and Orlean searching for a ghost orchid suggest opposite, but equally uninspiring, nostalgias toward nature. In the first, true to the book, Orlean and Laroche not only get lost, but also take nasty shots at each other, and do not even find the orchid. In the second, the first account is described by Orlean's voice-over as a lie, that in fact "something happened in the swamp that day," which is the fact that they did find the orchid and that this event catalyzed her sexual, as well as emotional, drug awakening with Laroche. But tellingly, when they discover the orchid in the alternate account, she muses, "it's a flower ... it's just a flower," as if to indicate the flower's complete demystification as it will soon become for her an object of profit and a metaphor for her illicit sensuality. And finally, of course, the role of the swamp in the chase and murder scene near the end of the film becomes simply a useful vehicle and a trite mechanism for suggesting the danger of trespassing in Laroche's world. That he is killed by an alligator is fitting, if not obviously suggestive of the easy metaphor that would permeate Donald's filmic universe, and which must take control of Charlie's narrative for him to successfully navigate the world. *Adaptation*'s emphasis on the almost prehistoric kind of natural world that is still alive, though appropriated, in Florida informs human struggles with the baggage of the past. In the end, human beings are not like plants, their happiness more complex and their suffering more tragic because of their ties to history.

The struggle to reclaim (or redeem) the past in a Florida setting is even more prominent in John Sayles' *Sunshine State*. The atmosphere is thick with nostalgia from the opening of the film, in which Buccaneer Days, an annual festival in the fictional Florida city of Delrona Beach (the name perhaps a cross between the two actual Florida cities of Delray Beach and Daytona Beach) that celebrates the city's "diverse heritage," is presented as the occasional frame for the narrative. That the opening scene depicts the burning of the pirate ship float, usually the lead float in the event's parade, gives an indication of the transience of these "traditions." The strained Southern belle event organizer, Francine Pinkney (Mary Steenburgen) tries her best to organize the festivities, her pronounced southern Georgia-northern Florida accent mellifluously making announcements and emceeing the staged events. However, even she, the representative of this contrived celebration, acknowledges its futility, her tired face slack during the presentation of the prizes awarded to scavenger hunt winners until she is called upon to congratulate them, and ultimately at the end of Buccaneer Days, to proclaim frustratedly to her husband, "People don't realize how difficult it is to invent a tradition." The ironic truth is that, regardless of Florida being one of the first locales in the U.S. to be "discovered" by European settlers and thus set upon the road toward colonial "civilization," the ethnic diversity of its population has made a coherent and consistent set of traditions impossible, thereby leaving it without a sense of a common history and with, instead, only a series of separate cultural memories and a sense of loss from the past.

The myriad characters in the film, with their peripherally intersecting lives, are grounded by two strong female characters: the African American Desiree Perry (Angela Bassett) — nicknamed "Hurricane Desiree" — and the white "cracker" Marly Temple (Edie Falco), each having significant stake in the development struggle occurring on Plantation Island. Marly refers to herself and the fellow patrons in the beach bar as "us crackers" to landscape architect Jack Meadows (Timothy Hutton), adding that her family has had "six generations on this sandpile," as opposed to Meadows' misconception that everyone on the coast is "a transplant from somewhere else." Though "cracker" has come to mean any southerner — usually a backward, racist, ignorant one — in the popular imagination, the term is usually thought to have originated as a descriptor for the "native" Floridian — usually poor and rural. In a 1997 *Halifax Magazine* article, researcher Rick Tonyan delineated some of the theories surrounding the origin of the name — from the Celtic braggart to the whipcracking early Florida cattleman — but there is no consistent explanation for the term. What is consistent, however, are the negative connotations associated with the term that have developed over time. Sayles characterizes Marly quite pointedly in this way to emphasize that even though it may not be apparent to the outsider (or even many state residents) Florida does indeed have a history and a cultural heritage worth remembering.

Similar to other characters in the film, Marly's feelings toward this heritage are complicated. As Susan Doll and David Morrow argue, the residents of the island "sift through their shared histories, struggling to determine which aspects of their heritage are worth preserving, which can be let go, and how far they should carry the fight" (229). Though she hates the life she leads as the manager of her father's SeaVue motel and restaurant, she also hates the idea of the "buzzards" like Meadows from the Exley Estates "mentally undressing" the land on which the motel is situated in order to perform a "feasibility study." "Don't you have enough of this coastline?" she irritably tells him. Her history is thoroughly bound up in Delrona Beach; she has been off the island, but only as far as Homosassa, where she worked as a "mermaid" swimmer for the Weeki Wachee tourist attraction. There, she learned how to "keep a smile on your face — even if you're drownin'." Marly is finding it hard to smile these days it seems, drowning as she is in frustration and inertia. One failed marriage behind her and a trail of uninspiring lovers too, she has not succeeded in finding love or satisfaction on the "sandpile" that is Delrona Beach, and the imposing images of her pioneer, but now diabetic and near-blind father, Furman Temple (Ralph Waite) and her Southernly genteel theatrical mother, Delia (Jane Alexander) haunt any impulses she may have to move in a different direction. For his part, Furman Temple is "hanging on for spite," wistfully recalling a time when the winner was "the strongest, smartest, swiftest ... a man could carve out something for himself and know he owned it," in contrast to the present, when everything has become "politically correcteded and environmentally sensitized." Delia, who has no love for the unromantic, run-down motel, tells Marly that her father has a "Darwinian attitude about what survives and thrives there and what doesn't." The ruthlessness (and racism) of the past are also oddly dignified, as it provided opportunity and did not take advantage of the land for simply mercenary sake. There was, it is implied, a healthy respect for the nature you could control and that you could not control, as Furman states about the ocean's undertow: "The trick is you don't try to fight it ... you swim parallel to the shore until it eases up ... otherwise you're a goner... [If] you try to take it head on, it'll pull you under." And perhaps it is the undertow of the future that convinces Furman to give Marly his blessing to sell the motel; it seems an organic decision, borne of a sense of the relentlessness of time moving forward. As it turns out, the land may not be sold because of Delia's savvy profit-sharing bargaining proposal, but Marly is clearly portrayed as having newfound release and freedom by the end of the film. Though she has been fascinated by the idealism of Meadows, whose goal is to transform nature by taming its wildness and making it "a place where everyone can go," he is nonetheless mired in a corrupt business and is not meant to remain part of her life after his company pulls out of the development project. One of the final scenes of the film shows a shot of surreal blue green water dissolving into a surface hit by droplets of rain, revealing Marly swimming again, after she had vowed not to since her mermaid days — now she is no longer an artificial mermaid, but something, symbolically, symbiotic with a real environment.

Like Marly, Desiree, who is a different kind of force of nature, has mixed feelings about her background on the island. She grew up on Lincoln Beach, a historically black beach community that is now being threatened by the Exley developers as well. She has in effect become a "transplant," having been pulled up by the roots when she became pregnant at age 15 (after being crowned the Pirate Queen of that year's Buccaneer Days celebration) and was sent to relatives in Georgia by her well-respected and upstanding parents. Back to visit her mother, Desiree must confront various ghosts from her past, including "Florida Flash" Phillips (Tom Wright), the college freshman football star father of her child who has now become a property-buying patsy for the development company. They are both damaged by their experiences: after her baby was stillborn, the complications caused Desiree's infertility, and a severe knee injury cost Flash his professional football career. The reversal of both characters parallels the explanation that Desiree's mother, Eunice Stokes

(Mary Alice) describes as her family's financial fall from grace after enjoying the heights of African American Jacksonville society life, including cotillions and coming-out parties. There is a loss of fundamental organic drive that Desiree and Flash each suffers now that causes them to alter the way they perceive the future. They both have found a way to make it in the world, but these ways lack substance (Desiree as an infomercial spokesmodel and Flash as a car salesman) and suggest a lack of closure with the past, as they encounter each other again amidst the turmoil surrounding Lincoln Beach's property crisis.

The defense of Lincoln Beach's heritage and the guardianship of its future fall to Dr. Elton Lloyd (Bill Cobbs) who hearkens back to the community's earliest days when it was founded in 1934 with the goal of providing the African Americans in the area a safe, owned place for recreation during the Jim Crow era. Lincoln Beach parallels the real American Beach on Amelia Island in north Florida, which was purchased by A. L. Lewis for the employees of his Jacksonville-based Afro-American Insurance Company in the 1930s and grew into a successful vacation destination for African American tourists (Mormino 310). Dr. Lloyd argues at city commission meetings, implores residents to remember the history of the community, and leads a protest that aims to stop the bulldozers from clearing the land. For all his efforts, though, the salvation of Lincoln Beach comes only through a random accident—that the main bulldozer, ironically driven by a transient Native American, plows up the remains of an Indian burial ground, and the beach therefore gains if not an ultimately protected status, then a significant delay. The legacy of history here, instead of bringing the thriving community longevity and pride that the African American entrepreneurs, including Desiree's father, had hoped for, has only brought abandonment and powerlessness. Dr. Lloyd laments the irony that the community had more value in the days of segregation, when the black citizens carved out a piece of ownership for themselves—similar to the kind of nostalgia that Furman Temple recollects. Now, the young people are "free" but they don't "own" anything—materially or ideally. This rootlessness is symbolized by Desiree's cousin, Terrell, who is drifting through life; he is a product of dysfunctional and violent parents and has a taste for arson. He is the one who burns down the pirate float at the beginning of the film. Eunice is his guardian at the moment, but the path that his life will take is clearly unknown. As part of his community service probation, he works for Delia Temple's theatre group, his main task to build a coffin for a production of *As I Lay Dying*. He uses as his materials the wood remains—presumably the strong and now nearly extinct Florida Heart Pine—of a burnt-out Lincoln Beach speakeasy, Buster's Place. The uncertainty of Terrell's future is bound up in these complex images. He destroys the Disney-fied symbol of

Delrona Beach's annual festival (which is an invented tradition based on plunder, rape, and murder) and as a consequence, is offered a fresh start by building a death-box for a dramatization of an old Southern story, using as his raw materials the failure of his own history. It is hard to imagine a more Southern narrative — the loss of self-respect by both blacks and whites and the insidious influence of the carpetbagger-like developers turn the future sour and the past bitter. As Kent Jones argues, "[h]istory is everywhere in *Sunshine State*, but it has no solidity, and it comes with no guarantees of stability. Everyone in the film is ... obliged to live beneath a bland aura of hope amidst an endless cycle of exhaustion and renewal, gleeful forgetting and soulful remembering, disintegration and preservation" (22).

The various ironies surrounding the island's history and future are framed by carefully inserted segments of pontificating golfers, who wax rhapsodic about the way that the land has developed. Led by Murray Silver (Alan King), they are like a humorous Greek chorus, one that illuminates in spite of itself. The golf course itself is a powerful image in its display of nature re-formed for human pleasure and the drain on natural resources, especially water, to keep it alive. Silver contrasts this image with the unspoiled land that they helped "civilize":

> In the beginning there was nothing. Wilderness ... worse than wilderness — endless raw acreage, land infested with ... alligators. The old name means in Seminole "You shouldn't go there." ... We bought there 'cause we knew... Dreams are what you sell. A concept ... you sell sunshine, orange groves. [We] took a land populated by white people who ate catfish ... and created this ... Nature on a leash.

The golfers represent another side to the island's history — the history of the developer, the "godlike" ancestors of the Exley company and current groups like them who transformed the "nothingness" of the wild state into civilized property. It is characterized, however, as not so much civilized in the lofty, philosophical sense as it is in the marketing sense. They congratulate themselves on their genius in selling basically uninhabitable land that became populated with transplants when they found themselves bilked in a real-estate scam. The developers got their money and disappeared, and out of those kinds of cons grew the communities of the state. A symbol of the de-fanged heritage of Florida is evident in the "fierce" alligator from Smoot's Gator Farm truck on display at the Buccaneer Days celebration; the gator is so sedentary, the observing children have to ask Smoot if he is alive. The transformation of the entire state is thus portrayed as a massive cheat, an idea that is consistent with the disillusion facing the Marlys and the Desirees and their families in the present. This idea is reinforced by the golfers' final exchange in the film, which recounts a story about how the Spanish were fooled into thinking that there was gold in Florida, when the "evidence" was from their own shipwrecked galleons. The golfers speculate that the future of capitalism in the state will rest with lotteries and the fruits of metal detectors — enterprises based on luck or chance, rather than drive or skill. When Silver muses, "What do our young people dream of? There's no mystery anymore," the camera pulls back to reveal the golfers playing in the median of a busy street. The implication is that the golfers, like everyone else who has a past in the "Sunshine State" must reap the results of what they sow.

The anchor of Florida's natural landscape, and the way that it has influenced the past, present, and future of the state's residents as depicted in these films inspire a complex brand of nostalgia. African American, Native American, and "cracker" cultures are entwined with longing reminiscence for the natural world in *Adaptation* and *Sunshine State*, and such filmic exploration conveys the richness of Florida's settlement history. Issues such as reconciliation with racial injustices and forward-looking plans for economic security are juxtaposed with fierce cultural pride and desire for preservation. What seems to be the most common thread in these depictions is the locus of nature in Florida life — it is a force that cannot be escaped and is alternately celebrated and reviled. Although the *Sunshine State* golfers scoff at global warming, argue about the futility about concern for the remaining wilderness, and proclaim, "Nature is overrated," even they must admit, "But we'll miss it when it's gone." This landscape and its attendant nostalgia thus becomes the "culture" of the state as it transcends individual race and ethnic concerns and binds the unlikeliest of characters together. In *Adaptation*, John Laroche both honors and exploits the native flora — and by extension, native American culture — of south Florida, his parasitic relationship with the Seminoles and also with Orlean breeding on the nostalgic perception of value in this domain. In *Sunshine State*, the fluid and sordid history of the state is a ghost that haunts both African American and "cracker" residents alike, whose heritage is tightly bound in the spoiled and exploited natural surroundings. What is perceived to be lost by the characters in both films is perhaps not something that had ever been found — only perhaps borrowed, from a Native American point of view, until later generations of residents redefine their identities and ownership from their relation to the land.

Works Cited

Doll, Susan, and David Morrow. *Florida on Film.* Gainesville: University Press of Florida, 2007.
Fernandez, Susan J., and Robert P. Ingalls. *Sunshine in the Dark: Florida in the Movies.* Gainesville: University Press of Florida, 2006.

Jones, Kent. "The Lay of the Land." *Film Comment* 38.3 (May/June 2002): 22–24.
Mormino, Gary R. *Land of Sunshine, State of Dreams: A Social History of Modern Florida.* Gainesville: University Press of Florida, 2005.
Rizzo, Sergio. "(In)fidelity Criticism and the Sexual Politics of *Adaptation*." *Literature/Film Quarterly* 36.4 (2008): 299–314.
Smith, David L. "The Implicit Soul of Charlie Kaufman's *Adaptation*." *Philosophy and Literature* 30 (2006): 424–35.
Tonyan, Rick. "Cracking Up Cracker Myths." *Halifax Magazine* (September 1997).

XIII.

Reel Horror: Louisiana's Vanishing Wetlands and the Threat of Hollywood (Mis)Representation

MARIA HEBERT-LEITER

In his review of the HBO series *True Blood* (2008), Joshua Alston describes the show as the place "where quaint, romantic notions of the South are recast with dread" (14). The show introduces a new threat in the world of rural Louisiana: vampires. Danger is not entirely new to the film and television representations of Louisiana, however, since alligators, venomous snakes, and isolated populations with different cultural practices have long suggested that a threat lurks in the wetlands of this particular southern state. In popular films set in Louisiana, the menacing swamps provide a staple of sensationalized entertainment for movie audiences. But what if such celluloid images affect national reactions to the loss of such geographical space? Contemporary films set in the swamps, such as *Southern Comfort* (1981), *The Skeleton Key* (2005), and *The Waterboy* (1998), demonstrate how Hollywood depicts the swamp as a dangerous and different space that must be controlled and contained. In reality, Louisiana swamps, marshes, and wetlands in general are ecological and cultural treasures because of the animal and plant species that inhabit them and the ethnic groups that live off of these fragile lands and their rich natural resources. The loss of such an area, an ongoing reality because of rapid erosion, would mean the loss of natural protection from hurricanes as well as the loss of vegetation, wildlife, and certain folkways of the Biloxi-Chitimacha-Choctaw Indians and Cajuns, among others. Through the popular images perpetuated in Hollywood films, the message of the swamp's danger to humans becomes a threat to preserving wetlands that are central to Louisiana's environmental preservation and the protection of cultural traditions.

In an attempt to comprehend why stereotypes about Louisiana exist, H.

Wayne Schuth has studied both Louisiana and specifically New Orleans films, which leads him to argue that "Filmmakers often choose the physical reality of New Orleans, but they ultimately create a symbolic reality colored by a personal vision" ("Image of New Orleans" 240), a conclusion he further supports in his study of Louisiana film in general. The "vast heritage of [film] images of Louisiana helps to create our mental map of the state" ("Images of Louisiana" 16). Filmmakers continuously use popular images that form the "vast heritage" of which Schuth writes, thus producing a "symbolic reality" that may have once extended from a "personal vision" but now arises from a collective imagined reality, a mental map of Louisiana. Such a theory illustrates the relationship between audiences and films about Louisiana, a relationship emphasizing viewers' desire for a familiar Louisiana and their impulse to replace the actual geographic area with Hollywood images created to induce fear, excitement, or humor. This shared vision allows for the entertainment of millions of people who make up a general audience of any given film. This theory, applied to Hollywood's representation of Louisiana swamps, proves useful in addressing why specific notions of the area are perpetuated, thus becoming the dominant image of the swamps for millions of Americans. It also reinforces the possible threat of such images to the protection and restoration of Louisiana wetlands. If audiences' assumptions about the vanishing wetlands are affected by popular film images of Louisiana swamps, then the real threat of losing such land is potentially misunderstood.

The swamp has long played a central role in Southern, especially Louisiana, literature and film. In *Shadow and Shelter: The Swamp in Southern Culture*, Anthony Wilson studies two tropes, "the swamp as the always present but always denied underside of the myth of pastoral Eden" and "the more recent figuration of the swamp as the last pure vestige of undominated but ever threatened Southern ecoculture," that while contradictory play out in representations of the swamp (ix). Popular Hollywood films, for the most part, continue to promote the concept of the Louisiana swamp as the anti-Eden even as Louisiana authors and documentary filmmakers favor the second trope.

In response to Hollywood's limited vision of this unique and culturally complex Southern state, Louisiana author Tim Gautreaux, who explores the significance of the swamp to Cajun culture in his fiction, has explained, "Hollywood is very superficial. So unless you're watching a documentary, you're not going to get any type of serious treatment of culture out of Hollywood. They just don't understand culture" (Hebert-Leiter 72). Mathé Allain studies such misrepresentations of Louisiana culture, specifically Cajun culture, in her essay "They Don't Even Talk Like Us: Cajun Violence in Film and Fiction." Her concern involves the altered image of Cajuns in film and literature from the early depictions of the religious heroine of Henry Wadsworth Longfellow's *Evangeline* and Edwin Carewe's 1929 film of the same title to the violent community in *Southern Comfort*. In the 1970s, Cajuns in film changed from a "tame, pious, peace-loving" people to "the quintessence of Southern violence and mindless bigotry" on screen (65). Allain's argument concerning Cajuns pertains to the geographic area, as well. As Schuth points out, in the 1929 film *Evangeline*, "The Louisiana swamps, bayous, and rivers shown in the film are indeed lovely, and very restful and peaceful" ("Images of Louisiana" 7). Walter Hill purposefully altered this peaceful image, however, when he "filmed the swamps in the winter, supposedly stopping when the sun came out, rather than in the lush spring, summer or fall" (10), in order to create "a deadly image of the swamps as gloomy and menacing" in *Southern Comfort* (10). Such changes to film images of Louisiana prove that representations of swamps are affected by the mood required by the script being filmed and do not reflect the reality of the people who live there or the geographical locations themselves. While such criticism of cultural and geographical representation is significant to any study of Louisiana films, the central question here is not how Hollywood misrepresents the area, but what consequences arise from these widely disseminated images.

While Hollywood movies do not necessarily determine political action, or the lack thereof, they both reflect and inform popular notions and stereotypes. Those who have studied the environmental crisis taking place daily along Louisiana's coast believe that restoration projects must be supported and funded on a national level, meaning that the nation, and not only Louisiana residents, must realize the serious consequences of losing this land. In *Bayou Farewell*, Mike Tidwell recalls his journey across coastal Louisiana as a means of arguing for conservation and restoration efforts. The battle to protect this area of the United States proves difficult because of the lack of national concern:

> Whatever the reason, virtually no one outside Louisiana was paying any attention even now. The Everglades, deservedly, was getting almost $8 billion in federal and state money for restoration. The city of Boston, deservedly or not, was getting $14 billion to build an underground highway, the notorious "Big Dig." For almost the exact same price, coastal Louisiana — the birds, the beauty, the seafood, the culture, the source of energy, the buffer against hurricanes — could be saved. Instead, as the twenty-first century dawned, it kept right on dying [Tidwell 135].

Tidwell's journey allowed him access to the riches of the area and his comparison between the lack of action taken towards restoring and protecting Louisiana's wetlands and the national funding provided for other areas in the United States reveals a disjunction between the state's reality and the national consideration of this situation at least as late as 2003 when his book was published.

By 2007, both the Louisiana Legislature and the United States Congress had taken action, perhaps a consequence of the destruction caused by the 2005 hurricane season that included two deadly storms: Katrina and Rita. In their article "Worry Over Wetlands," Melissa Savage and John Hill discuss recent legislation regarding hurricane protection and wetland restoration projects, including the Gulf of Mexico Energy Security Act signed by President Bush in 2007, which added $100 million per year for restoration and protection projects (42). In 2006, the federal government agreed "to pass along a substantial amount of royalties collected from oil drilling in the area to the nation's coastal energy producing states" (42), and before this action was taken, the people of Louisiana passed an amendment to use royalties from offshore production for restoration and protection projects (42). While such developments are positive, Savage and Hill argue that, at least in terms of the federal government, "the royalty payments will not begin to roll in for about a decade, and even then experts say it will not meet the needs" (42–43). In other words, the effort will be too little, too late. As early as 1990, Congress passed the Coastal Wetlands Planning program, but "because the program was not set up to do the massive, large-scale projects necessary to address the land loss, restoration projects in Louisiana over the last 15 years have received only about $33 million to $44 million a year from the federal government. One large-scale restoration project can cost as much as $200 million" (41). Furthermore, it was only after Hurricanes Katrina and Rita that the Louisiana Legislature passed the Coastal Restoration and Protection Act, which finally placed projects for both restoring and protecting the wetlands together to coordinate efforts (41).

Realizing the significance of this issue not only to Louisiana but also to the rest of the nation, Savage and Hill advocate for national education so that the general population may understand the tragedy that is unfolding around them. Unfortunately, such education has a formidable foe in the movie industry because the image of loss that must be realized continuously competes with images of darkness, evil, and ignorance. For this education to take effect, the "symbolic reality" created by films must be replaced with the actual reality of a vanishing world. Hollywood films starring popular actors, such as *The Waterboy* and *The Skeleton Key*, attract broad audiences. The average viewer who watches such films but has never been to Louisiana or taken a swamp tour understands the swamps through pop cultural images that offer only a superficial idea of the nature of the wetlands and their function.

Southern Comfort, with its violent Cajuns and shifting swamp waters, proves how difficult such a battle against the symbolic reality perpetuated by Hollywood may be. Directed by Walter Hill, this *Deliverance*-like film even comes with the tagline, "It's the Land of Hospitality ... Unless You Don't

National Guardsmen Pfc. Simms (Franklyn Seales), Cpl. Hardin (Powers Boothe), and Pfc. Spencer (Keith Carradine) battle the swamp and its Cajun inhabitants in this scene from *Southern Comfort* (1981, Cinema Group, Inc.).

Belong," immediately preparing the viewer for suspense and terror. These words also assume that the viewer does not belong, effectively separating the film's audience from any positive reaction to the swamp setting that frames the horrors to come. As nine Louisiana National Guardsmen travel through the swamp in 1973, they quickly discover that the area holds many dangers, both natural and human. While the Cajun trappers who terrorize the men remain the ultimate threat throughout the film, the swamp plays the central role of trapping the men, setting them up to be murdered in a variety of ways. In the end, the only way to live is to escape the swamp itself.

At the beginning of the film, the guardsmen start their "recon and security" patrol with a map, a compass, and guns full of blanks as they walk through cypress trees dripping with moss. The map quickly proves less than totally reliable when Sergeant Poole discovers a body of water where land should be. Once he realizes that the channel has expanded with heavy winter rains, the men are left with two choices: travel through the water or return to camp and travel another way. This one decision leads to several days of battling Cajuns and ends with only two men surviving the mission.

The film, with its fog-coated setting and echoing swamp sounds, constantly reminds the viewer of the strangeness and danger of this area. When the guardsmen locate pirogues, one of them explains that the boats belong to "an indigenous person" (*Southern Comfort*), and the same character even warns the men against taking such property, foreshadowing the peril the men will find themselves in as they travel through this strange land. This pivotal scene illustrates the assumption that swamp dwellers are strange, dangerous creatures, a people who remain other in the contemporary United States and to the majority of the film's audience. The "indigenous person" of the swamp must be similar to the swamp itself, which in this film means irredeemable and threatening. Such a belief proves true as Cajuns, the owners of the pirogue, do indeed hunt the guardsmen down and attack them.

As the men journey farther and farther into the swamp, they become not only impossibly lost but also more vulnerable to an attack and mentally unstable behavior, proving the swamp dangerous in a number of ways. Bowden (Alan Autry), a Louisiana high school football coach, even deteriorates mentally until his fellow guardsmen tie him up to maintain the other men's safety. Cribbs (T. K. Carter), another guardsman, chases after the helicopter that has come to rescue them and ends up in a sinkhole that becomes his grave. The cypress trees and shadows of the swamp prevent the rescuers from locating the men, making Cribbs's effort futile. The only way out comes from the mouth of a Cajun trapper who explains to the two survivors, Spencer (Keith Carradine) and Hardin (Powers Boothe), how to locate the road to town. Upon reaching "town" on the back of a Cajun couple's truck, the two men discover a rural community that still remains without a telephone as late as 1973. They partake of the beer and food, and Spencer even dances with a local woman to the Cajun music that sets the scene.[1] Hardin, however, refuses to believe that they are truly safe as they remain on the edge of the swamp itself. And indeed, the swamp encroaches on even this festive atmosphere as the Cajun trappers land nearby and hunt the men again. Finally, a truck with "US" painted on it saves the two men as the trappers force them back into the swamp. The camera's closeup of the truck's United States military identification reinforces the notion that previous to this moment, the men were no longer in an area controlled by the United States.

This film establishes the hazard of the swamp and swamp dwellers to the rest of the United States and emphasizes the nation's need to control and contain such threats. While the Cajuns quietly move through the waters of the swamp without need of compasses and maps throughout the film, the guardsmen become sitting ducks in the same environment. Ironically, the two survivors are the men who belong the least, since Spencer is a self-proclaimed "city boy" and Hardin hails from El Paso. For obvious reasons this film has developed into a source for criticism of popular Cajun and Louisiana representation. It should also be studied for its representation of the dangerous swamp and its peril to outsiders because such exaggerated representation allows film viewers to disregard the actual threat of losing this land since to do so, according to this film, would be to contain the danger within its moss-draped depths. The "indigenous" Cajuns of the film may pose a threat to the guardsmen, but the reality is that the choices of non-indigenous people affect the daily lives of Biloxi-Chitimacha-Choctaw Indians who choose to live on the edge of Terrebonne Parish in Louisiana even as they witness the washing away of their homes and lands year after year. While the film establishes an *us versus them* mentality with which the audience is supposed to relate, this mentality leads to dangerous assumptions about the wetlands of Louisiana, such as the assumption that such lands must be controlled and contained. It perpetuates the notion that such spaces are exotic and other, not a part of mainstream America, so perhaps not a source of real concern. History proves that the real danger that must be confronted lies in human action and inaction that has resulted in a tremendous loss of land.

The swamp that the guardsmen must confront and conquer is, in reality, part of a low lying landmass that is quickly disappearing because of decisions made at the national level to control Louisiana's waterways. Both Darran Simon and Mike Tidwell, along with many others, attribute this loss to two major causes: the construction of the Mississippi levee and of canals. Following the 1927 Mississippi River flood, the Army Corps of Engineers built the levee along the river to prevent such a flood from occurring in the future. This levee has, in Tidwell's words, "straitjacketed" the Mississippi River (6), creating a situation in which the river no longer deposits soil to rebuild the lands that act as a barrier against natural disasters such as hurricanes because the natural process has been permanently rerouted and prevented from doing so.[2] The oil industry also threatens the existence of the swamps and marshes because of the canals built to accommodate drilling in the coastal region. Such canals allow saltwater from the Gulf of Mexico to enter the freshwater wetlands, destroying natural vegetation and animal habitats (Simon A-1).[3] Furthermore, according to Tidwell, "Scientists at Louisiana State University (LSU) estimate that no less than a third of the total coastal-zone degradation can be traced directly to canals, and note that, once dug, these canals tend to *double their width every fourteen years*" (118). Fear of the waterways in Louisiana and the desire to control them can be paralleled to *Southern Comfort* and the fictional fear of a nature that will lead one to his demise until or unless the United States government steps in to save the day. While Walter Hill and his film would like American audiences to fear the swamps of Louisiana, the truth is that those who fight to save this area have more to fear from such popular images, the mental map created from them, and past national endeavors to contain this particular threat.

The Skeleton Key, a 2005 film directed by Iain Softley, starring Kate Hudson, and set in Terrebonne Parish, continues to exemplify "symbolic reality" and its reliance on the mysterious and threatening over twenty years after *Southern Comfort* was first released. The swamps southwest of New Orleans create an exotic atmosphere that remains central to the film's genres of suspense and horror. While *The Skeleton Key* begins in New Orleans and exhibits the typical images of the streetcar, the French Quarter, and jazz musicians, it quickly shifts to an isolated house located in Terrebonne Parish that is reminiscent of plantation homes.

Moss sways in the breeze as it hangs from heavy oak limbs in the opening scene of the film as Caroline, Hudson's character, witnesses the death of a hospice patient, immediately juxtaposing the wetland setting with a death scene. Choosing to continue her work as a hospice caregiver but disillusioned by the business atmosphere of the center where she works, Caroline decides to answer an advertisement for a nurse in Terrebonne Parish. Her roommate Jill (Joy Bryant), upon hearing of Caroline's intentions, exclaims, "This is Terrebonne Parish. This is the freakin' swamps." Then, Jill continues to warn her friend about the dangers that lie ahead: "They have gators in the swamp, and guys missing teeth." Anxious to escape from her previous experience, Caroline dismisses the warning and travels to the isolated home of Violet Devereaux (Gena Rowlands) where she cares for Violet's husband Ben (John Hurt), an invalid incapable of speaking. While working in the Devereaux home, Caroline uncovers evidence that the house has been occupied in the past by black hoodoo worshippers, specifically Papa Justify and Mama Cecile. The key to the story turns on an attic room where evidence of this worship remains and encourages Caroline's growing belief in the power of hoodoo, which, according to Jill, is an American folk magic which began in New Orleans.

The audience follows Caroline's movement from New Orleans to this dangerous place whose threat is foreshadowed when Caroline stops for gas at a rural gas station where she discovers the use of red brick dust in doorways, an indicator of hoodoo practice. The station appears to be empty, so Caroline searches for an attendant and instead discovers an old, blind woman who later in the film explains the power of hoodoo practitioner Papa Justify. When the attendant finally appears to accept Caroline's payment for the gas, he speaks French first before realizing that she does not understand the language as he shucks an oyster and sucks it out of its shell. Throughout this scene, oyster shells litter the counters, and alligator heads adorn the walls of the rusted-roofed shack. Furthermore, Caroline is immediately attacked by mosquitoes as she enters the building. From this moment forward, the audience is well aware that Caroline is no longer in familiar territory. The alligator head and the swarm of mosquitoes represent the creepy, natural swamp environment. While the attendant and the blind woman are native to the area and unbothered by such insects in this scene, Caroline is immediately attacked, reinforcing her status as an outsider and her entrance into a strange world.

When Caroline finally believes that hoodoo is indeed responsible for Ben's condition, she attempts to escape from Violet because she realizes her employer has used some sort of hoodoo spell to incapacitate Ben. The escape attempt occurs on a dark and stormy night when the waters of the swamp that lies directly behind the house threaten to flood the grounds. Caroline eventually discovers that the only way out is through the swamp, so she steals a boat and paddles through the dark, moss-draped waters until she sees lights and hears Cajun music. The swamp that borders the back of Violet's property constantly threatens the home as rainstorms arise throughout the film. Caroline must put on her rubber boots and slush through the muddy backyard while attempting escape, reminding her and the audience that the swamp waters create a barrier between her and the rest of the world. In order to free herself of whatever haunts the mansion, she must combat the swamp that isolates and thus protects the house's secrets. When Caroline finally does escape and believes she has reached safety, Violet's warning that "You'll never get out of here, child" proves true. She cannot escape because she trusts the wrong person who leads her back to the isolated house and its watery, uncertain path to supposed safety. Mama Cecile, in Violet's body and aided by Papa Justify, traps Caroline forever as she claims the young woman's body as her own, and the isolation of the swamp continues to protect the hoodoo worshippers from outside notice. Softley's images of moss-draped trees and rising muddy waters frame Caroline's passage into and out of Terrebonne Parish, reminding the audience of Jill's earlier warning of the dangers of the swamp.

With its collection of odd characters, one of whom speaks French more readily than English, *The Skeleton Key* creates an atmosphere of tension and suspense that not only maintains the interest of its audience but also perpetuates a popular national image of the Louisiana wetlands as isolated and dangerous. The violent Cajuns, the pseudo-"indigenous" folk of *Southern Comfort* who threaten the survival of the National Guardsmen, and the strange and superstitious characters of *The Skeleton Key* do not mimic the actual people who live along the wetlands and who struggle to survive on the edges of Louisiana, where unique ethnic communities battle yearly against the threat of loss. Such loss would entail not only the land itself but also the cultural traditions and history of the people who have called this land home. In Terrebonne Parish, about 80 miles southwest of New Orleans, the community of Biloxi-Chitimacha-Choctaw Indians remains to battle the hurricanes that endanger their homes on Isle de Jean Charles each year. Unlike Caroline who struggles to escape, these American Indian and Cajun descendants struggle to protect homes and a culture threatened by the vanishing wetlands.[4] Through his interview with Chief Albert Naquin, Darran Simon relates the increasing threat of hurricanes to the island because "saltwater encroaches the marsh on all sides of the island, taking the land where people farmed and gardened just 40 years ago" (A-3). Plans have been made to build a 72-mile levee that would protect Houma, the nearest city, but the levee will not shield Isle de Jean Charles since to do so would cost $100 million, as compared to the $8 million it would cost to relocate the community (McKay A-1). Instead of moving to higher and more protected ground, the approximately 150 to 175 people still living on the island refuse to relocate (Simon A-3).

In response to the debate regarding whether or not this community should be removed, Joel Waltzer, a tribal attorney for the Indians, explained that "losing the communities 'would mean the end of an entire lifestyle and, in this case, the end of an entire people'" (Simon A-3). This community thus continues to face the hazard of hurricane force winds and tidal surges in its attempt to preserve its rights to the land and a way of life. Its isolation from mainstream America, an isolation intensified by popular representation, forces the community to struggle to survive even as the isolation reinforces its otherness to an audience influenced by pop cultural film images.

Instead of portraying the swamps as a necessary and natural ecological system threatened by humanity's invasion and their populations as cultural treasures, *The Skeleton Key* once again addresses the unknown elements of the dense trees and watery banks as dangerous, as needing humanity to contain them. *Frankenfish*, a 2004 made-for-television film, exaggerates this danger even more as genetically-engineered fish torment and kill scientists and hunters who find themselves trapped on a houseboat in Louisiana.[5] B-movies, along with major productions like *The Skeleton Key*, continue to promote misunderstandings about this fragile place on the edge of the nation. Such wetlands and animal populations, actual endangered species and not genetically-engineered monsters for viewing enjoyment, require protection, but film audiences may view them in the opposite light because the deepest recesses of the swamps remain unfamiliar. Uncertainty and ignorance create tension, which promotes the reaction for which the producers are hoping: fear and excitement. While this portrayal of the world beyond New Orleans remains exaggerated, it is used in such a way to entertain the masses, most of whom may never enter a Louisiana swamp. By viewing films in this manner, one can study Hollywood images not in terms of what they reveal about an actual culture or place, but in terms of what they reveal about the cultural expectations of the viewers, of their "symbolic reality," and its consequences.

Both *Southern Comfort* and *The Skeleton Key* follow a contemporary tradition of representing the swamp as an isolated, thus disconnected, space in the United States. Often, Hollywood uses this space in conjunction with its stereotypical representations of African Americans, as in *The Skeleton Key*, and of Cajuns, as in *Southern Comfort*. The 1998 film *The Waterboy*, directed by Frank Coraci and starring Adam Sandler, follows in this tradition while also revising generic concepts of the Louisiana swamps. The film's plot unfolds around an ignorant Cajun character whose surprise football talent leads to his discovery of a world beyond his mother's superstitious teachings and isolated swamp home.

The story follows Bobby Boucher (Sandler) from his unappreciated position as the football team's waterboy to his rise as the team's key player and the MVP of the fictional Bourbon Bowl. This rise occurs not only because Bobby has the ability "to open a can of whoopass," but also because he realizes that a world exists in which he can become an educated man. As a means of guaranteeing Bobby's dependence on her because of her fear of losing him, Mama Boucher (Kathy Bates) home schooled her son and still warns him about the Devil if he mentions the outside world and its temptations. Mama's scheming effectively traps Bobby until Coach Klein (Henry Winkler) recognizes the usefulness of Bobby's pent up aggression. Coach offers Bobby more than a place on his team; he offers him the opportunity to receive a college education when he visits Bobby's swamp home. After a meal of snake and biscuits, Coach Klein asks Mama, "But don't you want the only part [of Bobby's father] you have left to get a college education?" Mama quickly replies, "Nah." Bobby, however, responds differently, and Coach continues to explain that with such an education "a whole new world will open to you." Openly disagreeing with his mother for the first time, Bobby expresses his desire for friends and acceptance, both of which he equates with college, which represents the world outside of his mother's isolated home.

In order to cut the string connecting him permanently to his mother and to juvenile behavior, he has to leave the swamp, both physically and metaphorically, by taking college classes and entering into a relationship with Vicki Vallencourt (Fairuza Balk). This film perfectly illustrates Glenn Conrad's argument that the Cajun is often "depicted as an ignorant, cunning, superstitious swamp dweller, living in squalor in a moss-draped, reptile-infested wilderness which is truly a backwater of American civilization" (1). Scenes set in Bobby's home emphasize the oddness of the area through meals of freshly cooked snake, grilled baby alligator, and frog-leg muffins topped fittingly with a frog-leg. To reach the rural shack complete with tires in the yard and Christmas lights around the roof and the door, Bobby must cross over a worn bridge, suggestive of the distance and division between Bobby's home life and the rest of the world.

Coach Klein (Henry Winkler) discusses game strategy with Bobby Boucher (Adam Sandler) and the other football players after Bobby decides to disobey Mama and join the team in *The Waterboy* (1998, Touchstone Pictures).

While *The Waterboy* chooses to represent the swamp and those who live there as isolated and ignorant, it departs from the sense of threat and danger promoted by *Southern Comfort* and *The Skeleton Key*, even allowing a view of the swamp in the sunlight. Instead, the threat is one against the emotional and intellectual development of the main character. If Bobby does not confront his mother, and if she does not allow him to live outside of her rigid and selfish boundaries, then he will remain an adult with a limited understanding of the world. Meanwhile, the mother maintains control over Bobby by keeping him firmly trapped in the muddy waters of the swamp that surround their home. He may leave the premises, but he cannot leave her control over him, as represented by his continual envisioning of her face and her words of warning. His awkward first day of class demonstrates her control over him when he responds to the professor's question about alligator aggression with Mama's explanation: alligators are "ornery because all them teeth and no toothpaste." In response, the professor and Bobby's peers laugh at him, forcing him to realize, if unwillingly at first, that Mama may not always have the answer. According to her, the swamp remains the safe zone in a menacing world, a message subverted by the lessons Bobby learns as the star of the college team.

By the end of the film, Mama Boucher allows Bobby to play football, even going so far as to drive him through the swamps in a fanboat to guarantee that he will make it to the Bourbon Bowl on time. This scene is one of escape from the ignorance and backward notions, as represented through the swamp setting, that have controlled Bobby throughout his life. Education, knowledge, manhood, and "a whole new world" exist beyond the swamps, not within them. Although Adam Sandler's film refrains from repeating the swamp horrors of other movies, it emphasizes the notion of the swamp as a distinctly inferior place that Bobby must escape to become a man.

The Waterboy thrives on various Louisiana stereotypes, including the representation of Cajun ignorance. Its use of the swamp, however, proves interesting because of the reality of these lands in south Louisiana and of the national ignorance that plagues efforts to restore and protect this area. If the "symbolic reality" of the swamps, as promoted by popular films, remains framed by images of danger, isolation, and ignorance, then the push to protect such lands and to educate a national audience about the realities of erosion faces a greater obstacle.

Mike Tidwell warns his readers that "the massive marshland coast of this watery southern state is vanishing from the face of the earth" and that this geographical loss is "an unfolding calamity of fantastic magnitude, taking with it entire Cajun towns and an age-old way of life" (6). What *Bayou Farewell* demonstrates is that while Hollywood would like for us to continue to fear such a place, as is evident in such films as *Southern Comfort* and *The Skeleton Key*, or to be convinced that those who dwell there would benefit from moving to "civilization," as indicated by such a film as *The Waterboy*, the reality is that while the swamps of south Louisiana may appear to threaten us in the popular imagination, we definitely threaten their existence.

While Hollywood suspense and comedy may not be directly responsible for this lack of national concern for a dying geographical area, and thus a way of life, the film industry's depictions of Louisiana swamps circulate widely and do reflect popular notions of the otherwise relatively unknown space. In reality, this area of the United States is different and dangerous, but not necessarily in the way Hollywood chooses to depict it. Even Tidwell describes the swamps as different: "I was a cynical traveler convinced that it was no longer possible to fall completely off the map in America, to get lost in an unfamiliar land among people barely recognizable as my countrymen. But hitchhiking through the bayou country ... has changed all that" (64). The "symbolic reality" of the swamps reflects this sense of the foreign, of difference, of an uncharted space. Tidwell's journey proves that being unfamiliar does not necessarily mean being dangerous, a significant distinction not encouraged by most films set in such Louisiana locations.

As a means of advocating for the restoration of the wetlands and realizing the difficulty of convincing a national audience of the problem, Savage and Hill promote not only education in general, but also an awareness of the centrality of these lands to the energy production of the nation. Such laws as the 2007 Gulf of Mexico Energy Security Act demonstrate the effectiveness of this argument. One positive movement, according to the authors, is the creation of America's Energy Coast initiative, "a group of government, private and nongovernmental organizations from the four energy producing states" whose goal is to "educate the public about the necessary co-existence of energy and ecology in the region and bring the varied interests together to work on solutions to the challenges along the Gulf Coast" (43). The irony is that to receive some of the attention necessary to rebuilding the wetlands, those attempting to increase federal funding for preservation and protection projects must first court one of the main culprits: big oil. Realizing the need to sell oil production, the Standard Oil Company commissioned Robert Flaherty's 1949 semidocumentary *Louisiana Story* (Schuth, "Images of Louisiana" 7). In the film, "The swamps, as well as the Cajuns, seem to remain basically untouched" (8). By the twenty-first century, Tidwell's journey and the Isle de Jean Charles community prove otherwise. While this image of the swamps does indeed alter during the twentieth century, it remains one that threatens the existence of the area because it promotes ignorance of the wetlands' cultural and environmental importance.

Perhaps the most effective way to counteract the dangers of such celluloid representations is to endorse more realistic films. As Gautreaux explains, documentaries primarily provide such depictions. One such documentary, *Haunted Waters* (1998), tells the story of Louisiana's vanishing coast and already fragile ecological systems. Glen Pitre, the writer, also produced the documentary *Hurricane on the Bayou* (2006) about the local experience of Hurricane Katrina. Born in Cutoff, Louisiana, Pitre's films reveal the realities of cultural and environmental loss without resorting to suspense, violence, or comedy to do so. The Barataria-Terrebonne National Estuary Program (BTNEP), established in 1991, has also produced videos about the wetlands in its effort to provide "avenues for the education of Louisiana citizens, as well as people around the country" ("BTNEP Resources"). Based on its realization that "for the Barataria-Terrebonne Estuary to be preserved, it must be understood and appreciated," the program has created such videos as *Vanishing Wetlands, Vanishing Future* (1996, 2001), *Haunted Waters, Fragile Lands* (2001), and *America's Vanishing Treasure* (2001). These titles emphasize three significant points: that the future of the wetlands remains uncertain, that these fragile lands are already haunted by loss, and that this calamity is a national, and not only a local, issue. The use of "haunted" by both Pitre and the BTNEP even reminds us that the true horror arises from the possible disappearance of this area and not from the people or animals that reside there. BTNEP attempts to counteract ignorance by endorsing education and understanding since such understanding can lead to appreciation. Unfortunately, popular films continue to perpetuate an opposing image of these fragile environmental treasures that encourages fear of the unknown. Unlike popular films that create suspenseful or humorous settings, Pitre and the BTNEP recognize that such appreciation may arise if their documentaries expose a national audience to the reality of the swamps, thus making them familiar. Pitre's films and programs promoted and sponsored by the BTNEP have continued educating the nation about the consequences of erosion, especially following the destruction caused by Hurricanes Katrina and Rita in 2005.

Contemporary Cajun authors have also captured the significance of the swamps to certain Louisiana cultural communities in their fiction, which often parallels the disappearance of the wetlands to fading Cajun culture as does Tidwell in *Bayou Farewell*. Tim Gautreaux's *The Next Step in the Dance* (1998) and Ken Wells's Meely LaBauve trilogy, among others, address the function of the swamps as a return to Cajun folkways, especially fishing and hunting traditions, even as the land continues to erode. In *Shadow and Shelter*, Anthony Wilson argues that *The Next Step in the Dance* "directly engages the clash between postmodern, consumerist values and traditional Cajun culture" (183). Contemporary films set in the Louisiana swamps are prime examples of such "postmodern, consumerist values," and Gautreaux's and Wells's works acknowledge the considerable loss that has already occurred. While such fiction reminds a national audience of the dangers of losing this land, popular films continue to oppose such images in a medium that reaches millions of viewers.

Even though Congress and the Louisiana Legislature had passed more significant plans for coastal restoration and protection projects by and during 2007, Hollywood continued to distribute films to popular audiences that counteracted these projects by inspiring fear instead of sympathy. While *The Skeleton Key* perpetuates the representations of swamp horrors, it was first released before either Katrina or Rita hit the coastal region. Released in 2007, *The Reaping*, directed by Stephen Hopkins and starring Hilary Swank, continues to inspire fear of the swamps even after the 2005 hurricane season proved the dire consequences of losing Louisiana's wetlands. In fictional Haven, Louisiana, the ten Biblical plagues have returned to terrorize the rural town. Attempting to debunk these seemingly miraculous occurrences, Katherine Winter, Swank's character and an outsider, discovers a satanic cult that uses local ruins at the edge of the swamp for the ritual sacrifice of their second-born children. Interestingly, the ruins of the original town of Haven, the site of the sacrifices in the film, remain as reminders of the destruction caused by multiple hurricanes over the years, which caused the townspeople to move to higher ground. Also, such natural destruction was one of the incentives for the townspeople to turn their backs on God and take up satanic worship. In reality, Louisianans such as the Isle de Jean Charles Indians have not abandoned their homes (or made them into places for human sacrifice) even after Katrina and Rita proved the hazards of living on the edge of the state (Simon A-1, A-3). *The Reaping* argues for the necessity of escaping this isolated and evil land, while reality continuously demonstrates the need to save it, not from the clutches of Satan, but from erosion, environmental and cultural, mostly caused by human actions, or lack thereof.

Unfortunately, films that create suspense and fear or that induce laughter continue to draw more viewers than most documentaries do. Besides, films are, for the most part, intended for entertainment purposes and not for educational endeavors. If Hollywood and films in general have the power to create a mental map of Louisiana wetlands, then perhaps it is time to create a different mental map in the national imagination. Films may be central to effectively educating a national audience about the horrors, not of Cajun violence and malicious swamp animals, but of a vanishing world.

Notes

1. For a critical analysis of this particular scene, refer to Chapter 3: "'J'ai Été au Bal': Cajun Sights and Sounds" in Charles J. Stivale's *Disenchanting Les Bons Temps: Identity and Authenticity in Cajun Music and Dance*.

2. John M. Barry's study of the 1927 Mississippi River flood, *Rising Tide*, relates the history behind the construction of this levee.

3. Ironically, some of the Cajuns who live along the bayous in south Louisiana have been major participants in the oil industry, thus actively contributing to one of the major causes of the erosion that now leaves them more exposed to hurricanes and environmental losses. For more on the story of Cajun involvement in the oil industry, refer to Woody Falgoux's *Cajun Mariners: The Race for Big Oil*. At the time this essay was being edited for publication, the nation watched in horror as a BP offshore oil rig exploded. About a month after the spill, the leaking oil made its way into the marshes of Louisiana, which will inevitably destroy already fragile wetlands vital to the protection and economy of the state.

4. In "Long Goodbye," Simon explains how the "island's original families grew from Frenchmen who married American Indian women," and that the tribal elders still speak in "their native Cajun French" (A-3).

5. This film, along with similar horror flicks set in the Louisiana swamps, can be viewed on the SyFy Channel, proving how widely such images of swamp terrors are disseminated through theater and television screens.

Works Cited

Allain, Mathé. "They Don't Even Talk Like Us: Cajun Violence in Film and Fiction." *Journal of Popular Culture* 23.1 (1989–1990): 65–75.
Alston, Joshua. "Give HBO Some Credit." *Newsweek* 22 Sept. 2008: 14.
Barry, John M. *Rising Tide: The Great Mississippi Flood of 1927 and How It Changed America.* 1997. New York: Touchstone, 1998.
"BTNEP Estuary Resources." Barataria-Terrebonne National Estuary Program. Jan. 2008. Web. 4 June 2009.
Conrad, Glenn R. "The Acadians: Myths and Realities." *The Cajuns: Essays on Their History and Culture.* 1978. Ed. Glenn R. Conrad. Lafayette: Center for Louisiana Studies, 1983. 1–18.
Falgoux, Woody. *Cajun Mariners: The Race for Big Oil.* Thibodaux, LA: Stockard James, 2007.
Frankenfish. Dir. Mark Dippé. Columbia-TriStar, 2004. TV.
Haunted Waters. Dir. Glen Pitre. Cote Blanche Productions, 1998. DVD.
Hebert-Leiter, Maria. "An Interview with Tim Gautreaux." *The Carolina Quarterly* 57.2 (Summer 2005): 66–74.
Hurricane on the Bayou. Dir. Greg MacGillivray. Written by Glen Pitre. MacGillivray Freeman Films, 2006. DVD.
McKay, Betsy. "After the Flood: In Louisiana, Diehards Cling to a Vanishing Isle." *Wall Street Journal* 17 Sept. 2008, Eastern ed.: A-1.
The Reaping. Dir. Stephen Hopkins. Warner Bros. Pictures, 2007. DVD.
Savage, Melissa, and John Hill. "Worry Over Wetlands." *State Legislatures* 34.7 (Jul./Aug. 2008): 38–43.
Schuth, H. Wayne. "The Images of Louisiana in Film and Television." *Southern Quarterly* 23.1 (1984): 5–17.
_____. "The Image of New Orleans on Film." *Southern Quarterly* 19.3-4 (1981): 240–45.
Simon, Darran. "Long Goodbye." *The Times-Picayune* [New Orleans] 22 Sept. 2008: A-1+.
The Skeleton Key. Dir. Iain Softley. Universal, 2005. DVD.
Southern Comfort. Dir. Walter Hill. Cinema Group. MGM, 1981. DVD.
Stivale, Charles J. *Disenchanting Les Bons Temps: Identity and Authenticity in Cajun Music and Dance.* Durham: Duke University Press, 2003.
Tidwell, Mike. *Bayou Farewell: The Rich Life and Tragic Death of Louisiana's Cajun Coast.* New York: Pantheon Books, 2003.
The Waterboy. Dir. Frank Coraci. Touchstone Pictures, 1998. DVD.
Wilson, Anthony. *Shadow and Shelter: The Swamp in Southern Culture.* Jackson: University Press of Mississippi, 2006.

XIV.

An Aesthetic of Play: A Contemporary Cinema of South-Sploitation

JAMES A. CRANK

In one of the main advertisements for the film *Black Snake Moan* (2006), Craig Brewer's huge and caricatured romp through the South's history of racial and sexual exploitation, the dual images on either side of the poster suggest a binary that Brewer reverses in many of his films. Christina Ricci, the white heroine of the film, is wrapped seductively in chains, while Samuel Jackson, Brewer's African American protagonist, menacingly holds the shackles before him: "Everything is hotter down South," reads the dime-store font. In a move that is both playful and disturbing, *Black Snake Moan*'s advertisement anticipates the way the film ostensibly calls into question the validity of Southern tropes. Significantly, though, *Black Snake Moan* does not offer a reversal of traditional Southern binaries such as slave/master in order to discredit racial assumptions or challenge traditional discourses on Southern femininity or sexuality. Rather, Brewer seems to insist throughout his film that these curious monoliths that represent cultural touchstones for reading the South in American cinema are no less valid because of their dominance. In fact, watching *Black Snake Moan*, one gets the distinct impression that Brewer does more playing than challenging, is more interested in ornamentation than identity.

Brewer's preoccupation with presenting the American South as a brutal, Christ-haunted landscape of sexual freaks and racial violence clearly belongs to a trajectory established early in the twentieth century: American cinema has a long tradition of using the South as both character and caricature. D.W. Griffith established the course for the cinematic South in his *Birth of a Nation* (1915), in which he articulated a mythology of the Southerner as beautiful loser, defender of a primitive and inimitably defensible culture. Griffith's presentation of the Southerner as honorable class warrior marked a shift in how American culture had perceived the people of the South in the early twentieth century. Griffith transformed the South, once the subject of ridicule, into a proud land full of a determined people, who fought bravely for the tenants of white supremacy. Film scholar Edward Campbell notes that in *Birth of a Nation*, Griffith successfully presented for the first time a "stereotyped South [that] finally became eminently respectable to many who before had shunned film." Such a success was noteworthy in that it pointed "to a unity of Northern and Southern whites, joined in an appreciation of the latter's adherence to tradition" (58). In short, in *Birth of a Nation*, Griffith popularized Southern nationalism and white supremacy by articulating a mythic South engaged in the important work of a continued racialized war. This South, the invented figment of white paranoia, dominated American cinema for half a century in films like *Gone with the Wind* (Fleming, 1936) and *The Little Colonel* (Butler, 1935). Through these movies, American audiences could simultaneously sympathize with and feel superior to the Southern people they encountered through the screen. Hollywood had found a golden formula that was immensely popular not just in northern states but throughout the South as well. By 1940, the creation of the mythic cinematic South became a popular commodity.

By the middle of the century, directors like Elia Kazan and Martin Ritt appropriated Griffith's vision with an extra twist: in films such as *Baby Doll* (1956) and *The Long, Hot Summer* (1958), cinematic representations of Southerners showed a people afflicted with not only a deep, racial anxiety but also a primitive, combustible and overpowering sexuality. The "lust-under-the-magnolias clichés" (Adams 144) that permeated American cinematic portrayals of the South from the 1950s to 1970s suggested the South as land of sexual taboo, a place where unquenchable homosexual, interracial and even interfamilial sexual desires were explored behind closed doors. Extremely popular with moviegoers (and excoriated by critics), films like *Tobacco Road* (Ford, 1941) and *Mandingo* (Fleischer, 1975) ran into problems with censors over their shocking content. *Baby Doll*'s trailer drew the ire of the Catholic Legion of Decency, which called for a full ban of the film based on its sexually promiscuous message, and *Mandingo*'s blend of sex and violence caused theater owners to pull it for fear of racial violence. Despite the inherent shock of sexual taboo (*Mandingo*'s advertisements contained the tag line: "Expect the savage, the sensual, the shocking, the sad, the powerful, the shameful. Expect the truth."), these films presented the South as a site where forbidden passions were given implicit authority, where incest, pedophilia and rape were understandable products of a primitive people and their sad history. Griffith's mythic South of lost causes and white supremacy had given way to an imagined modern landscape of savage sexual brutality and promiscuity, and American audiences again bought into the Southern spectacle of an invented and evolving outland. The cinematic portrayal of Southerners as an uneducated, savage people inhibited by their primitive religious beliefs yet bursting with sexual potency owed a good part of its creation to a perspective popularized by H. L. Mencken in his scathing article "Sahara of the Bozart" (1917). However, what Mencken criticized, directors like Ritt and Kazan revered. Mid-century cinema about the South largely transformed Mencken's land of artless and primitive people into an exaggerated celebration of all things backward and taboo.

For much of the twentieth century, American cinema addressed a South that is not so much a location as it is an idea — often a re-enforcing perspective of non–Southern American smugness, or an expression of cultural superiority written in broad strokes. What is particular, though, about these mannered and caricatured films is an often comical self-awareness of their vision of the South, a place simultaneously exaggerated and stark. From *Birth of a Nation*, to the mid-century lurid explorations of Southern iconography, to the explosion of sexual taboo in the 1960s and 1970s, these films might reasonably be grouped together as a cinema of South-sploitation,[1] a term that acknowledges the transformation of a real history and place into a site of outlandish grotesquery, a land of exotic, terrible violence, ignorance, and uninhibited sexual taboo. The cinema of South-sploitation thrives on entrenching the binaries that dogged Southern history — North and South, white and black, slave and master, Southern belle and whore — and has helped to create a mythic South, a place Houston Baker and Dana Nelson find necessary for the stability of American cultural memory: "In order for there to exist a good union, there must be a recalcitrant, secessionist 'splitter'" (235). South-sploitation cinema invents a South that as a matter of course denies complexity, resists sophistication, and relishes stereotype and singularity.

South-sploitation cinema's obsession with racial violence or the Southern primitive is, of course, not a unique preoccupation. Southern writers like Erskine Caldwell, Harry Crews and Flannery O'Connor often focused on the darkness inherent in Southern culture. In their novels, the Southerner's obsession with the past frequently manifested itself through a distortion in the present. Many times, so-called "Southern gothic" writers explored cultural myths about their homeland — the savagery of the Southern man, the promiscuity of the Southern woman, and the poor white Southerner paralyzed between the extremes of his desires and an unwavering religious faith — as a means of contradicting or deconstructing their validity. The connections between the cinema of South-sploitation and Southern writers like William Faulkner, Flannery O'Connor, and Tennessee Williams are clear, and the debt that these films owe to these authors certainly cannot be overestimated (*The Long, Hot Summer* was based very loosely on Faulkner's comic trilogy, and Williams wrote the screenplay for Kazan's *Baby Doll*). However, Southern writers expressed a vision that, for the most part, resisted binaries and monoliths as necessary tools to express the South's identity; those same tropes that Southern gothic writers denied, South-sploitation films like *Baby Doll* or *Deliverance* (John Boorman's campy 1972 adaptation of James Dickey's novel) largely embraced. Indeed, many films in the canon of what might be considered South-sploitation cinema are adaptations of Southern novels, absent the author's original vision. Critic Michael Adams notes of Ritt's *The Long, Hot Summer*, that the director dealt "only superficially" with the material he is given by Faulkner and was instead "attracted again and again to the region's backwardness" (153–154), while Campbell writes of the Southern novel's transition to the screen in mid-century that Hollywood "concentrated on the sensational effect [of the books], threatening any message the already emasculated adaptations retained" (159). If Southern writers from the 1930s to the 1960s engaged with and deconstructed the myths of their homeland, South-sploitation films from the beginning of the century to the 1970s, for the most part, re-affirmed the stereotype and mythology of the deep South.

In recent films such as *The Reaping* (Hopkins, 2007) and *The Skeleton Key* (Softley, 2005), directors have returned to the tradition, themes, tropes, and preoccupations of South-sploitation cinema. Instead of resisting or revising the perspective, many contemporary American directors have co-opted South-sploitation cinema as a way of actively articulating some concept of the South's identity in twenty-first century America. Brewer's *Black Snake Moan* ostensibly takes exception to the South's portrayal in contemporary popular culture as a savage and unfamiliar place. Brewer tells an interviewer, "I was looking to do a movie with my Southern obsessions and my Southern archetypes.... What blaxploitation movies were to *Hustle & Flow*, your dry then mud-slap honey moon shiner Southern girl in daisy dukes shorts ... gator bait ... visual aesthetic [is to *Black Snake Moan*]" (Carr). Brewer begins *Black Snake Moan* as an exercise in reclaiming some real notion of the South from the broad strokes of its own campy mythology.

Like Brewer's previous film, *Hustle & Flow* (2005), *Black Snake Moan* dialogues actively with the translation of African American experience into Southern music. *Moan* engages the blues in the same way *Hustle* explores hip-hop culture. *Black Snake Moan* follows the stories of Lazarus, a down-on-his-luck blues musician in the Mississippi delta, and Rae, an abused and battered woman who is also a violent and compulsive nymphomaniac. Finding her on the side of the road one morning badly beaten by her boyfriend's best friend, Lazarus takes in the woman and attempts to heal her. When she gets up enough strength to leave, however, Lazarus chains her to his radiator until he can "cure" her of her need for sex. Brewer admits that such a preposterous plot and broad characters invite criticism but claims, "I can't believe people are thinking this is, like, a documentary — that this goes on in the South every day.... It doesn't, but 'Tobacco Road' doesn't happen every day in the South, either. 'Baby Doll,' the Elia Kazan movie, doesn't happen every day either. But we give those movies a pass" (Zacharek).

Part of the reason that Brewer uses *Black Snake Moan* as a way to engage with the themes of South-sploitation cinema seems to be out of respect and admiration for the tradition itself. Of his style in the movie, Brewer says, "I look at movies like *Baby Doll* by Kazan and books by Flannery O'Connor and Faulkner and they take place in palpable, authentic looking worlds that people sometimes don't have any context or continuity to, especially when it comes to the South" (Brevet). In conflating contrasting visions of Kazan (a director) with that of Faulkner (an author), Brewer confuses his argument; more than that, by attempting to integrate the overdrawn world of Kazan and O'Connor into some meaningful representation of the South or Southerners Brewer contradicts himself in key moments.

Black Snake Moan eventually becomes a debate between authenticity (Brewer is a native of Memphis and considers himself a Southerner) and artifice. On one hand, Brewer wants to have something meaningful to say about the South's history or the culture of violence, misogyny and racism, but on the other hand, he uses the spectacle of South-sploitation cinema to address these real issues. Consequently, the film becomes a schizophrenic and disjointed attempt to have it both ways. At the beginning of the film, Brewer's character Lazarus is a deeply flawed man attempting to do the best he can. We learn in the opening scene that his wife has decided to leave him because of his obsessive need to control her life. By the end of the film, however, Lazarus becomes an over-the-top descendant of God's divine blessing; he cures Rae's sickness, builds her shattered confidence, and declares his controlling personality as a new kind of religious fervor. These shifts in character make Brewer's symbolic narrative muddy and contradictory. However, Brewer argues, "I'm not writing from a place of progress. I'm not writing a movie that I want people to necessarily intellectualize. And I think that really messes with people who feel that they need to make a statement against this, and they don't quite know what it is they're against." But, in the same interview, Brewer bemoans the fact that his audiences are not intellectual enough to understand the movie's symbolic narrative: "Because man alive, you look at this imagery on this poster, and I'm so obviously banging this drum. It's like, you really believe that I believe *this?* That women need to be chained up? Can we not think metaphorically once race and gender are introduced?" (Zacharek).

"Everything is hotter down South": Samuel L. Jackson stars as a struggling black man who reduces Christina Ricci to bondage in order to cure her nymphomania in Craig Brewer's *Black Snake Moan* (2007, Paramount).

By articulating his vision for the South through the lens of South-sploitation cinema, Brewer offers a difficult paradox. Throughout the film, he tackles real issues: Rae's horrific abuse at the hands of her mother's partner, the huge chasm between the world of the poor, Southern white and the African American, and the difficulty of imagining the Southern underclass. Throughout the film, though, while his obsession with larger than life imagery translates on the big screen as lurid and exaggerated posturing, his insistence on exploring meaningful ideas such as racial hatred and class conflicts (as well as presenting characters outside Lazarus and Rae's backlit world) undermines any meaning he creates. Brewer's profession of admiration for movies such as *Baby Doll* and *The Long, Hot Summer* makes clear that he is not deconstructing the myth of those films. If anything, his film is fanboy ode to the golden age of South-sploitation, an attempt to recover and re-invent the visual aesthetic of an era when the South was mysterious, shocking, and exotic. That Brewer does not succeed in making his viewer feel in any way connected with that South — a landscape that rivals the cartoonish and artificial world of Disney's *Song of the South* (Foster and Jackson, 1946) — contradicts what seems to be a central point of his first film, *Hustle & Flow*: that such a mythologizing perspective does unspeakable damage to the race and class consciousness of Southerners.

Samuel Jackson's character of Lazarus is at the opposite end of the spectrum from Brewer's major character in *Hustle & Flow*, Terrence Howard's Djay. Lazarus is a God-fearing man whose love life exposes a palpable need for control and stability. Djay, on the other hand, is an out-of-control pimp living on the margins of the urban decay of downtown Memphis. For Djay, music — more specifically crunk hip hop — is the only critical outlet that allows him to articulate and understand his identity. For Lazarus, his music — the dingy hoarse blues of his grandfather — is a sickness that he must cure through repetition. When Lazarus takes out his acoustic guitar during a critical scene in the movie, the thunder rolls and the lightning cracks. Brewer uses the blues as exorcism — driving both the demons of Rae's obsessive nymphomania and Lazarus's fear and depression into submission. But the music is double-dealing: it both heals and sickens; it is the reason behind and the cure for Lazarus's sickness. Even though by playing his song, Lazarus is able to deliver Rae, who clutches at his knees, to a safe harbor, the music stirs in him a simultaneous rage and depression. If music is a powerful force for redemption in *Hustle & Flow*, blues is an unshakable and haunting fever in *Black Snake Moan*. Brewer's own title suggests his ambivalence: "Black Snake Moan" references an actual 1920s recording by Blind Lemon Jefferson that articulates deep loss, anguish and depression, while simultaneously suggesting a distinctly racial sexuality. The song itself is an ode to ambivalence, and Brewer's sensationalized use of it throughout his film suggests that this particular expression of sorrow is colored with a dark sexuality.

Brewer's characters in *Hustle & Flow* deny the American perspective on Southerners through their reliance on sincerity, honesty and connection. *Black Snake Moan*, on the other hand, explores artifice, confusion and disconnection, and as a consequence, Brewer's use of South-sploitation imagery is less thematic than it is prescriptive: he ends his film in the same place it began, and suggests that a lazy obsession with mythologizing the South may actually reveal a truth it ostensibly obscured. In the end, *Black Snake Moan* becomes little more than one Southern filmmaker's struggle between his love for the spectacle of South-sploitation cinema and his genuine desire for substance and meaning.

Brewer's aesthetic in *Black Snake Moan* is only one in a number of many recent films that actively engage the perspective of South-sploitation cinema; like Brewer, these contemporary directors often offer South-sploitation's spectacle as self-conscious ornamentation. But, in the end, films like *The Skeleton Key* or *The Reaping* seemingly affirm South-sploitation's aesthetic as a valid perspective for articulating the South's identity. If Brewer has any anxiety over his debate between meaning and artifice as a Southern filmmaker (including questions of responsibility, perspective and metaphor), one hardly feels the consequences of that debate in *The Reaping*. Set in a small Louisiana bayou-town, *The Reaping* concerns Katherine Winter (Hilary Swank), a professor at Louisiana State University and a professional, scientific debunker of miracles and myths. The professor meets her match when the residents of small-town Haven, Louisiana come to her because their bayou has apparently been turned into blood. Believing the event to be one of the signs of the ten Biblical plagues, the townspeople hope Winter might disprove their suspicions.

As a movie that deals with the themes and preoccupations associated with South-sploitation cinema, *The Reaping* appears to be a tired and unimaginative piece of recycling; however, watching the film one cannot help but wonder: could this movie have been set outside of the American South? Throughout their exploration of small town Louisiana, the filmmakers suggest that the South's inherent religiosity is itself a kind of horror. As opposed to the enlightened, modern world of Baton Rouge — a world primarily shown through the lens of LSU and the academy — the small bayou town is creepy, strangely insular, and bleak. Professor Winter enters this backwoods outland with the smugness of her skepticism but is shocked to find that the "miracles" she comes to disprove have no scientific explanation. At the same time, the audience understands that Winter's own religious faith is in crisis (based primarily on her husband and daughter's murder by cult radicals during her time as a missionary in the Sudan). By the middle of the confused plot, the audience conceivably understands *The Reaping*'s inherent message as a strong suggestion that the South's obsession with religion represents a primitive savageness that exists nowhere else in America.

In the small Louisiana town, the ten plagues from Exodus are recreated locally, with the town's water supply turning to blood, an invasion of lice and frogs, and permanent darkness. Besides engaging the primitiveness of "the Saintly South," *The Reaping* expresses a somber obsession with the Southern gothic trope of religious zealotry connected to violence and terror. The true horror of the movie comes from a shocking psychic disruption between the natural world and the religious world. As the narrative pushes towards its climax, we learn that the biblical plagues are not (as we have been led to believe from the townspeople) a direct result of the coming of the antichrist in the version of a young girl, but in fact, a punishment for the town's evil. By the time we are treated to the plagues, the connection to another more personal narrative is obvious: the specter of Hurricane Katrina haunts the audience throughout the film.

The Reaping's filming in southern Louisiana, in fact, was interrupted by Katrina, and during that small break, the narrative of the film (including the engagement with the themes of South-sploitation cinema) seem heightened into ridiculous proportions; throughout the film, one finds a lingering and disturbing question over the responsibility of American intellectuals to the poor, backward, storm-ravaged folks of the South. One critic describes the mess as an "unsettling mix of Southern gothic and Old Testament huggermugger" (Rea D10), but the use of a term like "Southern gothic" here is troubling. The phrase, which once explained a certain tendency in Southern fiction writers, now seems to be reified not into just a genre, but a way to engage South-sploitation cinema's perspective. Contemporary Southern gothic cinema is less a set of themes or ideas than a glorified excuse to exorcise America's paranoia over issues of class, race and gender. For a film to engage with Southern gothic, it must first invert or eliminate a sense of realism; the cartoonish subversion allows the American filmmaker to re-define questions of class, race and gender in an unapologetic and largely exploitative way. Further, it presents an arena in which directors and screenwriters can present cultural stereotypes and racialized violence in a consequence-free environment. Southern gothic films, it seems, do little more than advocate and re-affirm South-sploitation cinema's artistic validity. Hiding under the guise of the Southern gothic, a contemporary cinema of South-sploitation disguises its meaning though it cannot hide its campy aesthetic.

The Skeleton Key offers a similar engagement with Southern gothic and the South's history of racial violence. The film follows Caroline Ellis, a hospice provider, who agrees to be the caretaker of Ben Devereaux, an invalid stroke victim in a tiny Louisiana parish. Caroline notices strange goings-on in the house between Ben and his wife Violet that she finds connected to hoodoo rituals. Originally from New Jersey, Caroline investigates the unfamiliar world of spells and curses only to discover that Violet Devereaux and the family lawyer Luke are really hoodoo priests Mama Cecile and Papa Justify, two African American servants who were supposedly lynched in the early twentieth century for performing rituals with white children. By the end of the film, Caroline (and the audience) discovers that the priests actually switched bodies with the children on the night they were lynched and continue to lure unsuspecting (white) dupes to their mansion in the tiny Louisiana parish in order to switch bodies, thus ensuring them eternal life. Mama Cecile exits Violet Devereaux's body for Caroline's, and the movie ends with the two hoodoo priests exchanging meaningful glances at one another in their new, young, white bodies.

The Skeleton Key's narrative shares striking similarities with that of *The Reaping*: Caroline must abandon her skepticism over inexplicable events and suffer through her unfamiliarity with the bleak world of small-town Louisiana by transforming her perspective. However, while *The Reaping* used the world of the poor, white Southerner as the site of the unknown, *The Skeleton Key* attempts to frighten its audience through the dark, mysterious and unknowable world of "primitive" African rituals. It is significant that Caroline is an outsider to not just the world of hoodoo but the South itself. Her naiveté about the mystery and darkness of the history of racial violence in the South makes her the perfect dupe for the double-dealing hoodoo priests. By the end of the film, we understand that the white perspective of disbelief is symptomatic of its inability to understand the primitive and dark nature of an African religion. Thus, the movie ends with the oppressed African Americans living on through the bodies of their white subjects, dark doppelgangers who threaten the normalcy of the modern, white South with their supernatural form of "passing." *The Skeleton Key* expresses a white anxiety about the inability to know the other, racialized self that could only have been set in one place, the cartoonish and caricatured landscape of South-sploitation cinema.

The Skeleton Key, The Reaping and *Black Snake Moan* all take an aesthetic of South-sploitation cinema as a starting place for an exploration of some real aspect of Southern culture. *The Skeleton Key* offers commentary on the consequences of racial naiveté. *The Reaping* attempts to create an entertaining and frightening experience that engages with our collective fears regarding mystery and faith, and *Black Snake Moan* begins as a dialogue with the cinema of exploitation and the silliness of Southern stereotypes. By the end of all of these films, however, we are left with a confusing and distorted idea of what the South means in American culture. While all these films engage with issues of real meaning — issues of class, race, religion, faith — and how those issues manifest themselves in unique ways in the South, none of them offer any conclusion beyond the easiest explanation: that the South is a victim of its own past, and continues to be the site of the violent, the savage, and the backwards. Southern critics should take exception, however, with how South-sploitation cinema distorts and subverts the American South and the Southerner into meaningless stereotype. Rather than deepening and re-invigorating the metaphorical landscape of the South — as I would argue Southern fiction writers like O'Connor or Faulkner did — such cinema reduces the South to a cultural anathema, a setting where all of America's latent and unspeakable anxieties are given authentication and validation through the unspeaking voice of place.

Southern filmmakers like Craig Brewer often articulate their desire to change the South's perception by exploring the very stereotypes and cultural myths that are embedded in American consciousness. In *Hustle & Flow*, Brewer engages the myth of the South's urban ghetto and redefines it as a site that produces creativity, beauty and art. In *Black Snake Moan*, Brewer claims, "look, you can't do a movie about the blues and not explore biblical imagery and Southern iconography.... *Hustle and Flow* is about discovering creativity about making art. *Black Snake Moan* is about being caught in that wicked place... It's this thing that's in your mind; that's in your soul, that's in your gut, that's coming to get you because it knows yourself" (Morales). But through his exploration of Southern iconography, Brewer provides little more than decoration. His film is a dazzling spectacle, but is, at best, an empty shell; at its worst, *Black Snake Moan* becomes essentially a vitriolic validation of the South's place in America.

What is remarkable is that an emphasis on presenting the South as an American outland where "all the race baiting yahoos" live (Baker 235) has persisted into the twenty-first century. Film scholars are quick to point out that a broadly defined cinema of exploitation engages race and ethnicity (see blaxploitation), or gender, but few Southern critics seem to be concerned over the South's place in American cinema. Such an oversight may be based on limited perspective; in the last six years, scholars of Southern culture and literature have begun to expand the conventional topics of what, to this point, has sometimes been an introspective and flat field of study. Southern studies mostly centered its debates over questions of regional geography and authenticity (What states belong in the South? Where is the authentic South?) and a frequently narrow white perspective. More and more, however, current scholars of Southern culture have complicated the notion of the South to include a broader vision, one that recognizes the Southern perspective as a global discourse that engages multiple perspectives. This new discipline, labeled by Baker as "new Southern studies," looks to Southern culture, literature and film to contest traditional and conventional notions of the South as a central idea perpetuated by its inhabitants; rather, it invites the disparities of culture, place and ethnicity to create a definition of the South that is constantly revised and expanded. It seems to me that scholars of Southern film are especially critical in this emerging discipline, for it is often in film that Southern life is misrepresented, exploited and misread, where its complexities and multiple perspectives are neutered and collapsed. New Southern studies offers a way of reading films like *Black Snake Moan* in order to point out what seems to be its central paradox: though Brewer invests himself in reversing traditional binaries of South-sploitation cinema, his film largely insists that those binaries are credible ways to engage Southern culture. More than that, the critical perspective of "new Southern studies" resists Brewer's black/white binary as the only monolithic perspective to reading racial matters in Southern literature, art, and film.

Though Brewer's films have some die-hard admirers, *Black Snake Moan* did not perform well at American box offices. The same is true for both *The Skeleton Key* and *The Reaping*, which critics attacked for their laughable and preposterous presentations of the South. And even though filmmaker Kevin Smith has compared *Black Snake Moan* to a Faulkner novel, most critics of the film agree with *New Yorker* critic David Brody, who labeled it a "heady rural stew of violence, race, lust and religion [that] strains after Faulknerian depth but is mostly Southern-fried hooey" (51). I hope that the current popular response to these movies articulates dissatisfaction with the state of American South-sploitation cinema in the twenty first century. In an era when we have Southern filmmakers attempting to project images of the South that engage Southern tropes and revise Southern identity—films like Duvall's *The Apostle* (1997), Morrison's *Junebug* (2007) or Gordon Green's *George Washington* (2000) and *Undertow* (2004)—South-sploitation cinema's playful spectacle seems quaint, decorative and outdated.

Notes

1. I want to differentiate between the term "south-sploitation" and what film critic Scott Von Doviak refers to as "hixploitation" in his *Hick Flicks: The Rise and Fall of Redneck Cinema* (McFarland 2004). Von Doviak's term refers to cinema centered on the Southern redneck, from 1970s trucker movies to the hillbilly horror movies of the 1980s; in Von Doviak's argument, hixploitation represents a specific cinema rooted in a historical moment (largely from 1960–1980) that exploits the stereotype of the Southern male "redneck" (and often his relationship with automobiles). South-sploitation cinema, however, engages a number of Southern tropes, including the "burden" of Southern history, racial oppression, gender roles, and sexuality in films throughout the twentieth century.

Works Cited

Adams, Michael. "'How Come Everyone Down Here Has Three Names?': Martin Ritt's Southern Films." *The South and Film*. Ed. Warren French. Jackson: University Press of Mississippi, 1981. 143–155.

Baker, Houston A., and Dana Nelson. "Preface: Violence, the Body and 'The South.'" *American Literature* 73.2 (2001): 231–244.

Brevet, Brad. "Craig Brewer Chats 'Black Snake Moan.'" *RopeofSilicon.com*. Web. 5 December 2009.

Brody, David. Rev. of *Black Snake Moan*. *The New Yorker* 83.4 (March 2007): 48–51.

Campbell, Edward D. C., Jr. *The Celluloid South: Hollywood and the Southern Myth*. Knoxville: University of Tennessee Press, 1981.

Carr, Kevin. "An Interview with Craig Brewer, Director of 'Black Snake Moan.'" *7M Pictures*. Web. 3 December 2009.

Morales, Wilson. "*Black Snake Moan* Preview." *Blackfilm.com*. Web. 6 December 2009.

Rea, Steven. Rev. of *The Reaping*. *The Philadelphia Inquirer* 4 April 2007. D1, D10.

Von Doviak, Scott. *Hick Flicks: The Rise and Fall of Redneck Cinema*. Jefferson, NC: McFarland, 2004.

Zacharek, Stephanie. "We're Bound to Each Other." *Salon*. Web. 5 December 2009.

XV.

"You Taste of America": *Talladega Nights, Deliverance,* and Southern Studies

TARA POWELL

My favorite movie of 2006 was a New South car racing parody featuring dysfunctional suburbanites from North Carolina crashing cars and fighting homosexual anxieties and big scary cats, both literal and figurative, in their back seats while driving fast to victory. Yet, despite relying for much of its humor on the vigorous use of hackneyed regional stereotypes, *Talladega Nights: The Ballad of Ricky Bobby* ultimately blurs regional and national identity in a manner that not only participates in interesting ways in NASCAR's twenty-first century remarketing campaign, but also in the selective revision of the Southern sense of its own exceptionalism on which redneck films and NASCAR's regional appeal both have historically depended. "Sir, you taste of America," declares French driver Jean Girard (Sacha Baron Cohen) after finally earning an unexpected kiss from Ricky (Will Ferrell) near the end of *Talladega Nights*. Indeed, the American journey, signified by Huck's great river and played on by Southern writers from Mark Twain to James Dickey to Lee Smith, has flowed to Talladega. The film opened far bigger than anyone expected and then just kept going, setting records for original comedy box office takes, as well as for product placement. Audiences loved *The Ballad of Ricky Bobby*, just as they gobble other mass-produced images of Southern spaces that suggest today's South has nothing to do with race or history, and everything to do with NASCAR and barbecue and SEC football. At the conclusion of *Talladega Nights*, however, the film suggests it has consciously been exploring—and exploiting—this hunger when, after the credits roll, we are treated to Ricky Bobby's sons' ambivalent reading of the portrayal of post-agrarian regional identity in William Faulkner's "The Bear." In this sense,

Talladega Nights is the *Deliverance* (1972) for our time, responding to white anxieties about the suburbanization of the rural South by commodifying and colonizing its stereotypes, thrusting them in the path of the modern world as a way of contesting traditional distinctions between American regional and national identities. Though film critics and scholars have not accorded *Talladega Nights* the same kind of attention as they have the adaptation of Dickey's novel, and certainly the creative boundaries *Talladega Nights* pushes are not the same as those bulldozed by the earlier film, still, the two films share a number of striking parallels as they both operate at the margins of so-called "serious" film to interrogate ways in which popular culture iconography can be self-consciously deployed to renegotiate regional identity in the postmodern South. Both films turn symbolically and literally on the threatened sexualities of anxious, straight white males, who respond to the pressures of suburban life by trying to reinhabit a mythical Southern past. By considering the respective places of these two films' performances of post-agrarian rage against middle-class American suburbia in the history of redneck film iconography, I suggest that the projects intersect in a mutual erasure of historical measures of Southern distinctiveness, including both rurality and race consciousness — the erasures of which permit the nationalization of contemporary markers of regional identity.

At the beginning of Dickey's 1970 novel *Deliverance*, the epigraph he chooses from French mystic Georges Bataille suggests that the common human condition is to feel inadequate. Both the novel and the film directed by John Boorman that followed it two years later rely upon their audiences' ability to relate to that feeling of frustration as a motive for the adventure on which protagonist Ed Gentry embarks with his friends. In order to move the viewer to understand both Ed's dissatisfaction with what Walker Percy might have called the "everydayness" of his middle class life in Atlanta as an advertising executive, and his belief that a remedial trip into a doomed wilderness might somehow ameliorate that dissatisfaction, Dickey's novel and Boorman's film must both tap into the reservoir of three centuries of American redneck iconography that portrays poor whites as what Anthony Harkins has called "the white other [that] has served ... as a continually negotiated mythic space through which modern Americans have attempted to define themselves and their national identity and to reconcile the past and the present" (4). Though sometimes the hillbilly is portrayed as evil and other times innocent, his redneckery is almost always seen as granting access to a lost American self because of its closeness to wilderness. Jim Goad's *Redneck Manifesto* (1997) asserts that, either way, Southern rednecks are "America's id" (89), pointing out, "the redneck rapists in *Deliverance* rise from the bushes spittin' evil, no explanation (besides domicile) is given for their degeneracy" (98). Further, Steven Knepper's essay "Do You Know What the *Hail* You're Talkin' About?" suggests that, in the novel, both Ed's demonization of poor whites and Lewis's romanticizing "of the Appalachian rural poor have little to do with reality and much to do with personal preoccupations and phobias" (23). In part because the film elides much of the novel's backstory and conflates Ed's and Lewis' different stereotypes of mountain people, audiences and readers have tended to believe that *Deliverance* foregrounds only the viciousness of its two most famous redneck characters. Still, in both versions, it is Lewis's concurrent romanticizing of mountain people and their surroundings that not only gets him and his friends all out on the river in the first place, but then colors Ed's interpretation of Drew's death and all his subsequent choices, and ultimately, permits him to reinhabit his suburban life with a re-authenticating sense of joy about his secret triumph in the struggle of life and death.

Dickey commented that though he had mixed feelings about the filmmaker's decision to represent "the hand of the past reaching up out of the lake in a nightmare" (Thesing and Wright 38), he felt that it was in general in keeping with the main idea of his novel. In Pamela Barnett's essay, "James Dickey's *Deliverance*: Southern, White, Suburban Male Nightmare or Dream Come True?" she persuasively suggests, however, that the lake contains more Southernness than simply Ed's hillbilly id reaching up out of the past. She writes, "Ed explicitly associates his sense of emasculation with his Southernness" because "While Ed's crisis is contemporaneous with a host of national challenges to white male power, these challenges were felt most deeply in the Southern states" since "the South was a microcosm of the nation's most anxious responses to civil rights, black nationalism, and feminism" (146). Barnett connects Ed's need to "perform ... masculinity" directly with some of the markers of Southern identity that are written out of the novel's verbal space, including race, suggesting that only by considering the social climate of the 1960s South can one fully explain what Ed and the other white yuppies are doing out in the wilderness trying to live a version of masculine power that they see as disappearing. The idea of "performing" masculinity runs throughout the novel and echoes in the movie version, as well, as Ed's career in advertising makes him especially sensitive to questions of authenticity, the necessity of playing roles, and the differences between appearance and reality. Though he deals in appearances, he has the sense that reality has a texture all its own, and he is torn between the need to play roles and the desire to write his own life in a way that conforms to his sense of maverick Southern masculinity as celebrated in the frontier South as he understands it. He successfully defends his sexuality, saves the lives of two of his friends, and controls the narrative of his own life by both creating the "truth" for the outside world, as well as an internal narrative that explains and justifies his actions. In *Deliverance*, the frontier Southern past as represented by the redneck or hillbilly is literally wiped off the face of the earth at the end so that the physical and moral wilderness it represents live on only in Ed's mind, no longer visible beneath the still waters of suburbia or its recorded history.

Historians of what Scott Von Doviak dubbed "Hick Flicks" in his 2005 book by that name, point out that a "Southern" genre of film never emerged to compete with the western as such for a national audience, though there was a rise in hixploitation films in the 1970s whose success hinged on and ultimately died with the demise of the drive-in regional theater (French, Von Doviak). *Deliverance* was a highlight of hick horror in this period—a strain of popular film that eventually would be supplanted by automobile films such as *Smokey and the Bandit* (1977), which was part of what John Shelton Reed has identified as part of a pop culture rehabilitation of the South in the late 1970s (286). In 1981, Warren French suggested that perhaps *Smokey and the Bandit* and other "gasoline operas" represented "the South's best chance for rising again—this time cinematically" as "resourceful producers find new challenges for the 'bandits' who have traded in their stallions for thundering wheels" (13). Although the genre French envisioned never emerged as such, popular film and television have continued to work with redneck stereotypes, and there have been a number of interesting racing movies in the past 25 years that turn on Southerners' belief that, as Hazel Motes suggests in Flannery O'Connor's *Wise Blood* (1952), "Nobody with a good car needs to be justified" (113). Among the Southern gas opera's recent installments, *Talladega Nights* distinctively fetishizes the redneck not in terms of labor or association with a literal wilderness as in *Deliverance*, but in terms of stereotypical traits of poor or newly-monied whites that evoke a suburban version of that wilderness—tacky taste, tackier manners, bad hair, outsized Southern accents, bad diet, a propensity for alcohol and violence, stupidity and ignorance, and an obsession with masculinity as represented by sex and physical danger—in this case, "hot, nasty, badass speed." In this sense, the Bobby family is Dickey's hillbillies all cleaned up. In a parody of the familiar communal dinner scene that often represents the best of hillbilly extended family life in popular culture artifacts ranging from *The Waltons* to *Deliverance*, Ricky prays before a family meal:

> Dear Lord Baby Jesus, or as our brothers to the south call you, Jésus ... we thank you so much for this bountiful harvest of Domino's, KFC, and the always delicious Taco Bell. I just want to take time to say thank you for my family, my two beautiful, beautiful, handsome, striking sons, Walker and Texas Ranger, or T.R., as we call him. And of course my red hot smokin' wife, Carly, who is a stone cold fox ... who, if you would rate her ass on a scale of 100, it would easily be a 94.... Dear Lord Baby Jesus, we also like to thank you for my wife's father Chip. We hope that you can use your baby Jesus powers to heal him and his horrible leg. It smells terrible and the dogs are always bothering with it.

Although, on the one hand, the scene is a helpful shorthand for communicating the Bobby family's gross materialism and satirizes the hypocrisies of their version of evangelical Christianity, by operating in the rhetorical space of that familiar shorthand, it reinscribes the ways in which the film moves the redneck "wilderness" portrayed by *Deliverance* into a New South suburbia that has paved over the old wilderness, but remains in many ways unchanged. Though the prayer verbally acknowledges the realities of the twenty-first century multi-ethnic South, and director Adam McKay visually removes the family from the physical wilderness and even the rural communities in which those other dinner scenes took place, the portrayal of class here, as well as the image of physical deformity, suggest Ed and Lewis's view of their country cousins from *Deliverance* is very much alive, and only superficially updated, in 2006.

In scholar Hugh Ruppersburg's blog, "Films about the South," he makes clear in his entry on *Talladega Nights* that he does not mean by his attention to it to suggest that the movie "operates in a serious dimension, or that it seeks to be anything more than what it is, a comedy about American stock car racing, a satire of the American dream of personal satisfaction." Yet, I find this film, like *Deliverance*, quite eloquent in its way on all the hot topics in the field of Southern studies, including the global South, the reexamination of Southern exceptionalism, the commodification of regional identity, and the contested space of the Southern, even postsouthern self. In James Annesley's 1998 study *Blank Fictions*, he draws on the language of metafiction to recover popular urban fiction such as *Less Than Zero* (1985) and *American Psycho* (1991) as serious topics of academic concern, arguing, "Instead of regarding the presence of this range of mass cultural reference points as a measure of the novel's banality and an index of its weightlessness, these allusions can be interpreted as elements that root the text firmly to a precise material situation" (91). *The Ballad of Ricky Bobby* chronicles the life of a man whose prayers are sponsored by PowerAde, and it foregrounds its material situation so consistently, it might even be viewed as a pastiche of advertising strategies. Ricky's home and car are littered with products, as are the movie's credits and outtakes, and one of the film's key moments is when it is literally interrupted by an Applebee's commercial, further underscoring not just the film's time and place, but the story-ness of the film as text. The film's visual strategies not only spoof NASCAR's notorious commercialism, but also emphasize Ricky's bland, store-bought sense of his own national and regional identity. Like the urban novels Annesley considers, *Talladega Nights* participates in cultural work that requires one to be, in NASCAR terms, "dialed-in" to recognize. Though many of the film's reviewers debated over the purpose to which the film was skewering its Southern characters and their approval or disapproval of the movie depended at least in part on how they felt about the ethics of its use of redneck stereotypes, all recognized that the film was working with Southern stereotypes, despite its never referencing racial prejudice or rural life — and reviewers, like audiences, by and large took no interest in the ways the South buried beneath the parking lots of *Talladega Nights* shaped its audience's recognition of the cultural markers that propel the movie's sense of humor.

As Ricky dozes in the sun, discouraged and emasculated by losing his job, money, lady, car, and, most of all his nerve, his father Reese wakes him up by dousing him with three buckets of water and a pop quiz about the beginnings of NASCAR. Without a moment's hesitation, the usually clueless Ricky passes the test, automatically spouting the widely accepted tale — that it was born in the southeast out of the carryings-on of bootleggers trying to evade cops with cars full of moonshine during Prohibition. What follows is an archetypal *Smokey and the Bandit* style gas opera car chase that Reese initiates by telling his son that, to sharpen Ricky's driving skills, he has stashed heroin in the car and called the cops, so Ricky better drive fast. Then, we cheer Ricky on as he gets back to the sport's outlaw roots. It is a fun sequence that pays deliberate homage to redneck gas operas of the late 1970s by reifying the regional identity of the sport. Yet, sports historians and geographers tell us that this version of NASCAR's beginnings is mostly a durable bill of goods, that despite some early high profile drivers' connections to the world of moonshining, in fact people have been racing cars as long as there have been cars, that there was no particular Southern dominance to the sport when it was first organized in the late 1940s, and that the identification of stock car racing with the rural, working class South dates to a period in the 1960s which began for a set of fairly specific economic reasons and began to erode as soon as the organizers had the cash to run more races outside the region and started getting national sponsors in the 1970s — though not nearly fast enough for those national sponsors.

Recent work by sociologist Joshua Newman and his colleagues has illustrated how, "In contemporary sport culture, NASCAR is made important, and simultaneously problematic, by its Southern dialects and dialectics" ("NASCAR and the 'Southernization'" 482). Newman and Adam Beissel's essay, "The Limits to 'NASCAR Nation': Sport and the 'Recovery Movement' in Disjunctive Times," reveals, among other things, that NASCAR founder Bill France and his heirs deliberately worked to promote racing as a "localized sport enterprise" (521) in the early years, an enterprise that

> celebrat[ed] ... the economic (and cultural) logics of industrialism and of the localness of this emergent "Southern" sporting subculture.... Juxtaposed against a pervasive lynch mob vigilantism, Ku Klux Klan-led public spectacles, and

spectacles of political racism of the US Civil Rights Era, NASCAR emerged as an insatiably conservative sporting and cultural space during the late Civil Rights Era... [522–523].

In short, as Newman has illustrated in several studies of Southern sporting spectacle, the "Southernness" of NASCAR, and the neo-Confederate signifiers that have gone with it since the 1960s, especially the Confederate flags that are ubiquitous at racing events inside and outside of the South, all emerged in the 1960s as a marketing tool that consciously responded to social upheaval by affirming white Southern community amidst and against social change at an opportune moment of white anxiety. "Through the propagation of Old South conservative values and exclusionary practices," Newman writes, "NASCAR races brought to life a contextually important, racial homogeneity that not only excluded those nonwhite Southern subjects, but *created symbolic value out of that exclusivity*" (523).

Though NASCAR has spent several decades trying to detach itself from the racially-derived "symbolic value" of that market, Von Doviak observes in his discussion of representations of stock car racing in American film, "The change in NASCAR's demographics continues to outpace the change in NASCAR's image by several laps" (102), and numerous others have recorded the objections of white Southern fans and drivers over the past twenty years to advertisers and organizers' attempts to sanitize stock car racing's image in terms of class and regional identity. Richard Pillsbury observes, "The mythology that has always bound stock car racing to the rural Southerner is clearly in jeopardy, just as the entire Southern mythology itself moves toward the brink of absolute change" (294). Indeed, Jim Wright, upon visiting the track where much of *Talladega Nights* was to be filmed a few years later, wrote, "For the most part, Charlotte's 'Southernness' is a caricature.... The track — one of the few meaningful links that remain between the modern city and its own legacy — is about the only thing left in Charlotte that would make one think of it as a Southern city" (15). Though I think this is probably an overstatement, Wright's basic point, that Southern fans' investment in the sport's symbolic mythology is considerable, is a good one. In Scott Poole's essay, "'White Knuckle Ride': Stock Cars and Class Identity in the Postmodern South," he describes how anxious Southern yuppies use stock car racing as a way to "purchas[e] identity" via "a tie to a rough-neck Southern past, even if they themselves have little connection to that past" (8), and colorfully terms the phenomenon "post-agrarian road rage" (7). Wright, somewhat more approvingly, with an example that makes me think of *Deliverance* and the city boys heading into the wilderness, explains, "NASCAR people are unambiguously, defiantly, proudly country folk — and that's true even if they live in downtown Atlanta" (156).

The process of broadening the appeal of stock car racing in the United States and abroad has been one of trying to hang onto traditional fans invested in the mythological version of its supposed Southern roots, while at the same time shedding enough of the negative associations with redneckery to appeal to mainstream America, including women and people of color likely to feel a less romantic attachment to the Southern past and the sense of white community on which NASCAR's marketing strategy once depended. Part of that project has required sanitizing Southern redneck iconography to be less exceptional, a project that has placed racing and films like *Talladega Nights* at an interesting crossroads in terms of the renegotiation of Southern identity. As geographer Derek Alderman and his colleagues note,

> Rather than being removed from issues of regional culture, stock car racing is increasingly an arena for defining and debating southern identity. The complete desegregation of Winston Cup racing involves more than simply NASCAR transcending its connection with the South. On the contrary, it requires that the association address how southernness is open to multiple and competing interpretations [244–245].

Diversity drives, ad campaigns, the visibility of nonsouthern drivers such as Jeff Gordon and even the rare nonwhite driver such as Juan Pablo Montoya, as well as efforts to decrease the visibility of Confederate flags in favor of American ones on cable TV, have all met with some limited success over the past decade and change. Scholars, however, have identified a kind of "consumer backlash" as the traditional "local" fan base resists the globalizing market strategies that threaten to take their sport away from them. Newman and Beissel point out that finding a way for these strategies to work together is essential to the sport's future and observe that "selective remembering of the sport's history speaks to the complex plasticity of a globalized NASCAR local that extracts elements of the 'traditional,' while emphasizing a *faux* cultural maturation of its contemporary cosmopolitanism" (532). Newman with Giardina in fact specifically call out *Talladega Nights* for the fact that although "the Talladega venue is notorious in NASCAR circles as one of the most Confederate-flag-saturated tracks on the circuit, the symbol is strangely absent from Hollywood mediations of the space. Moreover, the track is transformed into a site of tolerance...." They call the South of *Talladega Nights* a "Southern simulacra" and a "dream world" that superficially proposes a multi-ethnic South, all the while "situating heteronormative White masculinity at the center of power" ("NASCAR and the 'Southernization'" 492–493).

Just as Barnett suggests knowledge of the social upheaval of the 1960s is necessary for contemporary readers to understand why white Southern yuppies would feel the need to head into the woods to prove their manhood in *Deliverance*, Newman and others who unpack the history of NASCAR give us con-

All-American NASCAR driver Ricky Bobby (Will Ferrell) poses in front of the American flag (2006, Sony Pictures).

text for understanding Ricky's desire to "wanna go fast" and bust up white suburbia in 2006 — even as the film participates in NASCAR's efforts to mainstream its own Southernness. The bulldozed history beneath the lake in *Deliverance* that drives the action of both the novel and film is the same lost history that puts Ricky behind the wheel and NASCAR fans in the stands in *Talladega Nights*. Howell writes that the sport's "roots in rural Southern America have been transformed by the public at large into stereotypes reflecting the outlaw nature of moonshiners and the aggressive nature of men who make their living going fast and turning left" (11). Fans are encouraged to see drivers as modern-day "frontiersmen" who use everyday machines in a heroic way (110). Throughout *Talladega Nights*, the more positive signifiers of Ricky Bobby's Southernness are articulated as distinctively American, and he is cast in the role of that quintessential headstrong, rugged American adventurer — the "cowboy," or maverick masculine ideal. The head of Dennit Racing exhorts his son to be more like Ricky, saying he wished Larry "had a little more stupid cowboy" in him. Ricky calls himself a "big, hairy, American winning machine," and, as he rear-ends his nemesis's Perrier car, he quips, "Hey, it's me, America!" Later, as Susan exhorts Ricky to run the film's final race, she asks him to imagine himself as a saint riding through hell on a skeleton horse.

> Ricky Bobby is not a thinker. Ricky Bobby is a driver. He is a doer, and that's what you need to do. You don't need to think. You need to drive. You need speed. You need to go out there, and you need to rev your engine. You need to fire it up. You need to grab ahold of that line between speed and chaos, and you need to wrestle it to the ground like a demon cobra. And then, when the fear rises up in your belly, you use it. And you know that fear is powerful, because it has been there for billions of years! And it is good! And you use it! And you ride it; you ride it like a skeleton horse through the gates of hell, and then you win, Ricky! You WIN! And you don't win for anybody else. You win for you, you know why? Because a man takes what he wants. He takes it all. And you're a man, aren't you? Aren't you?!

Audiences cheer as the Bobby family literally and figuratively uses the race car to smash up suburban life and the everydayness that goes with it — not just driving to victory on the track, but driving right through someone's living room, making a family tradition of getting thrown out of Applebee's, subverting even NASCAR rules by racing not for points or even to win, but just to go as fast as they can for as long as they can while waving and wearing American flags. When Ricky does finally defeat his fear and the French driver, we see an American flag on his visible sleeve, and another one waving ghostlike behind him as all his dreams come true. As the family heads into the sunset for a celebratory meal at Applebee's, the lyrics of Lee Ferrell's song "Goodbye, Cowboy," evoke the conventions of the great American western. By sanitizing the racial dimensions of NASCAR's history and present, and laying the conventions of the American western over those of the Southern gas opera, *Talladega Nights* nationalizes the most appealing aspects of Bobby's regional identity, while still softly lampooning his backward regional shortcomings and ironing them out of his sons entirely.

Talladega Nights performs redneckery in terms of a romantic, headstrong frontier individualism that reminds me of nothing so much as W. J. Cash's *Mind of the South* (1941), and yet does so while writing race out of the issue of class. The film's one black character, Lucius Washington, has few if any regional, or even racial markers in the final version. Further, the material in deleted scenes where he references his "black behind" and treats Donna Summer as an icon suggests the absence of such markers was a deliberate editorial decision. (His angry admonition to Ricky not to "put that evil on me" when Ricky curses his future sons in the hospital scene is such a veiled reference to hoodoo that my students tend to accuse me of making it up.) Like the black ambulance driver in Dickey's novel, Lucius is a comforting and nonthreatening foil to the main character. His presence in the film helps it to posit a kind of biracial New South, while at the same time excluding Lucius's ethnic experience from the film's categories of acknowledged Southern experience. People are "cowboys," "Americans," and "winners" at the race track, rather than black or white. As Wright observes, "race is the skeleton in the NASCAR family closet" (280), and so Lucius's presence in *Talladega Nights* is an oblique, but in some ways unsatisfying acknowledgment of that. The post-agrarian road rage that drives Ricky to want to go fast, his anxieties about his masculinity and his place in modern culture, are tied historically if not explicitly to his whiteness and the related anxieties represented by the cougar riding in the backseat of his car — the same world that swims at the bottom of *Deliverance*'s Lake Cahula, the hand of the past in Ed's nightmares.

After Ricky masters his car and reconstitutes his family, regains his confidence and position in the community, subverts Dennit Racing and the NASCAR establishment, and tames the cougar in his backseat and names her Karen, he is secure enough in his masculinity to plant a public kiss on his gay opponent. Jean, who is supposedly so moved by Ricky's masculinity that he cannot resist trying for a second smooch, responds admiringly, "Sir, you taste of America," awarding Ricky the position that he and NASCAR corporate sponsors both crave: redneckery mainstreamed, no longer the regional margin and the exceptional Southern past, but at the center of the American tradition, a position gained by eliding parts of the racist, rural redneck iconography with which we began — perhaps entering into what Jim Goad has called "a perverse form of minstrelsy" (33–34). This is further illustrated in the subplot of Lucy Bobby's taming of Ricky's sons, as it lets her be more specific about some of the less appealing aspects of "Southern" being written out of the New South (though she still avoids race). While they are initially introduced as out-of-control kids "all hopped-up on Mountain Dew" and threatening their grandfather that they will "come at [him] like a spider monkey," when Lucy Bobby declares "Granny Law," the boys quickly recognize that she will "break [them] like wild horses"— that language setting up the nod to Faulkner in the film's final sequence. After the *Talladega* credits roll, filled with outtakes of Ricky and his buddy Cal using their celebrity to advertise commercial products, the film doubles back to Ricky's family life, and we are treated to Ricky's sons' ambivalent reading of their own investment, or lack thereof, in post-agrarian regional identity. Lucy is seen reading her grandsons the end of "The Bear" from a beat-up copy of Faulkner's *Three Novels* and asks, "So, what do you think that story was about?" Texas Ranger responds, "Doesn't the Bear symbolize the Old South, and the new dog the encroaching industrialization of the North?" and Walker chides him, saying, "Duh! But the question is: should the reader feel relief, or sadness at the passing of the Old South?" They conclude the ballad of their father's life by acknowledging its "moral ambiguity" in a scene from which he is conspicuously absent. Granny Law has introduced Walker and Texas Ranger to contemporary versions of a variety of traditional icons of Southern life that differ from the way their father raised them — a church choir experience replaces the Baby Jesus prayers sponsored by PowerAde, a chain gang-like experience picking up trash along the highway replaces a frontier without consequences, and an encounter with a "mangy grandfather" who, instead of taking them fishing and telling them stories about his childhood à la *The Old Man and the Boy* (1957), replaces that version of Southern boyhood by telling them to "dig a hole" while he finds another beer. Ricky and the redneck South may have driven right through the living room into the sunset, but Walker and Texas Ranger are able to see them as both heroic and ridiculous, their dad's regional legacy a moral question mark, barely intelligible as Southern in postmodern suburbia. Their father's success unexpectedly becomes a cautionary tale about how not to pursue an authentic life.

In William Ferris's "Preamble" to *Bridging Southern Cultures* (2005), he suggests that the methodology of Southern Studies requires attention to both "inner" and "outer," or objective and artistic, views of Southern life. Yet *Deliverance* and *Talladega Nights* both beg the question of how to think about those categories, as they depend on satisfying their audiences' need for more appealing, mainstreamed versions of Southern history for their success, at the same time as a closer look at both films illuminates the ways in which they critique that need. I have found these films instructive in large part because, even as they participate in that historical revision to seek a wider audience, they also both expressly acknowledge the moral ambiguity of colonizing Southern redneck typology. Both the novel and the film of *Deliverance* require the worst sort of stereotyping to drive the action, but they do ethical work as they resist letting Ed sleep easy. He goes to the wilderness seeking to re-authenticate himself as a man in a mythical Southern landscape, and he returns having written his own myths to sell to the outside world, continuing in the uncomfortable knowledge not only that has he told himself and the world a story, but also that such stories invite consequences. *Talladega Nights* deploys more banal stereotypes, but like *Deliverance*, ultimately finds a way to illuminate some of the limitations of those stereotypes. It invites audiences to consider what makes a suburban redneck Southern other than his own fetishized sense of history, and what "nationalized" redneck iconography that equates him with a "stupid cowboy," means for the postmodern South. Possibly it means that it is all over down here — that, as Jean suggests, the "matador shall dance with the blind shoemaker," that it is all nonsense for sale, and that the South on the screen, like the history Ed records or the ballad version of Ricky's life, has become more real than the one in which real people live. I resist that conclusion, though, and am heartened by a contemporary popular film that closes on a note of moral ambiguity. As with *Deliverance*, the careful viewer will find a cautionary tale in what is not there in *Talladega Nights*— validation of an authentic, singular experience of region.

Works Cited

Alderman, Derek H., et al. "Carolina Thunder Revisited: Toward a Transcultural View of Winston Cup Racing." *The Professional Geographer* 55.2 (2003): 238–249.
Annesley, James. *Blank Fictions: Consumerism, Culture, and the Contemporary American Novel.* New York: St. Martin's, 1998.
Barnett, Pamela. "James Dickey's *Deliverance*: Southern, White, Suburban Male Nightmare or Dream Come True?" *Forum for Modern Language Studies* 40.2 (2004): 145–159.
Deliverance. Dir. John Boorman. 1972. Warner Home Video, 1999. DVD.
Dickey, James. *Deliverance.* New York: Dell, 1970.
Ferris, William. "Preamble: The Study of Region." *Bridging Southern Cultures: An Interdisciplinary Approach.* Ed. John Lowe. Baton Rouge: Louisiana State University Press, 2005. 29–36.
French, Warren. "'The Southern': Another Lost Cause?" *The South and Film.* Ed. Warren French. Jackson: University Press of Mississippi, 1981. 3–13.
Goad, Jim. *The Redneck Manifesto.* New York: Simon and Schuster, 1997.
Harkins, Anthony. *Hillbilly: A Cultural History of an American Icon.* New York: Oxford University Press, 2004.
Howell, Mark D. *From Moonshine to Madison Avenue: A Cultural History of the NASCAR Winston Cup Series.* Bowling Green: Bowling Green State University Press, 1997.
Knepper, Steven. "'Do You Know What the *Hail* You're Talkin' About?': *Deliverance*, Stereotypes, and the Lost Voice of the Rural Poor." *James Dickey Newsletter* 25.1 (2008): 17–29.
Newman, Joshua, and Michael Giardina. "NASCAR and the 'Southernization' of America: Spectatorship, Subjectivity, and the Confederation of Identity." *Cultural Studies, Critical Methodologies* 8.4 (2008): 479–506.
Newman, Joshua, and Adam Beissel. "The Limits to 'NASCAR Nation': Sport and the 'Recovery Movement' in Disjunctive Times." *Sociology of Sport Journal* 26 (2009): 517–539.
O'Connor, Flannery. *Wise Blood: A Novel.* 1952. New York: Farrar, Straus, & Giroux, 1990.
Pillsbury, Richard. "Stock Car Racing." *The Theatre of Sport.* Ed. Karl B. Raitz. Baltimore: Johns Hopkins University Press, 1985. 270–295.
Poole, W. Scott. "'White Knuckle Ride': Stock Cars and Class Identity in the Postmodern South." *Studies in Popular Culture* 25.1 (2002): 1–10.
Reed, John Shelton, and Dale Volberg Reed. *1001 Things Everyone Should Know about the South.* New York: Doubleday, 1996.
Ruppersburg, Hugh. "William Faulkner and *Talladega Nights.*" *Films About the South.* 25 Sept. 2006. Web. 11 Nov. 2010. <http://filmsaboutthesouth.blogspot.com >.
Talladega Nights: The Ballad of Ricky Bobby. Dir. Adam McKay. Columbia Pictures, 2006. DVD.
Thesing, William B., and David Wright. "Dealing with 'Immortal Works': James Dickey's Last Public Discussion of *Deliverance.*" *James Dickey Newsletter* 24.2 (2008): 36–42.
Von Doviak, Scott. *Hick Flicks: The Rise and Fall of Redneck Cinema.* Jefferson, NC: McFarland, 2005.
Wright, Jim. *Fixin' to Git: One Fan's Love Affair with NASCAR's Winston Cup.* Durham: Duke University Press, 2002.

About the Contributors

Thomas R. Britt is a graduate of Ohio University and teaches in the Film and Video Studies Program at George Mason University. He has presented papers at the Conference of Film & History, Cine-Excess, the Cultural Studies Association, the Literature/Film Association, and the Appalachian Studies Association. He is a staff writer for *PopMatters* and has also been published in *Americana: The Journal of American Popular Culture*, *Bright Lights Film Journal*, and *Cinephile: The University of British Columbia's Film Journal*.

Stephen Broomer is a filmmaker and graduate student in communication and culture at Ryerson University in Toronto. He is completing a dissertation on urban ruins and the philosophy of preservation. He is an active media preservationist and has exhibited his restorations of Canadian experimental and student films of the 1960s throughout Canada. His documentary films concentrate on social and environmental issues in his immediate environment.

C. Scott Combs is an assistant professor of film and English at St. John's University in Queens, New York City. He has published articles on early film's interest in the death moment and on film noir. He is finishing a book titled "Deathwatch: American Film, Technology, and the End of Life."

Amy Corbin is an assistant professor of film studies at Muhlenberg College. She holds a Ph.D. from the University of California, Berkeley, and writes on race and cultural geography in American film. She is writing a book, "Traveling Spectators: Cinema, Geography, and Cultural Difference in America," in which she theorizes about the geographical relations inherent in film spectatorship, and the way these relationships reveal racial and cultural hierarchies — in Indian Country, the South, the inner city, and the suburbs.

James A. Crank is an assistant professor of American literature and the director of Undergraduate Studies at Northwestern State University in Natchitoches, Louisiana. His articles have appeared in *The Mississippi Quarterly* as well as the collections *Agee Agonistes: Essays on the Life, Legend, and Works of James Agee* (University of Tennessee Press, 2007) and *Agee at 100* (University of Tennessee Press, 2010). He is editing *The Morning Watch and Collected Short Prose of James Agee* (forthcoming).

Phillip Lamarr Cunningham is a doctoral candidate in American cultural studies at Bowling Green State University in Ohio. His primary research interests are in black American popular culture, particularly film and television, music, and professional sports. His work has appeared on FlowTV.com, in the *Journal of Graphic Novels and Comics* and the *Journal of Sport & Social Issues*, and in anthologies on Captain America and Southern film.

ABOUT THE CONTRIBUTORS

Courtney George received a Ph.D. from Louisiana State University and teaches composition and Southern literature at Columbus State University in Columbus, Georgia. She has published articles on Southern literature and music in the *Southern Literary Journal* and *Studies in American Culture*. She is writing a book on the ways contemporary women writers use popular music like blues, gospel, and country in their fiction in order to formulate new conceptions of Southern identity.

Bryan Giemza is a North Carolina native who teaches American and Southern literature at Randolph-Macon College in Ashland, Virginia. He is the coauthor of *Poet of the Lost Cause: A Life of Father Ryan* and an editor of *Southern Writers: A New Biographical Dictionary*. He is writing on "The Irish Outliers of Southern Literature," a comprehensive history of Irish American writers of the region that includes such writers as Kate (O'Flaherty) Chopin, Flannery O'Connor, and Cormac McCarthy.

Oliver Gruner is completing a Ph.D. and teaching at the University of East Anglia in the UK. His disertation is focused on the representation of the 1960s in 1980s and 1990s American cinema.

Maria Hebert-Leiter received her Ph.D. from the University of North Carolina at Chapel Hill. She is the author of *Becoming Cajun, Becoming American: The Acadian in American Literature from Longfellow to James Lee Burke*, which studies the literary history and development of Cajun representation in American literature (Louisiana State University Press, 2009). She is writing a second book that studies New Orleans detective fiction.

Andrew B. Leiter received his undergraduate degree from the University of Alabama, and he completed his graduate work at the University of North Carolina at Chapel Hill. He currently teaches English and American studies at Lycoming College in Williamsport, Pennsylvania. His research specialties include literary and popular representations of the American South as well as multicultural intersections with other regions. He is the author of *In the Shadow of the Black Beast: African American Masculinity in the Harlem and Southern Renaissances* (Louisiana State University Press, 2010).

Landon Palmer is a Ph.D. student in the department of Communication and Culture at the University of Indiana–Bloomington. In addition to studying the representation of the South in mainstream cinema, his other research interests include the aesthetic and cultural functions of classical and popular music in cinema and other forms of audiovisual media. He wrote an essay on the role of classical music in the films of Michael Haneke for the anthology *The Cinema of Michael Haneke: Europe Utopia* and is cofounder of the media studies e-journal *Movement*.

Tara Powell is an assistant professor of English and Southern studies at the University of South Carolina at Columbia. Her book on literary representations of Southern intellectual labor is forthcoming from Louisiana State University Press, and her other research interests include studying New South verse memoirs, Italian-American experiences in southern Appalachia, and portrayals of the South in contemporary literature and film.

Hugh Ruppersburg is the senior associate dean of arts and sciences and a professor of English at the University of Georgia. He is the author of studies of William Faulkner and Robert Penn Warren, and the editor of a series of anthologies of Georgia literature. He is writing a book on films about the American South.

Marlisa Santos is an associate professor and the director of the Division of Humanities in the Farquhar College of Arts and Sciences at Nova Southeastern University in Fort Lauderdale, Florida. She has published essays on film in numerous anthologies, and her areas of research and teaching include film noir, classic film studies, and food and film. She wrote *The Dark Mirror: Psychiatry and Film Noir* (Lexington, 2010).

Usame Tunagur is an award-winning filmmaker born and raised in Istanbul. He has a B.A. degree in broadcasting and mass media from Temple University and an M.F.A. degree in film from Ohio University. He produces shows for Ebru-TV, which creates programming that promotes diversity and multiculturalism. His films have been screened and received awards at numerous festivals such as Big Muddy, Urbanworld, and Athens International Film and Video Festival.

Index

Numbers in ***bold italics*** indicate pages with photographs.

Absalom, Absalom! 160*n*
Adams, Amy 100, 155, 158–159
Adams, Michael 207
Adaptation 8, 12, 175–180, 185
Adventures of Huckleberry Finn 10, 66–68
affirmative action 19, 40–42
African American: Christianity 54–56, 60*n*; community 48, 50–60, 133, 181–184; erasure in civil rights films 16–20; family 123–133; identity on film 5–7, 11, 194–197, 204, 213, 215, 226–227; masculinity 47–48; patriarchal attitude toward women 131; *see also* affirmative action; "black brute"; blues; civil rights movement; hip hop; integration; minstrelsy; multiculturalism; segregation; slavery
Alderman, Derek 224
Alexander, Jane 181
Alexandria, Virginia 32, 36–37, 41
Alice, Mary 124, 183
All the King's Men 88*n*
Allain, Mathé 188–189
Allen, Woody 140
Alston, Joshua 187
Altman, Robert 11, 76–88
American Dreamz 173
American Gangster 50
American Psycho 221
America's Energy Coast initiative 200
America's Vanishing Treasure 200
The Andy Griffith Show 8, 9
"Angel Band" 69
Annesley, James 221
Anthony, Alexandra 135
Apfel, Oscar 4
The Apostle 8
Army Corps of Engineers 193
As I Lay Dying 183–184
ATL 10, 48, 56–61
autobiographical film 144–146
The Autobiography of Miss Jane Pittman (film) 5

auto-ethnographic film 135, 145–146
Autry, Alan 192
Avedon, Richard 137
Avnet, Jon 10, 19
Ayler, Ethel 124
Ayres, Agnes 164, ***165***

Baby Doll 205, 207, 208, 210
Bachofner, Simone 7
Backyard 11, 134–138, 140
Badalucco, Michael 63
Baker, Aaron 38
Baker, Houston 206, 215
Balk, Fairuza 197
Bamboozled 7
Barataria-Terrebonne National Estuary Program 200–201
Barber, Bryan 10, 54
Barnett, Pamela 219, 224
Barry, John M. 202*n*
Barton Fink 66
Bassett, Angela 181
Bataille, Georges 218
Bates, Kathy 197
The Battle 4
Bayou Farewell 189, 199, 201
"The Bear" 217, 227
Beatty, Ned 116
Beissel, Adam 222, 224
Benjamin André 54
The Beverly Hillbillies (series) 2
The Big Lebowski 66
Biloxi-Chitimacha-Choctaw Indians 187, 193, 195–196, 202; *see also* Native American
Binet-Simon intelligence test 113, 115
The Birdcage 175
The Birth of a Nation 4, 5, 7, 47, 50, 65, 94, 102–103, 112–113, 118, 144, 204–206
Bjerre, Thomas Ærvold 66
"black brute" 47–48, 50–52, 60, 93–94, 112–113

Black Like Me 94
Black Masculinity and the U.S. South 60*n*
Black Natchez 144
Black Panthers 32
Black Power movement 19
Black Snake Moan (film) 12, 204, 207–211, 213–215
"Black Snake Moan" (song) 210
Blakely, Ronnee **82**
Blank Fictions 221
blaxploitation film 207, 214; *see also* African American, identity on film
Blood and Wine 175
Blue Collar TV 2
bluegrass 1, 53, 68, 69
blues 49, 53, 60*n*, 63, 69, 123–124, 126, 207, 210–211, 214
Bogle, Donald 5
Boorman, John 1, *3*, 114 **117**, 118, 164, 207, 218
Boothe, Powers **191**, 192
Bowling for Columbine 112
Boyz n the Hood 47, 50, 61*n*, 132
BP oil spill 202*n*
Brakhage, Stan 144
Branch Davidians 140
Braxton, Charlie 49
Breen, Bobby 4
Brenon, Herbert 4
Brewer, Craig 10, 12, 50, 54, 204, 207–211, 214–215
Brewster McCloud 76
Bright, Matthew 120
Bright Leaf 142–143
Bright Leaves 11, 135, 142–144
Britt, Thomas R. 11, 161–174
Brody, David 215
Brokeback Mountain 95
Brooks, Richard 124
Broomer, Stephen 11, 134–146
Brown, James 49
Bryant, Joy 194
Bryant, Paul "Bear" 38
Bugs Bunny 2
Bull-Durham Tobacco 142
Burnett, Charles 11, 123, 126, **130**, 132
Burns, Ken 44
Burr, Ty 153, 160*n*
Bush, George W. 103, 190
"busing" 19, 41–42; *see also* integration
Butler, Paul 123

Caddyshack 175
Cage, Nicolas 176
Cajun identity on film 2, 12, 187–202
Cajun Mariners 202*n*
Caldwell, Erskine 2, 206
Cameo Kirby 4
Campbell, Edward D.C., Jr. 4, 5, 7, 65, 205, 207

Canby, Vincent 22
Canton, Steven 169, 170
Carewe, Edwin 189
Carradine, Keith *191*, 192
Carroll, Pat 170
Carson, L.M. Kit 144
Carter, Jimmy 15, 77, 87*n*
Carter, T.K. 192
Cash, Johnny 87; *see also* Johnny Cash Show
Cash, W.J. 226
Cassavetes, John 94
Catholic Legion of Decency 205
Cawelti, John 16–17
The Celluloid South 7
Chadwick, Bruce 7
Chandler, Karen 128, 130, 131
Chaplin, Geraldine 88*n*
Charleen or How Long Has This Been Going On? 135
Charley 177
Cheshire, Godfrey 135, 138, 143, 146
Chireau, Yvonne 127, 132
Christianity 69, 70, 149–150, 152–155, 158–160, 220–221, 228; and conjure 123, 127, 129–130, 132–133; and Islam 163, 170–171; and multiculturalism 24, 26; and satanism 201–202; and South-sploitation 204, 206, 208, 210–212, 214
civil rights movement 10, 32–46, 93–94, 96, 99, 135, 144, 223; and white violence 17–19, 222–223; *see also* "busing"; integration; King, Martin Luther, Jr.; Ku Klux Klan; segregation
Civil War 64–65, 93, 101–103, 135, 138, 139–142, 143
Civil War (documentary) 44
Civil War dramas 4, 144
Claiborne, Jerry 38
Clemens, Samuel *see* Twain, Mark
The Client 29*n*
Clinton, Bill 40, 43, 151
Clooney, George 62, 63, **64**, 65
Clover, Carol 16, 115, 118, 120–121*n*
Coach Carter 39
Coal Miner's Daughter 16, 29*n*
Coastal Restoration and Protection Act 190
Coastal Wetlands Planning program 190
Cobbs, Bill 183
Coen, Ethan 9, 11, 62–73
Coen, Joel 9, 11, 62–73
Cohen, Sacha Baron 217
Combs, C. Scott 3, 11, 106–122
Coming Apart 144
Comolli, Jean-Luc 95
Confederate flag 92, 96, 102, 223–224
conjure 11, 123–133, 194–195, 213, 226
Conrad, Glenn 197
Contemporary Southern Identity 102

The Content of Our Character 41
Cook, Greg Russell 170
Cookie's Fortune 87
Cool Hand Luke 62
Cooper, Chris 176, **178**
Cooper, Gary 142
Cops 120
Coraci, Frank 12, 197
Corbin, Amy 10, 15–31, 71
The Cotton Club 55
country music 11, 69, 76–88
Country Music Hall of Fame 78
Coward, Herbert "Cowboy" **3**, **117**
"cracker" *see* redneck
Crank, James A. 12, 204–216
Crews, Harry 206
Crockett, Davy 82
Crosby, Bing 4
Cunningham, Phillip Lamarr 11, 123–133
Cunningham, Sam 38
Curtiz, Michael 142

Darwin, Charles 113
Dash, Julie 47
Daughters of Dust 47
David Holzman's Diary 144
Davidtz, Embeth 100, 151, 154–155, 158
Davis, Bette 5
"The Dead" 153–154, 157
The Dead Eye Boy 154, 156
Deliverance (film) 1–3, 9, 11, 12, 68, 72, 107, 114, 115–118, 164, 190, 207, 218–228
Deliverance (novel) 164, 207, 218–228
DeMent, Iris 173
DeMille, Cecil B. 144
Democratic National Convention (1968) 110, 112
Dempsey, Patrick 97
The Descent 164
desegregation *see* integration
Diaries: 1971–1976 144
Diawara, Manthia 5
Dickey, James 107, 164, 207, 217, 218, 219, 226
"Didn't Leave Nobody but the Baby" 69
Dirty Harry films 119
Dirty Mary Crazy Larry 28*n*
Dirty States of America 49
Disenchanting Les Bons Temps 202*n*
Doll, Susan 181
Domination and the Arts of Resistance 104*n*
Donley, Kerry 32
Douglas, Andrew 8
"Down to the River to Pray" 69
Drew, S. Rankin 4
Driving Miss Daisy 16, 17, 28*n*, 94
D'Souza, Dinesh 40
Dubliners 147–148, 152–154, 157–158
"Dueling Banjos" 1
Dugdale, Richard 114

Duke, Daryl 11, 83
Duke, James B. 142–143
The Dukes of Hazzard (film) 3, 172
The Dukes of Hazzard (series) 2, 28*n*, 134
Dunne, John Gregory 112
Duvall, Robert 8, 215
Dyson, Michael Eric 50

Eastwood, Clint 115, 119
Easy Rider 3
Ebner, David 7
8Ball 53
8 Mile 48
Elliott, Sam 66
Ellison, Ralph 69, 78
Embry, Ethan 104*n*
Eminem 48
The End of Racism 40
environment: and coastal development 176–178, 181–185; and ethnicity 175–185, 187–202; and Louisiana wetlands 12, 187–202; as pastoral ideal 175–176, 188; restoration efforts 189–190, 200–202
Esu-Elegbara 126
ethnicity *see* African American; Biloxi-Chitimacha-Choctaw Indians; Cajun identity on film; multiculturalism; Native American; Seminoles
eugenics 113–115
Eugenics Records Office 113, 114
Evangeline (film) 189
Evangeline (poem) 189
Eyes on the Prize 34

A Face in the Crowd 88*n*, 135
Falco, Edie 181
Falgoux, Woody 202*n*
Faulkner, William 66, 81, 138, 145, 148, 151, 160*n*, 206–208, 214, 215, 217, 227
Fernandez, Susan J. 176
Ferrell, Lee 226
Ferrell, Will 217, **225**
Ferris, William 228
Field, Sally 22, **23**
Field Mob 50, 58
50 Cent 48
Filene, Benjamin 72
Fisher, Antwone 56
Flaherty, Robert 172–173, 200
Fleischer, Richard 6
Flowers for Algernon 177
folk music 10–12, 63, 68–73, 163, 172–174
football 197–199; and integration 37–44
Ford, John 118
Framing the South 7, 87–88*n*
France, Bill 222
Frankenfish 196
Freeman, Jason 53

Freeway 115, 120
French, Warren 7, 220
Freud, Sigmund 163
Fried Green Tomatoes 10, 15–29

Gable, Clark 5, 65
Gaines, Ernest 5
Galton, Francis 113
Gator 28*n*
Gautreaux, Tim 188, 200, 201
gender: African American masculinity 47–48; African American men and white women 93–94, 97, 100, 104*n*, 204, 207–211; heroines and multiculturalism 15–31; homosexuality 95, 217, 223; lesbianism 119; subordination of women 93–94, 131, 167–170; white female identity on film 11, 97–104, 163–171; white male anxieties 12, 218–227; *see also* African American, family; "black brute"; redneck, and sexual deviance; Southern belle
George, Courtney 10, 47–61
George, Nelson 48, 60
George, Susan **6**
George Washington (film) 215
"Georgia" (song) 50, 58
Get Rich or Die Tryin' 48
Ghosts of Mississippi 35, 94
Giardina, Michael 224
Giemza, Bryan 11, 147–160
Gilmore, Glenda 93, 98, 100
Ginsberg, Milton Moses 144
Gleason, Ralph 83
Glory Road 39, 94
Glover, Danny 123, **130**
Goad, Jim 108–109, 134, 218, 227
Goddard, Herbert 113–118
Goddu, Teresa 124
God's Little Acre (novel) 2
Gone with the Wind (film) 1–2, 4–5, 7, 10, 16–17, 47, 63–70, 98, 112–113, 144, 205
Gone with the Wind (novel) 4, 112–113
"Goodbye, Cowboy" 226
Goodman, John 62
Gordon, Jeff 224
gospel music 50, 53, 55, 60*n*, 80, 158
gothic 12, 123–127, 133, 206–208, 211–213
Gould, Stephen Jay 113–114
Graham, Allison 7, 18, 33, 71, 87, 88*n*
Graham, Nathan Lee 104*n*
The Great Debaters 94
Great Depression 11, 62–64, 66–68, 72–73
Great Migration 90
Green, Gordon 215
Green, Harvey 37
Green, Tony 49
Greenwald, Maggie 11, 163, 170
Griffith, D.W. 4, 5, 47, 65, 93, 102–103, 118, 121*n*, 144, 204–206

Griffith, Edward H. 5
Groening, Matt 3
Gruner, Oliver 10, 32–46
The Guerrilla 4
Gulf of Mexico Energy Security Act 190, 200
Gullah 47
Guy, Buddy 53

Haberle, Stephanie Roth 170
Haggard, Merle 84
Hairy Man 126, 129
Haley, Alex 6
Hall, Jacquelyn Dowd 35
Hannah, Darryl 107
"Hard Time Killing Floor Blues" 63, 69
Harding, Michael 170
Harkins, Anthony 3, 9, 162, 170, 218
Harlem Nights 55
Harold & Kumar Escape from Guantanamo Bay 173
Harold and Kumar Go to White Castle 116, 119
Harris, George Washington 2
Harris, Tip "T.I." 49, 56
Haunted Waters 200
Haunted Waters, Fragile Lands 200
Hayes, Taylor 171
Heart of Dixie 33–34, 35
The Heart of Maryland 4
Hebert-Leiter, Maria 12, 72, 187–203
Hendrix, Jimi 87
Henry, John 128
Hentz, Caroline Lee 4
Her Father's Son 4
Hick Flicks 215*n*, 220
Hicks, Ray 156
Hill, George Roy 109
Hill, John 190, 200
Hill, Walter 11, 12, 189, 190, 193
hillbilly *see* redneck
Hillbilly: A Cultural History of an American Icon 162
Hillbillyland 121*n*
hip hop 10, 47–61, 210
His Trust 4
"hixploitation" films 215*n*, 220; *see also* redneck
Hollywood Film and the Cultural Memory of the Civil War South 7
Homer 62
"hood" films 47–61
hoodoo *see* conjure
Hooper, Johnson Jones 2
Hope, Bob 77
Hopkins, Stephen 12, 201, 207
Hornaday, Ann 156
Horwitz, Tony 65, 68
Houston, Jordan 53
Howard, Terrence 50, 210
Howell, Mark D. 225

Hudson, Kate 194
Hunter, Stephen 36
The Hurricane 94
Hurricane Katrina 190, 200, 201–202, 212
Hurricane on the Bayou 200
Hurricane Rita 190, 201–202
Hurst, Ryan 39
Hurt, John 194
Hurwitz, Jon 173
Hustle & Flow 10, 47–61, 207, 210–211, 214
Hutton, Timothy 181

"I Am a Man of Constant Sorrow" 69, 70
Ice Cube 47
Ice T 47
Idlewild 10, 48, 54–60
In Slavery Days 4
In the Heat of the Night 33, 94
Ingalls, Robert P. 176
integration 19, 36–38, 41–42, 102; *see also* civil rights movement; segregation
Intruder in the Dust (film) 45n
Invisible Man 78
Iraq War 112
Islam 163–164, 169–171
"It's Hard Out Here for a Pimp" 50

Jackson, John Wyse 150, 152
Jackson, Samuel L. 107, 204, **209**, 210
jazz 54–56
Jefferson, Blind Lemon 210
Jenkins, Philip 15
Jezebel 5
Johnny Cash Show 84
Johnson, Robert 126
Johnson, Tommy 126
Jones, Jacquie 123–124, 126, 128, 132
Jones, Kent 184
Jonze, Spike 8, 175, 176, **178**
Joplin, Janis 87
Joyce, James 11, 77, 147–154, 157–160
Juice 47
Juke family 114, 120
Junebug 9, 11, 89, 96, 100–104, 147–160, 215

Kael, Pauline 80, 88n
The Kallikak Family: A Study of Genetic Feeble-mindedness 113–118
Kaufman, Charlie 176
Kazan, Elia 88n, 205–208
"Keep on the Sunny Side" 69
Kennedy, John Pendleton 4
Kennedy Square 4
Kentucky Fried Chicken 15
Kierkegaard, Søren 153
Kill Bill 2 107
Kim, Sojin 126
King, Alan 184

King, Burton 4
King, Chris Thomas 63
King, Coretta Scott 58
King, Martin Luther, Jr. 34–35, 38, 40–41, 58
Kirby, Jack Temple 5, 7, 88n
Knepper, Steven 218
Koehler, Julie 68
Ku Klux Klan 17, 19, 24, 40, 62, 64, 69, 70, 72

Landsberg, Alison 43
Langman, Larry 7
The Last American Hero 28n
"Latitudinarianism" 152
Leacock, Richard 139, 141
Lear, Norman 24
Lee, Spike 7
Leibman, Ron **23**
Leigh, Vivien 5
Less Than Zero 221
Let Us Now Praise Famous Men 66
Levine, Marilyn 143
Lewis, A.L. 183
Lhamon, W.T. 6
Light in August 81
"Li'l Abner" 2
Lil Wayne 49
The Little Colonel 4, 205
The Littlest Rebel 4
Livengood, R. Mark 126
London Museum 82
Long, Walter 93, 165
The Long Hot Summer 18, 205, 207, 210
The Long Walk Home 34, 35
Longfellow, Henry Wadsworth 189
Longstreet, Augustus Baldwin 2
Louisiana Story 200
Loury, Glenn C. 41
Love Field 35
Lucas, Josh 97
Lucia, Cynthia 136
Ludacris 49, 53, 58
Lumbly, Carl 124
Lynde, Francis 162
Lynn, Loretta 81
Lynyrd Skynyrd 96–97

MacLachlan, Angus 148, 151, 153, 154, 155–156
Make Mine Music 2
Man of the West 114
Mandingo 6, 205
Mann, Anthony 114
Marcus, Daniel 34
Marsh, Mae 93
Martin Luther King Day 34
Marxist film theory 95
M*A*S*H 76
Masterson, Mary Stuart **25**
McBride, Jim 144

McCabe and Mrs. Miller 76, 115
McCullers, Carson 138
McElwee, Adrian 143
McElwee, John Harvey 142–143
McElwee, Ross 11, 44, 134–146
McFarland, Douglas 71
McGinley, Bernard 150, 152
McKay, Adam 12, 221
McKenzie, Ben 100, 155
McPherson, Tara 1, 44, 65, 91–92, 98, 102
McTeer, Janet 163, **169**
Media-Made Dixie 7, 88n
Medium Cool 110, 112
Meer, Sarah 6
Mekas, Jonas 144
Melford, George 11, 164
melodrama *see* multiculturalism: and melodrama
Men of Honor 94
Menace II Society 47
Mencken, H.L. 206
Micheaux, Oscar 5, 121n
Milk 95
Million Dollar Baby 119
Mind of the South 226
minstrelsy 6–7
Mississippi 4
Mississippi Burning 10, 15–29, 33–34, 35, 36, 94
Mississippi Freedom Summer 34
Mississippi River flood (1927) 193, 202n
Mitchell, Margaret 112
modernization of South 8–9, 63–66, 72–73, 147–150, 153, 170, 218–229; and African American family 123–133; as commercialism and commodification 76, 147, 149–150, 172, 201, 220–221, 227; and urban development 181–185; *see also* civil rights movement
Mohammed 164
Monteith, Sharon 33, 35
Montgomery bus boycott 34
Montoya, Juan Pablo 224
Moonshiner of Fact 162, 166
Moore, Michael 112, 145
Morel, Pierre 172
Morrison, Jim 87
Morrison, Phil 11, 89, 147–160, 215
Morrow, David 181
Motif Index of Folklore 126
The Moviegoer 157
Muller, Matthias 146
multiculturalism: and melodrama 10, 15–29, 167; and redneck identity 106–121, 217–229
music 10–11, 207; *see also* bluegrass; blues; country music; folk music; hip hop, jazz
Muslim stereotypes 11, 161, 164–165, 169–171
My Lai massacre 109, 111, 119

NAACP 5
Nanook of the North 173

Naquin, Albert 196
Narboni, Jean 95
NASCAR 12, 217, 221–227
Nashville 11, 76–88
The Nashville Chronicles 88n
Natchez Trace 125–126
National Civil Rights Museum 34
Native American 109, 177–179, 183, 185; *see also* Biloxi-Chitimacha-Choctaw Indians; Seminole
Natural Born Killers 115, 120
Neale, Steve 39
Negroponte, Michel 135
Nelson, Dana 206
Nelson, Tim Blake 63, **64**
New Jack City 47
New Woman 167–169
Newitz, Annalee 25, 108, 112, 120
Newman, Joshua 222, 224
The Next Step in the Dance 201
Nivola, Alessandro 155
Nixon, DeVaughn 124
Norma Rae 10, 15–29, 167
Norton, Ken **6**
Notorious 48
Notorious B.I.G. 48

O Brother, Where Art Thou? (film) 9, 10, 62–75, 88n
O Brother, Where Art Thou? (soundtrack) 68–70, 72
"O Death" 69, 70
O'Brien, Ellen L. 126, 127, 128, 129
O'Connor, Flannery 66, 206–208, 214, 220
The Odyssey 62
oil industry 200, 202n
The Old Man and the Boy 228
Orientalism 161–174
Origins of the New South 93
Orlean, Susan 176
Out of Time 175
Outkast 49, 50, 54, 55, 56
The Outlaw Josey Wales 115

Page, Thomas Nelson 4
Palmer, Landon 11, 89–105
Palmer, R. Barton 62, 71
Palmetto 175
Panettiere, Hayden 39
Panola 144
Parker, Alan 10, 17, 19
Parsons, Gram 87
Parthenon (Athens) 81–82
Parthenon (Nashville) 76, 78, 81–83
The Partisan Leader 4
Party Girl 167
Patton, Antwan 54, 56
Patton, Will 39

Payday 11, 83–87
Peckinpah, Sam 11, 109, 111
Penley, Constance 112
Penn, Arthur 109
Percy, Walker 140, 157, 218
Perfumed Nightmare 145
Pierce, J. Kingston 125–126
Pillsbury, Richard 223
Pincus, Ed 144
Pinky 45*n*
Pitre, Glen 200–201
Places in the Heart 29*n*
plantation South 1–5, 62–73
The Planter's Northern Bride 4
"Po' Lazarus" 69
Poe, Edgar Allan 157
Poole, Scott 223
Poor White Trash, Part II 110
Pope Benedict XVI 164
Powell, Tara 12, 217–229
Presley, Elvis 87, 150
"Pretty Saro" 173
Pride, Charley 81
The Pride of the South 4
The Prince of Tides 17, 22
The Princess and the Frog 2
Pulp Fiction 3, 106–108, 114, 115, 119, 120–121*n*

Quinn, Aidan **169**, 170

Rainer, Luise 4
Raising Arizona 66
Ralph, Sheryl Lee 124
rap *see* hip hop
Reagan, Ronald 118
The Reaping 12, 201–202, 207, 211–213, 215
Reconstructing Dixie 44, 91–92
Redden, Billy 116
Redding, Otis 53
redneck: and car films 15, 134, 215, 217–218, 220–229; and civil rights 17–18, 33; comedy 8–9, 12, 62–73, 197–199, 217–219; as "crackers" 181, 185; identity on film 1–3, 9–10, 11, 161–174, 217–229; and multiculturalism 106–121, 217–229; and sexual deviance 1, 10, 106–121, 164, 205–206, 207–208; and violence 9, 10, 70, 97, 106–121, 164, 170–171, 189, 190–193, 195; and Westerns 107, 109, 111–112, 115; *see also* South-sploitation
Redneck Manifesto 218
Reed, John Shelton 90, 99, 101, 104*n*, 220
The Reel Civil War 7
Reeling 88*n*
Reid, Mark A. 5
Remember the Titans 10, 32–46, 94
Rendleman, Pat 139–140
Resident Exile 135–136

Reynolds, Burt 15, 28*n*, 116, 134–135, 139–140, 143
Rhames, Ving 106
Ricci, Christina 204, **209**
Richardson, Riché 48–49, 60*n*
Rising Tide 202*n*
Ritt, Martin 10, 20, 205–206, 207
The River of Romance 4
Rizzo, Sergio 177
Robert Altman: The Oral Biography 88*n*
Roberts, Davis 124
Robinson, Bill "Bojangles" 4
Robinson, Chris 10, 56, 57*n*
Rogers, Buddy 4
Rogin, Michael 112–113
romantic comedy 96–100
Roots (miniseries) 6
"Rosa Parks" (song) 50
Rose, Tricia 49
Rossum, Emmy 170
Rowlands, Gena 94
Ruppersburg, Hugh 11, 62, 76–88, 221

Sago Mine accident 166
"Sahara of the Bozart" 206
Said, Edward 163
Sandler, Adam 197 **198**, 199
Santos, Marlisa 12, 175–186
Sartain, Gaillard **77**
Savage, Melissa 190, 200
Sayles, John 12, 175, 180, 181
Scarface 50
Schlossberg, Hayden 173
Schluer, Ulrich 164
Schumacher, Joel 10
Schuth, H. Wayne 187–188, 189
Scott, James C. 104*n*
Scott, Sir Walter 66
Scum of the Earth see Poor White Trash, Part II
Seales, Franklyn **191**
The Searchers 118
Searching for the Wrong-Eyed Jesus 8
segregation 92, 135, 137–138; *see also* civil rights movement; integration
Selznick, David O. 1, 10, 65, 68, 112–113, 144
Seminoles 177–179, 184, 185; *see also* Native American
Sergeant York 110
Shadow and Shelter 188, 201
Shadows 94
Shaheen, Jack 164
Shakespeare, William 55
Shakur, Tupac 47
Shaw, Stan **25**
The Sheik 11, 161–171
Sherman, William Tecumseh 139, 141–142, 143, 145
Sherman's March 11, 44, 135, 139–146

Shohat, Ella 171
Show Boat 5
Sidney, George 5
Siegel, Janice 62
Simon, Darran 193, 196, 202*n*
Simpson, Jessica 172
The Simpsons 3
Singleton, John 50
Six O'Clock News 141, 146
The Skeleton Key 12, 187, 190, 194–199, 201, 207, 211, 212–213, 215
slavery 4, 6, 138, 140–141, 151
Slotkin, Richard 107, 109, 111
Smith, Ayana 126
Smith, David L. 176
Smith, Howard K. 80
Smith, James "FLX" 49
Smith, Kevin 215
Smith, Lee 217
Smith, Wonderful 129
Smokey and the Bandit 15, 23, 134–135, 220, 222
"Snuffy Smith" 2
Softley, Iain 12, 194, 195, 207
"Softly and Tenderly" 160
Someone Like You 166
Song of the South 5, 210
Songcatcher 11–12, 161–163, 166–174
Sonic Youth 149
The Sound and the Fury 145
The South and Film 7
South-sploitation film 204–215
Southern belle 4–5, 16–17, 97–98, 101, 140, 180
Southern Comfort 11, 12, 112, 187, 189, 190–195, 197, 198, 199
"Southern Man" 97
Southerners: The Social Psychology of Sectionalism 90, 104*n*
Space Coast 135
Speakerboxxx/The Love Below 55
Spears, Britney 172
Spiro, John-Paul 71
Spivey's Corner Hollering Contest 157
Stam, Robert 171
Standard Oil Company 200
Steel Magnolias 16, 28–29*n*
Steele, Shelby 41
Steenburgen, Mary 180
Stephen Hero 150
Stevenson, Diane 138
Stivale, Charles J. 202*n*
Stone, Oliver 120
Stowe, Harriet Beecher 5, 47
Streep, Meryl 177
Stuart, Jan 88*n*
Sullivan's Travels 62, 71
Summer, Donna 226
Sunshine State 12, 175, 180–185

Sutherland, Kiefer 120
Swallow Barn 4
Swank, Hilary 201, 211
Swansea, Charleen 135, 142
Sweet Bird of Youth 88*n*
Sweet Dreams 29*n*
Sweet Home Alabama (film) 9, 11, 89, 96–104
"Sweet Home Alabama" (song) 96–97

Tahimik, Kidlat 145
Taken 172
Talladega Nights 12, 217–218, 220–229
Tarantino, Quentin 3, 106–107, 116, 120–121*n*
Tavare, Jay 178
Taylor, Charles 66
Taylor, Elizabeth 144
Taylor, Frank Hoyt 102, 156
Taylor, Helen 1
Taylor, William Desmond 4
T.C. Williams High School 42, 43
Temple, Shirley 4
Tennant, Andy 11, 89
Tennessee Valley Authority 73
Tewkesbury, Joan 78, 80, 88*n*
The Texas Chain Saw Massacre 3
Thompson, Stith 126
Thorpe, Richard 4
Three 6 Mafia 50, 53
Thunder and Lightning 28*n*
Thunder Road 28*n*
Tidwell, Mike 189, 193, 199, 200, 201
Timber Falls 164
Time Indefinite 142
A Time to Kill 10, 18, 71
To Kill a Mockingbird 18, 33, 45*n*, 94, 135
To Sleep with Anger 11, 123–133
tobacco industry 142–144
Tobacco Road (film) 205, 208
Tobacco Road (novel) 2
Tol'able David 3
Tonyan, Rick 181
Torn, Rip 83, 84, 144
The Toy Wife 4
True Blood 187
Tucker, Beverly 4
Tunagur, Usame 11, 161–174
Turner, Otis 4
Turturro, John 63, **64**
Twain, Mark 10, 63, 66–68, 71, 73, 217
Twitty, Conway 84

Ulee's Gold 175
Ulysses 62
"Uncle Tom" image 47–48, 59, 60
Uncle Tom's Cabin (novel) 5
Undertow 215
University of Alabama 38
University of Southern California 38

Valentino, Rudolph 164, **165**, 171
Vanishing Wetlands, Vanishing Future 200
Vietnam War 11, 76, 108–112, 119
Virginia 5
Voight, Jon 116
Von Doviak, Scott 215*n*, 220, 223
voodoo *see* conjure

Waco, Texas 141
Waggner, George 171
Waite, Ralph 181
Wallace, James H. 114
The Waltons 8, 15, 220
Waltzer, Joel 196
Washington, Denzel **38**, 39
The Waterboy 12, 72, 187, 190, 197–199
Watergate 76
Watt, Montgomery 163
Watts, Rebecca Bridges 102
Way Down South 4
Weinlich, Barbara P. 62
Weitz, Paul 173
Welles, Gwen **77**
Wells, Ken 201
Welty, Eudora 140
Weston, Celia 155
Wexler, Haskell 110
White Lightning 28*n*
"white trash" *see* redneck
White Trash: Race and Class in America 108
"Why I Live at the P.O." 140
The Wild Bunch 11, 111–112, 115
The Wild Palms 66

Williams, Hank 87
Williams, Linda 18
Williams, Tennessee 206–207
Williamson, J.W. 3, 121*n*
Willis, Bruce 106
Wilson, Anthony 188, 201
Wilson, Scott 155
Wilson, Woodrow 65
Winkler, Henry 197, **198**
Wise Blood 220
Witherspoon, Reese 96, 120
Within Our Gates 5, 121*n*
Wizard of Oz 62
Wolfe, Thomas 140, 149
Woodward, C. Vann 93
Wordsworth, William 152
Wray, Matthew 25, 108, 113, 115
Wright, Jim 223, 227
Wright, Tom 182
Wrong Turn 164
W.W. and the Dixie Dancekings 28*n*
Wyler, William 5
Wynette, Tammy 81
Wynn, Keenan **77**

Yakin, Boaz 10, 32
Yo La Tengo 148–149
York, Alvin 110
"You Are My Sunshine" 70
Young, Neil 96–97
YouTube 2, 144

Zuckoff, Mitchell 88*n*

www.ingramcontent.com/pod-product-compliance
Ingram Content Group UK Ltd.
Pitfield, Milton Keynes, MK11 3LW, UK
UKHW041939140426
5217IPUK00014B/562